CRIMINOLOGY

Sara Miller McCune founded SAGE Publishing in 1965 to support the dissemination of usable knowledge and educate a global community. SAGE publishes more than 1000 journals and over 800 new books each year, spanning a wide range of subject areas. Our growing selection of library products includes archives, data, case studies and video. SAGE remains majority owned by our founder and after her lifetime will become owned by a charitable trust that secures the company's continued independence.

Los Angeles | London | New Delhi | Singapore | Washington DC | Melbourne

TONY MURPHY

CRIMINOLOGY

A CONTEMPORARY
INTRODUCTION

Los Angeles | London | New Delhi
Singapore | Washington DC | Melbourne

Los Angeles | London | New Delhi
Singapore | Washington DC | Melbourne

SAGE Publications Ltd
1 Oliver's Yard
55 City Road
London EC1Y 1SP

SAGE Publications Inc.
2455 Teller Road
Thousand Oaks, California 91320

SAGE Publications India Pvt Ltd
B 1/I 1 Mohan Cooperative Industrial Area
Mathura Road
New Delhi 110 044

SAGE Publications Asia-Pacific Pte Ltd
3 Church Street
#10-04 Samsung Hub
Singapore 049483

Editor: John Nightingale
Editorial assistant: Eve Williams
Production editor: Sarah Cooke
Copyeditor: Lynda Watson
Proofreader: Katie Forsythe
Indexer: Silvia Benvenuto
Marketing manager: George Kimble
Cover design: Francis Kenney
Typeset by: C&M Digitals (P) Ltd, Chennai, India
Printed in the UK

© Tony Murphy 2020

First published 2020

Library of Congress Control Number: 2019937294

British Library Cataloguing in Publication data

A catalogue record for this book is available from the British Library

ISBN 978-1-52641-140-2
ISBN 978-1-52641-141-9 (pbk)

At SAGE we take sustainability seriously. Most of our products are printed in the UK using responsibly sourced papers and boards. When we print overseas we ensure sustainable papers are used as measured by the PREPS grading system. We undertake an annual audit to monitor our sustainability.

CONTENTS

ABOUT THE AUTHOR

Tony Murphy is a Staff Tutor in Criminology, and Associate Lecturer at the Open University, and until recently, a Senior Lecturer in Criminology at Sheffield Hallam University. He has also held positions at Birkbeck (University of London); Kaplan / University of Essex Online; the University of Westminster, Manchester Metropolitan University, and the London School of Economics and Political Science (LSE). Tony is currently studying for a D.Phil at the University of Oxford, researching penal transportation. He previously studied at LSE and the Open University.

ONLINE RESOURCES

Criminology: A Contemporary Introduction is supported by a wealth of online resources for lecturers and students to support teaching, learning and studying. They are available at **https://study.sagepub.com/criminologyintro**

FOR INSTRUCTORS

PowerPoint Lectures provided for each chapter can be utilised as guidelines for course presentations and adapted as needed for the module's necessities.

The Testbank is designed to elaborate on chapter contents and further critical analysis on the key issues. It is multipurpose, to be used as a tool for class discussion, and take-home and in-class examinations.

FOR STUDENTS

An exciting series of Author-led Videos where key issues in criminology are explored in detail, alongside case study examples, with an academic or practitioner who has engaged in that area.

The videos include:

- 'Crime, Recovery and Desistance' with Professor David Best, Professor of Criminology, Sheffield Hallam University
- 'Probation, and Controversies of Punishment' with Dr. Jake Philips, Reader in Criminology, Sheffield Hallam University
- 'Military Veterans, Crime, and Theory' by Dr. Katherine Albertson, Senior Lecturer in Criminology, Sheffield Hallam University
- 'Comparative Criminology, police accountability, and child soldiers' with Dr. Bankole Cole, Reader in Criminology and Human Rights, Sheffield Hallam University

A list of Web Links including blogs, datasets, specialised video and audio materials – carefully curated to directly compliment the subject matter for every chapter and provide the most relevant research material.

ACKNOWLEDGEMENTS

I was fortunate enough to study at a true pantheon of the social sciences: the LSE. I am particularly thankful to the following people there who taught and inspired me: Chris Husbands; Julian LeGrand; David Manlow; Tim Newburn; David Piachaud; Robert Reiner; and Anne West, plus others whose mere presence at the School was a great stimulus, such as Stan Cohen, Tony Giddens and my dear friend Alan Sked. At Oxford I am grateful to Jonathan Healy, Jane Humphries, Mark Smith and, particularly, my ever-supportive, patient and inspiring D.Phil supervisor, Deb Oxley.

My career in academia owes a lot to my close friend David Manlow, who taught me at LSE and gave me my opportunity at Westminster. It was there I undertook my *academic apprenticeship* of sorts under his tutorage. Thanks also to colleagues at Sheffield Hallam who are a constant source of support and ideas, and so too my colleagues at the Open University over the past 10 years.

Thank you to the team at SAGE, for their confidence in me, and their patience and encouragement in dealing with me – thank you Natalie Aguilera, Delayna Spencer and Eve Williams.

Finally, a special thanks to Camille, Maisie, Verity and Lilah, who collectively are my anchor in the turbulent waters upon which I exist.

Tony Murphy, December 2018

CHAPTER CONTENTS

1 INTRODUCING THE *LANDSCAPES* OF CRIMINOLOGY

Image 1.1

LEARNING OUTCOMES

After reading this chapter you will be able to:

1. recognise the nature of what 'criminology' is, and its focus around crime and law and order issues;
2. recognise the different areas of concerns and issues within criminology;
3. recognise and understand different ways of defining 'crime';
4. understand possible consequences of how we think about crime;
5. recognise different labels used to describe types of crime and bunch them together.

1.1 INTRODUCING THE TEXT

Criminology has been, and continues to be, a popular and growing area of study at all levels. The number of undergraduate degrees that in some way cover criminology is a testament to this. This is perhaps because at its core, criminology is meant to be *real-world* and applied in nature, and it encourages students and academics alike to think about the world in different ways, often challenging taken-for-granted ideas. It is a truly exciting area of study to be involved with, and I hope that I am able to do justice to it within this text. The text has been inspired by my teaching of undergraduate students across different abilities and backgrounds, and as a part of this I have developed introductory criminology courses. This text is designed to serve as an introduction to criminology for all students of the subject, whether this is via a single honours route, or a combined honours route. The intention behind it is to offer students a concise and yet strong foundation in criminology in terms of the following key areas:

- key questions and issues of concern for those engaging in criminology;
- key debates of the past, present and future of criminology;
- exposure to some important authors who have shaped criminology in some way;
- key theoretical models of offending and the nature of society more widely;
- an international or 'globalised' understanding of crime and justice matters;
- a discussion of policy matters and the relevance of criminology for understanding the world around us more broadly; and
- the implications of how we think about law and order issues and processes, in terms of seeking to study and research those issues and in relation to policy and practice.

BOX 1.1   ADDITIONAL INFORMATION

You will encounter a number of key terms in this chapter that you might not be familiar with. Any key terms presented here will be covered and fully explored in subsequent chapters, but for now jot down a list of any you come across in the chapter.

The approach taken within this text is one of trying to show fluid connections between areas of study that have been traditionally made separate within the introductory literature. This approach is embedded across the various chapters. All of that sounds quite complicated, but in essence, I seek to introduce students to the exciting world of criminology in a brief but thought-provoking way. The text is not intended to cover every single topic and aspect of criminology, but instead provide a foundation. When looking back on your studies in the future, you will be able to recognise links to those bullet point items above, but for now, it is enough to know that by engaging with this text and using it to support your studies, you will be building a strong foundation for understanding the nature of criminology.

The principles you learn at this stage are building blocks that you will come back to time and time again within your further reading, and should you follow a career related to the subject in some way. If your engagement with criminology is briefer than that, you will at least come to look at society and the world around you in different ways and you will be able to employ the processes of analysis and evaluation you develop here in whatever context you find yourself.

1.2 STRUCTURE OF THE TEXT

The book is split into three strands. The first strand (Chapters 1 to 5) sets out basic ideas upon which the rest of the book is built. The second strand (Chapters 6 to 8) explores critical issues within criminology, and demonstrates the ways in which some criminologists challenge the taken-for-granted ideas often held regarding law and order processes, and how they question the workings (and even the purpose) of criminal justice processes. Finally, the third strand (Chapters 9 to 11) is concerned with exploring the ways in which we respond to crime, the ways we currently do this, and broader ways in which we might do this; where the criminal justice in itself is not always the answer. There is also a focus on critical issues such as corporate crime, State crime, human rights, and social justice within that final strand, to demonstrate the globalised nature of crime and justice/injustice processes.

The early chapters (strand one) introduce 'criminology', the relevance of it, and ideas linked to how we understand the nature of crime and offending, and how we go about trying to measure or record this in some way. Later in Chapter 1, the very idea of 'criminology' is considered, and competing ideas regarding what 'crime' is are explored, and how some criminologists seek to move beyond that very concept through a focus on 'harm'. There is also a consideration of the different forms of crime, and different categories of crime. Chapters 2 and 3 are concerned with theory, mostly exploring the different ways in which criminologists have sought to account for the existence of crime, in terms of why people commit crime, or how processes of criminalisation shape and define what activities and which groups are deemed to be criminal. Aetiological theories are a key focus of those two chapters; in essence, they are concerned with seeking to explain why crime occurs, and therefore, what we should do about it. How you tackle crime depends on what you view as being the *cause*.

Chapter 4 explores research within criminology, covering different approaches to understanding issues such as why crime occurs, and various other questions criminologists might have. Basic ideas about the research process and the different types of research undertaken by criminologists are considered. Chapter 5 is related to this, because its central theme is that of measuring crime, and related processes such as victimisation. In order to understand crime and justice issues, and to make a positive change in some way, it is important to know something regarding the scale of the problem; how such things are measured are crucial within this, but also, some of the problems associated with doing this.

The next series of chapters build on this, and seek to explore the ways in which social divisions relate to crime and justice in some way. Thus here, issues of class, power, and inequality are important ideas. Chapter 6 examines the ways in which politics (politics in the widest sense) can play an important role in terms of what is defined as 'crime', and who might be deemed to be problematic or 'criminal', and also the responses to crime we see. Chapter 7 takes a critical approach to exploring what is meant by an 'offender' and a 'victim', moving the discussion beyond taken-for-granted ideas, and just traditional forms of offending and victimisation. Such a critical approach points to how it is often the poorest or marginalised groups of some kind who are disproportionately affected by offending and victimisation (including 'harms'), and indeed, by law and order systems.

Chapter 8 examines the important relationship between the media and crime and justice issues. The media often shapes attitudes towards, and understandings of, law and order issues, and can even shape policy-making in this area. The inaccuracies with which the media (of various types, across news, television, film, social media, gaming, and so on) often depict law and order issues, and their decision to focus on specific issues, and present them in the way they do, has profound implications.

In the final strand, Chapter 9 explores responses to crime, particularly the notion of punishment, considering aims and rationales, different ways of punishing, and the outcomes of punishment. It considers broader patterns across punishment, including a tougher approach taken in recent decades. The use of imprisonment and the death penalty are key examples developed within the chapter. Chapter 10 moves the debate away from thinking about the criminal justice system and formal mechanisms of punishment in dealing with crime, by linking crime to a range of other social issues which need to be addressed through other areas of policy-making. Thus, going beyond the criminal justice system to deal with crime is important. The relationship between criminology and social policy is a central feature of the chapter.

Chapter 11 then focuses on global justice/injustice, through discussions of social justice and human rights, and a focus on offending and victimisation (building on discussions developed in Chapter 7), which are 'globalised' in nature, and are often not formally criminalised through law. The notion of 'harms' is once again important in such contexts. A range of topics such as State crime, corporate crime and cybercrime are explored in that chapter. Chapter 12 then summarises the key points from the text, and points towards the present and likely future directions within criminology.

Overall, there is an attempt to lay down foundational ideas in chapters which are subsequently revisited in later chapters. This means that many of the early chapters deal with a range of issues and themes that lay foundational blocks of knowledge for subsequent accounts. For example, the first five chapters deal with key developments, questions, themes, and theories in criminology, which subsequently inform some of the work within the later chapters.

Criminological theory is a crucial part of any introduction to criminology, and Chapter 2 sets out the reasons why this is so important. With that in mind, theory is not limited to one chapter; Chapters 2 and 3 are dedicated to initially setting out the role, value and types of theory used by criminologists ('aetiological' theories are important within this), and exploring actual examples of them within the field. But more than that, each subsequent chapter draws on theoretical models to make sense of the issues being examined; whether this is who we see as offenders, or the role of the media. This is also the case in relation to thinking about research, policy-making, and implications for criminal justice processes.

When working through the chapters, seek to recognise connections across the material and the ways in which much of what we think about in terms of criminology is fluid or connected in some way. Engaging with the listed follow-up materials and review activities will help with this. It is strongly advisable that you engage with the activities and do the follow-up reading in order to get the most out of the text, and this includes the materials and activities on the accompanying website.

1.3 WHAT IS 'CRIMINOLOGY'?

BOX 1.2 ACTIVITY

Before reading on, have a think about what you understand 'criminology' to be, and even attempt to come up with a definition of it. Do also try to come up with a list of issues or topics which you think are explored within criminology. You can then compare this to discussions below.

Criminology might be defined in relation to the topics or issues of concern dealt with within the field. Or it might be defined in the context of the methods or tools employed in seeking to understand issues, and to do something about them. There is no one correct definition, nor is there an exact type of person who might be described as a 'criminologist'. Criminology means different things to different people, but in considering most descriptions or definitions of it, the following can be noted:

> Criminology is the study of crime, justice, and law and order issues, and the broader dynamics of societies in terms of informing how those things exist and are experienced.

That might seem complicated, but in essence, within criminology, in addition to studying crime, justice, and law and order processes, there is also consideration of wider processes which in some way have an impact on those things. Thus, the social and cultural context, the political climate, the nature of the economy, processes such as globalisation and technological progress, a human rights agenda, and so on, must also be considered when seeking to explore and understand the nature of crime and justice.

By looking at the list of chapters in this book, or indeed any criminology textbook, it is possible to recognise the broad range of topics that are core features within criminology. But beyond those, criminology, and thus criminologists span a wide range of areas of interest and topics, all of which relate in some way to above definition. Table 1.1 demonstrates some of these. It is often written that criminology is interdisciplinary in nature: as a field of study it draws in the expertise and knowledge of people working across many academic disciplines, as well many different areas of employment. This then means that a richness of experiences and knowledge can be employed in seeking to understand issues. Typically, criminology tutors and researchers come in to the field from different study backgrounds covering sociology, psychology, law, social policy, economics, geography, history, and criminology itself, and related professions. This is then reflected within the type of research undertaken within criminology, where background can influence the areas of criminology and specific issues a researcher concerns him – or herself with.

1.4 SKILLS AND COMPETENCIES OF A CRIMINOLOGIST

As a student, engaging in criminology requires a range of skills and competencies. These skills and competencies will develop over the course of a degree, but aspects of these will be increasingly recognisable from early on. Here is a short list to keep in mind when moving through the text, and your studies in criminology more generally:

* Finding appropriate materials: using 'credible' sources within your work is important. This means that sources have been produced by recognised and checked sources, and should be at an appropriate level. Typically, this will include journal articles, academic books and book chapters, government and NGO (non-governmental organisations) reports and statistics, academic blogs, and so on. You will become more familiar with good sources and bad sources with experience. But, initially, the reading lists your tutors create for you should be your main sources because they have been chosen for a good reason.
* Using materials in an appropriate way: regardless of the actual source used, it is important to ask from where has it come: is there a purpose, agenda or preconceived position influencing what is written; what are the main points being presented; what is the evidence to support the discussions; does it fit in with what other sources tell us about the issue or topic being dealt with, and so on. Criminology is evidence-driven. This means that any claims or arguments need to be supported by appropriate evidence. So essays or any other assessment exercises should be approached in that way, this also involves appropriate referencing.

BOX 1.3 ADDITIONAL INFORMATION

Referencing is an important academic skill. There are different styles, but your department will usually specify which one they want you to use. Common styles are '**Harvard**', '**APA**', and '**Chicago**'. Regardless of style, they all do the same job. In essence, this is about giving credit to the sources you use, but also, helping to evidence your points and demonstrate your research to those reading your work. Referencing is not dealt with in this text, but you should consider this early on in your studies and make use of any guide you receive from your university. Plus, there are key skills texts which also help you with this, and lots of online guides.

Finch and Fafinski (2016) offer a good overview of skills within criminology. Chapter 8 focuses on referencing.

- Being a critical enquirer: this means approaching topics, arguments and sources of material (as described above) with a natural curiosity for what it tells us, but also what it does not tell us: how arguments and discussions are put together; the evidence presented; alternative ways of thinking about the issue or understanding it; possible gaps or flaws to an argument or analysis; underlying motives of the author/commentator, and so on. Again, this becomes a more natural process with practice.
- Being a reflective learner: this means actively stopping and taking stock of your own learning, work, skills and skills gaps, and ask what has gone well, and what has not gone well. This is related to improving study habits and skills, and changing things that are ineffective. There are different models of reflection to help with this, and there are specific ways of action planning to improve practice (see the box 1.4).
- Being a pragmatic researcher: this entails approaching/investigating issues using different approaches and methods, and thus utilising the best tool for the job being undertaken – being able to work with different types of material, different types of data, different research methods, and so on. The example of digital material, below, is a good example of recent changes to the field, and the need to be pragmatic and adaptable.
- Being digitally competent: increasingly, criminologists must engage with the digital world in terms of using online materials, social media, databases and applications for the purpose of accessing information, undertaking research and disseminating (spreading) the results of their work. As a student, this also extends to assessment processes and tuition strategies, which are increasingly innovative and e-based. Thinking about this early on is useful, and taking all opportunities available to use specialist technologies and databases.
- Being an advocate for change: some criminologists talk about being an activist of some sort, or agent for empowering the marginalised and holding the powerful to account. This is undoubtedly a political choice and not something that all criminology students need to buy in to, although some do. However, at some

level, it is important to want to see positive change in some way. This could be in terms of improving the ways in which criminal justice systems work, ensuring peoples' rights and access to justice, challenging corruption or harmful processes, and so on. As a student, this might drive engagement with the subject, inform dissertation projects, or foster engagement with the wider world through social media, getting practical experience, and so on.

BOX 1.4   ADDITIONAL INFORMATION

Gibbs' cycle of reflection:

1. first **describe** what happened in a situation →
2. consider your **feelings** and thoughts at the time →
3. **evaluate** what was good and bad about the experience/s →
4. do an **analysis** in terms of what sense you can make of the situation? →
5. form a **conclusion** in terms of what else could you have done →
6. develop an **action plan** for what would you now do. (Adapted from Gibbs, 1988)

Action planning: This is a crucial skill linked to being a reflective learner, concerned with putting specific steps in place to become a more effective student. This process can be aided by following the **SMART** process, whereby you set actions or targets for improvements that are **S**pecific, **M**easurable, **A**ppropriate/**A**chievable, **R**ealistic and with a specific **T**ime attached to it.

1.5 KEY TOPICS WITHIN CRIMINOLOGY

The concerns of criminology are incredibly diverse, but Table 1.1 is a useful summary of many of the key concerns and topics within modern-day criminology that are dealt with in this book in some way. It is also noted within the table where these are explored in the various chapters of this text. This is not exhaustive, but it should prove useful in reflecting the breadth and plurality of criminology. Within each entry, there are often several sub-topics, but what is presented here is a useful starting point.

The criminal justice system

In addition to those various areas of focus in Table 1.1, the nature of and the workings of criminal justice systems (i.e. the CJS) is an important feature of criminology. It is therefore worth briefly setting out an overview of a typical such system, such as that in the UK. Barbara Hudson (2013: 100) offers a useful starting point to understanding this:

Topic or issue	Key points	Where in the book?
Causes of crime	Related to explanations and arguments for why people commit crime, in terms of individual and social processes, and a consideration of aspects such as decision-making, biology, psychology, culture, the economy, and so on. And also more critical ideas related to power, control and 'criminalisation'.	Chapters 2 and 3 explore this in some detail. Other chapters come back to these ideas in some way, e.g. Chapter 9 on punishment.
Class, power and inequality	What role do 'class' and inequality play in relation to law and order issues? Who has 'power' in a society, and to what end do they exercise such power? Many criminologists consider issues of class, power and inequality in the context of thinking about law and order processes.	These are central ideas within Chapters 3, 6 and 7, and also considered directly in Chapters 9, 10, and 11.
Crime	Crime can be defined and understood in different ways: a common-sense legal definition versus a focus on morality, social construction and harm.	Implicitly considered in a number of chapters, but dealt within in detail later in Chapter 1. 'Harm' is a focus within Chapters 7 and 11.
Researching crime and justice issues	Criminologists use a diverse range of tools to gather information on crime and justice issues.	Chapter 4 focuses on this and Chapter 5 is closely connected.
Crime statistics	There are multiple ways of measuring crime and other law and order processes, such as victimisation, fear of crime, and so on. Different mechanisms for counting each have strengths and limitations.	Chapter 5 focuses on this in detail and is revisited in some form in Chapters 7, 8, 9, 10 and 11.
Criminalisation	Why is it that some groups interact with the criminal justice system more than others? Some criminologists focus on how it is that some behaviours and groups become labelled as 'criminal'.	Chapters 6, 7, 8, 9 and 10 consider this in some way, and Chapter 3 raises the issue in relation to 'critical approaches'.
Criminal law, criminal justice processes and institutions	What law is and how it is created are important questions to consider. Some criminologists question the intentions and workings of aspects of criminal law. The police, prisons, probation and other elements of law and order processes are in themselves important areas of focus for criminologists.	Chapter 1 gives a brief overview of the criminal justice system in the UK, while Chapters 6 and 9 cover this in relation to the politics of law and order and the nature of punishment.
Desistance from crime	The processes that move an offender from an offending status, to a non-offending status. The issues of identity and social capital are important within this.	This is discussed in Chapter 3 and later in Chapters 9 and 10 on responding to crime.
Differential experiences of crime and justice	Inequality in relation to offending, victimisation and law and order processes are important for criminologists. Matters of class/status, wealth, ethnicity, gender, religion, sexuality, legal status, age, disability, can seemingly shape CJS interactions.	Central within Chapter 7 on victimisation and offending, and re-visited in Chapters 8, 9, 10 and 11.
International processes of crime and justice	Crime and justice can no longer be thought about simply in a 'local' way: the world is connected and integrated (globalisation). Aspects of offending (and so too justice) have evolved through the emergence of cyber-crime, organised crime activity and other international forms of offending.	Chapter 11 directly tackles this, while it is also important in the context of Chapters 6, 7, 8 and 9.

Topic or issue	Key points	Where in the book?
Human rights	Basic and universal rights and freedoms, which governments have an obligation to ensure. Breaches of human rights might be witnessed in relation to policing immigration and terrorism, and mass imprisonment.	Chapter 11 focuses on this in detail and, to a lesser extent, Chapter 7.
Media and crime	A well-established topic within criminology, considering how law and order issues are selected and presented by different media forms and the implications this can have for perceptions and attitudes, and even offending itself, and policy-making around crime and justice.	This is the focus of Chapter 8 and there are also close links to Chapter 6 on the politics of law and order.
Politics of law and order	What is viewed as a problem, who is viewed as problematic, and what ought to be done about all this, is linked to things beyond simple objective reality and evidence. Politics plays an important role and 'penal populism' is a key idea within this.	Chapter 6 is explicitly focused on this, but Chapter 8 also closely links to it on media and crime.
Responding to crime/ punishment/ penology	How do we respond to crime and why? Are there specific rationales or purposes of how we respond, or crudely, how we punish? We respond in different ways, yet, the criminal justice system itself cannot deal with crime in its entirety, especially when considering wider social influences on offending. Patterns of punishments must also be considered.	Chapter 9 is focused directly on punishment, while Chapter 10 is focused on responses to crime beyond the CJS. Chapter 11 explores the notion of 'global justice'.
Social justice	Some groups in society face processes of injustices, as a consequence of their status, their ethnicity, gender, and so on. Systematic processes of injustice and victimisation (including 'harms') are explored by criminologists in relation to sexual exploitation, working conditions, civic rights, welfare benefits systems, and so on.	Chapters 7 and 11 use this concept in a significant way.
Types of crime	There are many different forms of crime. It is possible to separate these out crudely between 'acquisitive' and 'expressive' acts. We can also point to labels such as crimes against the person, property crime, sexual offences, and so on, and also point to events such as genocide, cybercrime, war crime, corporate crime, and so on.	Considered later in Chapter 1, but other chapters also focus on specific types of crime, e.g. corporate crime, state crime, and cybercrime in Chapters 7 and 11.
Victimisation	What is a 'victim' of crime, and how do people become victimised? How is this experienced, and does it vary between groups, crime types, and so on?	Chapter 7 explores this topic in detail and so too does Chapter 11 on global justice.
Youth justice	The nature of policing, law-making and punishment specifically in the instance of children. This can often be highly controversial, given the possibility for needlessly criminalising young people and drawing them into the criminal justice system.	Considered, briefly, in Chapter 9 and alluded to in other chapters.

Table 1.1   The concerns of criminology

The process through which the state responds to behaviour that it deems unacceptable. Criminal Justice is delivered through a series of stages: charge, prosecution, trial, sentence, appeal, punishment, these processes and the agencies which carry them out are referred to collectively as the criminal justice system.

The various processes and agencies include law-making, enforcement of laws through agencies such as the police, and then the processing, defence and sentencing of suspects via a system involving the crown prosecution service and the court system, and the instruments for delivering punishment, such as prisons and probation. And also, there are various agencies whose role it is to manage or inspect those processes, namely Her Majesty's Inspectorates.

Each element of this is of interest to criminologists for a number of reasons, but partly because of the potential for controversies and inequalities to operate within processes of criminal justice. Hudson, for example, remarks how: 'Unemployment, race and gender have been shown to influence criminal justice decision making. The role of gender specifically for example, in shaping criminal justice processes is much debated and contested by criminologists' (Hudson, 2013: 101). The need to think in terms of intersectionality for instance, becomes relevant here. That is, how the combination of dynamics such as gender, class and ethnicity can interact with one another to create or exacerbate issues such as criminal justice inequalities. For a detailed examination of the CJS in the UK see Case et al. (2017 – specifically Chapter 20) and, generally, Hudson (2013).

1.6 WHAT IS 'CRIME'?

A legal definition

The concept of crime might seem straightforward. However, it is more complicated than perhaps you might have imagined. A common-sense way of talking about crime often entails linking it to law, defining *crime as an intentional act which breaks or goes against a law of some sort*, or phrased in a way similar to this. This could be a domestic (national law), or an international law. Thinking in that way is not necessarily wrong; technically, it is correct. But only seeing 'crime' in that way is very limited. Criminologists point to a range of problems associated with this, the legal definition. This is (usually) a transparent and clear guide for society to follow, and a clear framework then for law and order practitioners to work with. The law after all, might be seen as a set of tools in place to protect the public, and ensure that society runs in an orderly (and fair?) manner. But a range of issues must be considered:

* Where have laws come from, who creates them, and for what purpose?
* Is the law effective at criminalising all behaviours or events that are damaging or harmful?

- Are some laws needless?
- What are the consequences of the laws we have?
- Who is affected by the laws we have? Do some laws, intentionally or not, victimise specific groups?

It must also be consider that laws are not fixed or static. New laws can be made, and old laws repealed. This, then, means that what is understood to be 'crime' must then also be fluid. When thinking about how laws are made, this happens at the level of the State. Government must create new legislation in order to do this. The process can be lengthy, but arriving at the very decision to criminalise certain behaviours in the first instance can take much longer, meaning that certain damaging behaviours are not considered in law for some time, and so, are not acted against.

Also, the decision to criminalise certain behaviours has to be influenced by something. This could be pressure from the public, the media, from pressure groups, a political or ideological agenda, changing social and cultural attitudes towards behaviours, technological development which creates new problems, and so on. This, then, means that things only become defined as 'crime' once there has been enough of a reason for the State to react to it, and, even then, criminalising some behaviours might be slowed-down or blocked by powerful actors with vested interests. Consider here the slow progress of environmental laws, financial regulations, those which provide workers' rights, and those related to tobacco and alcohol consumption.

BOX 1.5   ADDITIONAL INFORMATION

Some 'critical' criminologists (see Chapter 3) link the creation and use of laws (and indeed a reluctance to create some necessary laws) to the **control and subjugation of populations**, and maintaining **capitalist** economic interests.

The moral and social context of crime

Many damaging behaviours are not criminalised, while some groups in society are seemingly disadvantaged by the needless criminalisation of certain behaviours. A good example of this is the criminalisation of homosexuality in many countries. In places such as the UK, the social and political climate changed over the course of the twentieth century, which meant that the law eventually changed to make homosexuality legal at that time. Similar processes can be recognised in relation to acts such as abortion. Often, then, there is a moral component to how we understand behaviours and whether they are viewed as being problematic.

Of course, this can work in the other direction also, whereby certain behaviours were not previously defined as illegal, but become criminalised as the public begin to see them as problematic or immoral. Yet even then, it can take some time for the law to catch up. 'Rape within marriage' is an example of this; it was only made illegal in the UK in 1991. Another example relating to changing social attitudes is that of the banning of smoking in public buildings and enclosures in Ireland (from 2004) and the UK (from 2007), which accompanied a gradual decline in the number of people smoking in such countries, and a recognition of the harmful consequences for smokers and those around smokers alike.

This also relates to what some criminologists describe as the socially constructed nature of crime, that is, how much of what is viewed as 'crime' is a product of the dynamics of a given society at a given point in time (see Muncie, 2009). Here, the notion of deviancy is important, and describes acts that are outside of the mainstream values and norms of a society. They may be illegal or legal behaviours, but where they are legal, deviant behaviour can often eventually become formally criminalised, once there is enough of a reaction against it. This links to the work of writers such as Howard Becker, and labelling theory, which is covered in Chapter 3. Some criminologists (often those from a sociological background) prefer to use the term deviancy over that of crime.

Beyond a legal definition of crime: harms

Furthermore, some criminologists point to the harms caused by various behaviours that are often not dealt with by law. Thus, instead of focusing explicitly on crime, some criminologists prefer to utilise a harms-based approach to thinking about offending (e.g. Steve Tombs and David Whyte). This, then, means that criminologists can consider a range of issues such as working conditions, environmental damage, health damage, and so on, whereby there is clearly harm being carried out against people and groups (social harms in the context of groups), and this demands some form of attention and action.

The more harm done, the greater the severity of the response required. Eventually, the formal law can/does tend to catch-up, albeit sometimes not going far enough. Governments, institutions, corporations and others can then all be implicated in offending more easily than they otherwise might be as a result of adopting a harms-based approach.

1.7 TYPES OF CRIME

Thus, as is evident in the above, the very understanding of the concept of 'crime' is significant in terms of who is thought of as an offender, which acts are considered, who is a victim, and what should be done about it; all which are key focal points for later chapters in this text. Although 'crime' is, then, not a straightforward concept, it is possible to point to a number of different forms of crime, and this is aided through also considering harms within the list. Such labels are used by criminologists, policy-makers and others, and it is important to be aware of them because of their use within literature, crime statistics and academic debate. The following is not exhaustive, but a useful introductory overview:

Label	Notes
Acquisitive crimes	Acts that involve the 'acquisition' or gain of property, money or anything else that is a tangible reward. They might include theft, robbery, burglary, fraud, and so on.
Expressive crimes	Acts that do not, seemingly, involve the acquisition of goods, but instead, are linked to emotions and emotional release: anger, frustration, etc., where the act itself is the goal. They are often violent or sexual in nature.
Property crimes	Acts involving the acquisition of property or damage to property. So in addition to acts such as theft and robbery, this includes criminal damage, vandalism, and so on.
Crimes against the person	Crimes that directly involve an act against an individual of group of people, such as a violent or sexual act.
Sexual offences	Acts covering all manner of unwanted or inappropriate sexual behaviour against a person, or group, physical or otherwise.
White-collar crime	Acts committed by people usually in a work context, for their own personal gain, e.g. theft and fraud; offending within respectable or status-based professions, as opposed to 'blue-collar' workers (manual workers).
Corporate crime	Acts committed by/on behalf of a company that in some way benefit company goals. This includes financial transactions, but also negligence, 'industrial espionage', not adhering to health and safety or environmental regulations, etc.
Crimes of the powerful	Acts committed by those in positions of 'power', such as governments and business figures, where they are abusing their position of power, and acting with some form of corruption and impunity.
State crimes	Acts committed, or commissioned, or advocated in some way by States (government and associated institutions of government) to achieve their goals.
'Peace crimes', including crimes against humanity	Acts that are so abhorrent or terrible, that they go against humanity as a whole, and they have their own label. The United Nations sets out what these entail, but they include things such as genocide, systematic torture, and so on.
Social harms	Linked to the 'harms'-based definition of crime, above. Acts that harm communities or specific groups of people and are often not dealt with by formal laws.
War crimes	Acts committed during conflicts and wars, whereby State actors (usually the military and intelligence agencies) breach domestic or usually international laws regarding warfare, and usually involve a disregard for human rights.
Status offences/ crimes	Acts that are prohibited, usually only for certain groups or in the context of certain conditions. Often, this is in the instance of young people having their behaviours regulated.
Hate crimes	Acts committed where the victim or victims are targeted because of their personal characteristics: age, gender, religion, ethnicity, culture, sexuality, and so on.
Cybercrime	Acts committed using or facilitated by emerging information and communication technologies, typically the Internet.

Table 1.2   Types of crime

Note: Please be aware that there is often overlap between these labels, whereby an act can be placed under several of the labels.

It is also important to be aware that, as was demonstrated in the context of defining crime, new forms of crime can be identified over time, and so new labels appear. For example, cybercrime and hate crime have emerged in recent decades as new crime categories. One feature of both has been their close link to emergent technologies. For example, even though hate crimes can occur anywhere, there are increasing patterns of offending and victimisation online. This links to a wider issue regarding the extent to which new technologies can create new forms of crime, or at least allow older forms of crime to occur in different ways, or evolve. In considering this, Grabosky (2001) seeks to assess the actual relationship between a crime and technologies, and uses the analogy of wine, asking: *'is the act being committed fundamentally a new act of crime: would it be impossible in all senses, without the electronic platform or network? Or, is it simply an older act occurring through a new medium?'* The analogy of 'new wine or old wine in a new bottle' is used by Grabosky.

Finally, and linked to the above, the now pervasive nature of social media must be explicitly considered, in terms of the opportunities this can afford for offending, and victimisation; the extent to which social media platforms can both facilitate offending, and also be used directly for an act of crime. This includes acts such as hate crimes, where direct victimisation can occur through social media platforms. Other examples include behaviours such as terror recruitment and propaganda, and also 'digital dealing', whereby illicit drugs (and other illicit items) are traded using social media platforms (see BBC, 2017); such examples represent instances of how social media can facilitate offending.

1.8 SUMMARY AND IMPLICATIONS

This opening chapter has presented an overview of the remainder of the text, and pointed to the key areas of discussion to be encountered within each chapter. It has also shown how 'criminology' is an incredibly varied, but exciting field of study, and the range of topics highlighted in this chapter reflect that point. 'Crime' is a complex idea, and the various ways of thinking about it here, and its different forms, also add to the complexity of criminology. The different ways of thinking about 'crime' each entail a set of implications in terms of responding to crime. But also, 'criminology' and 'crime' are not static, they are instead fluid, and how they are understood and where this leads to must be continually re-thought – for example, new crime categories. Crucially also, the concept of 'harm' has emerged within criminology as an alternative to the label of 'crime', and this has expanded the focus and remit of criminology in allowing for examination of damaging processes of victimisation beyond the narrow confines of legal understandings of crime, and the criminal justice system.

RECOMMENDED READING AND
FOLLOW-UP MATERIAL

Read

- Muncie, J. (2009) 'The construction and deconstruction of crime', in Newburn, T. (ed.), *Key Readings in Criminology*. Cullompton, Devon: Willan.

  (This offers a more detailed coverage of the various ways of defining/understanding crime.)

- Dorling, D., Gordon, D., Hillyard, P., Pantzias, C., Pemberton, S. and Tombs, S. (2008) *Criminal Obsessions: Why Harm Matters More than Crime* (2nd edn). Centre for Crime and Justice, available at: www.dannydorling.org/wp-content/files/dannydorling_publi cation_id1047.pdf

  (This is a lengthy document but do have a look at Chapter 1 as a minimum, and then any others you might have time to read. This offers a wide exploration of the concept of 'harm'.)

Watch

- Dr. Steve Wakemman's SAGE video, 'The Sociology of Crime and Deviance', available at: http://sk.sagepub.com/video/crime-and-deviance

CHAPTER REVIEW QUESTIONS

1. What is 'criminology'?
2. What are the different ways in which we can define 'crime'?
3. What sorts of issues do criminologists research and write about?

REVIEW ACTIVITIES

1. If you did not do this as you read through the chapter, go back through and list the names of authors mentioned throughout the text (there are not that many), and write down in what context their name was mentioned. You can

come back to this list and add to it as you work through the subsequent chapters.

2. Homosexuality was illegal in the UK until 1967, but in many countries today this is still illegal, including in Iran and Saudi Arabia. Use the Internet to research which other countries criminalise homosexuality, and think about the reasons why this might be the case in those countries. Is it linked to wider social or cultural values, religion, the nature of the government/politics in those places, and so on?

3. Think about behaviours that are damaging to groups of people, or society as a whole, which are not actually criminalised. Try to list at least a few. Think about the damage or 'harms' these things do, and also, what ought to be done about them?

4. Consider the following list of behaviours, and think about:

   a. Whether they are legal or not.
   b. Whether they should be legal or illegal.
   c. Does it depend on the context in which the behaviour occurs?
   d. In what ways do they impact people or groups?
   e. How might the various definitions of crime help us to think about these behaviours, and their legal/illegal status?

- Downloading the latest music albums and films for free.

- Killing a person.

- Taking illicit drugs.

- Suicide.

- Ridiculing a person's religious beliefs.

PART 1

UNDERSTANDING THE CAUSES AND PREVALENCE OF CRIME

CHAPTER CONTENTS

2 'THEORY', AND ITS USES

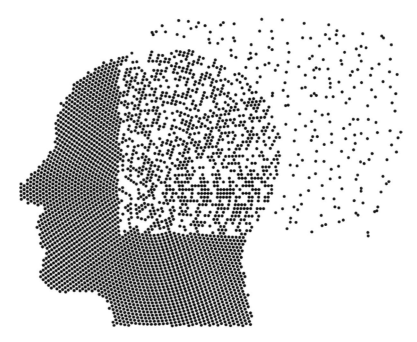

Image 2.1

LEARNING OUTCOMES

After reading this chapter you will be able to:

1. understand what 'theory' is, and how it is used within criminology;
2. understand the application of theory for various crime and law and order issues;
3. recognise some basic distinctions between theories within criminology;
4. understand the relationship between theory and other aspects of the web of knowledge, such as questions, concepts, research, and evidence.

2.1 WHAT IS THEORY?

Theory is a very broad term, simply meaning:

An explanation, or a model, or framework for understanding particular events or processes.

Thinking about theories as frameworks for analysis, or explanations, is a useful thing to do; it can be helpful to translate the word 'theory' into something more meaningful and straightforward. This is something to think about more widely within your studies; translating difficult terminology into something more familiar to you. Theory is considered throughout the entire book; this is embedded within each chapter in some way because there are different types of theory and different uses of it, that is, in each chapter we are always seeking to understand and account for things, and this usually means that some form of explanation is offered.

Usually however, when people talk about theory within criminology, they are thinking about how to understand the nature of offending, that is, why people engage with crime. This is certainly a crucial aspect of theory, and one of its main uses, but in fact it is only one aspect. In the literature, such theories that allow us to talk about how crime comes about are labelled as aetiological theories of crime. This simply means that they are concerned with *causes* of crime, and the discussions in Chapter 3 are mainly focused on this.

Yet that in itself is complicated a little by the fact that seeking to understand why people commit crime, or account for crime in some way, is rested on the assumption that crime is something that exists, and something that we can therefore work out motivations towards. It seems strange to note this, but remember towards the end of Chapter 1, it was demonstrated how what is understood as 'crime' can be contested because its meaning can vary between different groups, between space, and over time. Therefore, accounting for why people commit crime, for instance, is based on assuming that certain things are deemed to be 'criminal', and that's that. More generally, all theories are based on a series of assumptions of some kind. In reality, what these aetiological theories do, mostly, is to take the legal definitions and thus what is presented in law, as their starting point. But of course, Chapter 1 demonstrated that there are other definitions. The critical approaches examined in Chapter 3 challenge this, and ask questions of the taken-for-granted positions of the other theories, and so they are distinctive in what they do and how they approach law and order issues.

In addition to being concerned with why people commit crime, theory in criminology can help us to consider and understand a range of different issues connected to crime, law and order, and the broader nature of society.

BOX 2.1   ACTIVITY

Think about some of the concerns and topics within criminology, as explored in Chapter 1, and think about the sorts of questions that can be asked in relation to those concerns or topics. Which aspects of those topics might be explored? Start

(Continued)

(Continued)

by looking at the example below. As a result of completing this activity, it will be become apparent that there are a great range of issues that criminologists might want to explain or make sense of in some way.

Example: *Focusing on the issue of victimisation, it would be useful to understand who becomes a victim of crime, and why, and whether victimisation is experienced differently in relation to different types of crime, and in relation to different groups.* Chapter 7 explores this, and presents some relevant theories concerned with victimisation.

Listed below are a series of questions and concerns criminologists grapple with, where theories have been developed to aid understanding, and offer explanation. This is not exhaustive, but a useful starting point. It might be useful to compare this list to the notes made within the previous activity.

- What is crime?
- How are laws made, and what purpose do they serve?
- Who commits crime, and why?
- What is the nature of the world around us, including the State and the Criminal Justice System?
- Is society fair? And how does this relate to crime and law and order processes?
- Who becomes a victim of crime, and why?
- How is victimisation experienced? Is this different across groups?
- Why do we punish? And how is this done?
- What should be done about crime?
- How do offenders stop offending?
- What are the connections between the media and crime?
- What role do politics play within law and order issues?
- How can we know about/research law and order issues?

Thus, theories within criminology are developed and used extensively in relation to a range of different issues and concerns, particularly in relation to offering understanding or explanation. They also, crucially, afford the opportunity for policy-making, i.e. the creation of laws, strategies and specific measures to tackle crime, or deal with law and order issues in some way. Thus, policy-makers of various types (in government, charities, Local Authorities, public services, and so on) might want to know why people engage in offending for instance, so that they can create policies to stop offending. Similarly, academics who teach and research around law and order issues, as well as students of course, engage with theory as part of their work

2.2 THE 'PROBLEMS' WITH THEORY

Often when students are introduced to theory, they approach it with some trepidation. Unhelpfully, theory within criminology is all too often over-complicated by those teaching students, and one of the main issues is that the language and specific terminology used in books, lectures and workshops is as much a barrier to student engagement and understanding, as are the actual ideas themselves. Students often find this area of criminology a challenge, but mostly, I would argue, this is because the emphasis and the approach to covering the material are misplaced.

For example, students are often given far too much information, too early within their studies and academic careers. Yes, detail is important, but when setting-out on an academic journey, it is enough to recognise that there are various ways of understanding law and order issues, such as why people commit crime, and sometimes these different ideas can conflict with one another, or overlap, or even complement each other. Also, knowing basic arguments and a few key ideas associated with each of these ways of thinking about law and order issues is sufficient. First-year undergraduate students do not need 20 pages of discussion around the intricacies of a few early authors such as Jeremy Bentham, Cesare Beccaria, Cesare Lombroso, and so on, as is sometimes presented.

Those three authors named above are important in the context of early thinking around crime and justice issues, but the emphasis should be on the contemporary relevance of their ideas. Thus, another problem sometimes evident within teaching and textbooks at this level, is assuming that students need to have a complete historical record of authors and their writing. In reality, students will need only be aware of where ideas have come from in so much as this demonstrates how thinking on crime and justice are products of context and particular social and political climates, and how modern thinking owes something to the pioneering work of those writing and researching in earlier periods. This chapter, and the subsequent ones, attempts to avoid some of the pitfalls mentioned here, presenting a basic and overarching view of these theories without the reams of detail often provided. Where there is too much detail, the most significant messages can be lost among the noise.

Finally, another 'problem' in terms of how theory is sometimes presented is that there is often a black and white separation of the theories, and what they can tell us. Theories are all too often seen as models for understanding things that are quite separate from one another; if you want to understand something, such as why people commit crime, then you have to subscribe to one of those models and reject the others. In reality, these theories or models are simplified efforts at explanation, and rarely is it the case that one of the models can completely explain or make sense of events and processes on their own. I like to refer to theories in criminology as heuristic tools; this simply means that they are mental short cuts or simplifications for making sense of something. They are usually unrealistic simplifications, but they nevertheless allow for understanding by offering different viewpoints from which to look at the matters of crime and justice.

A helpful way of thinking about this is looking at a crime scene from different positions, as in Figure 2.1. From each of those positions, the viewer might be able to get the same information, by seeing the same features and aspects of the event, but potentially, they might also view different aspects according to where they stand; a different injury, a different clue, a different perspective on what happened, and so on. A person looking from position 'A' has a very different view from that of someone looking from position 'D', and so on. It might not matter, but equally, it could make a big difference in terms of how they think about the events that unfolded. This is a still shot, but imagine the added complexity of the situation in a live and moving event.

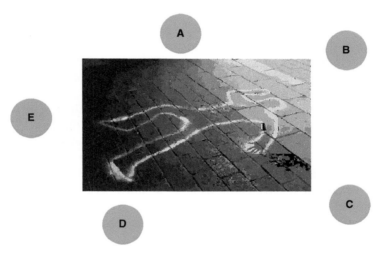

Figure 2.1   Seeing events from different theoretical positions

In essence, criminological theories can be used together to overcome the fact that they are simplifications, in a process of synthesis to make sense of events in the real world. Different theories might help us to understand different aspects of events and processes, and quite often, using more than one theory fills in more of the gaps than using one in isolation. And in the context of the history of criminology, this is what has happened. Commentators have taken previous theories, and added to them, or amended them, or fused them with different explanations in order to make better sense of events. Some examples of this are explored in the next chapter. Of course, in some situations, a particular model can seem to make much more sense of events than others might, and could go a long way in affording explanation.

Synthesis of entire theories and key aspects of theories has become increasingly common within criminology. **Cultural criminology** is a useful example of this because it is, in essence, created out of the coming together of several pre-existing theories, perhaps forming a fuller model of crime and justice. This is discussed in Chapter 3 in more detail within the **integrated approaches** block of theory. Also, a useful recent example where synthesis is a crucial feature within the analysis is that of Murphy (2019), writing on organised crime and terrorism in South Asia. Here, **routine activity theory** is fused together with considerations often outside of that model, such as social, economic, political and cultural aspects of communities, and processes of globalisation.

Recent writing on rational choice models of crime reflect this approach of synthesis, whereby writers have recognised that the assumptions of early writers in this area, such as Bentham and Beccaria whose work still influences modern writers, did not take into account the full complexity of human behaviour and decision-making processes. Their analyses of the world were overly simplistic. For example, some early writers within the Classicist tradition of theory, such as Bentham and Beccaria, who are examined in Chapter 3, over-emphasised the extent to which humans act in a rational way, and they largely underplayed the extent to which judgement can be clouded by external and internal factors. More modern writers in this tradition, such as Cornish and Clarke (1986) through using concepts such as bounded rationality, now often accept that people act rationally in relation to what they actually know, and their ability to process the information they have. This might not be completely rational at all, but rational in relation to that person and how they see and understand the world. This is explored further in the next chapter, so for now, it is enough to understand the wider point regarding synthesis, and theories evolving over time.

2.3 KEY EXAMPLES OF THEORIES WITHIN CRIMINOLOGY

The field of criminology has evolved immeasurably since its early origins, but some of the early thinking about crime and law and order have persisted and still influence criminologists today. Classicism and Positivism are foundational schools of thought within criminology. This means that not only were they significant in terms of the formation of criminology, but also the origin of many more recent theories can be traced back to them in terms of how they approach issues of crime and justice.

In brief (because this is dealt with in detail in Chapter 3), Classicism positions offending as a consequence of people *choosing* to commit crime, based on them weighing-up situations and likely outcomes. Individuals are viewed as rational actors, who are self-interested/selfish in their actions. Crime can be a chosen behaviour if the situation presents it as a rational act. Positivism on the other hand – Individual Positivism and Social/Sociological Positivism are two different strands of this – presents an opposite account of offending; people engage in offending because they are influenced by forces outside of their own control. Some people do not have the capacity to act rationally, but instead, internal forces of biology or psychology, or external forces of social conditions and culture can influence actions. Classicist principles might be described as a first block of theory within criminology, which I label more expansively as choice and decision-making. The analyses of Positivism can be labelled as a second block, related to individual/internal influences; and a third block related to social influences. I label these in a more expansive way as individual pathologies, and social pathologies.

A fourth school of thought, which I label as critical approaches, emerged a little later, but now has a major impact on the field of criminology. These positions are often, but not always influenced by Marxism in some way (influenced by the work of Karl Marx). In short, Critical theories challenge the status quo, and, ask questions of the role of the State, laws, and the Criminal Justice System. They, in some form, point to conflict in society, and inequalities based upon things such as class, ethnicity and gender. Within critical theories, how crime is defined, who are labelled as offenders, and how crime is responded to, are often said to relate to inequality, power and even social control. It is possible to argue that most criminologists are in some way 'critical' in their approach to the field.

A fifth way of thinking about offending is not necessarily a distinctive and separate block, but rather, a mixture of influences from the first four, which links to the earlier point on synthesis of ideas. This block can be labelled integrated approaches, because they integrate aspects of the other blocks, in a process of synthesis, to present a more holistic explanation. The five 'blocks' outlined here have spawned a large range of individual different theories, but banding theories together into broad bands, as is done here, can be useful in terms of affording appreciation for the big overarching arguments that transcend individual theories.

The blocks of theory

Presented below is a crude overview of the main 'blocks' of theories within criminology. In each case, the important aspects are what they suggest about *why crime occurs; and therefore what we should do about crime;* and *the wider nature of society.* Remember, the theories that sit within each block of theory can be diverse in nature, but they share fundamental arguments in common, hence the value of gathering them together into blocks.

Theories that present offending in relation to choices and decisions made by an offender, often as part of a rational decision-making process in some form: people actively choose to commit crime because of the expected outcome. Here, Classicism is a key area of theory, and can be broken down into traditional or early Classicist ideas, and modern interpretations and re-workings of it. Understanding crime this way means that in responding to crime we should look to make offending more difficult, and make the punishment outweigh the gains of crime to discourage offenders. This could involve making targets of crime tougher, such as improving security measures in residential areas. Or, it could involve tougher sentencing practices to dissuade would be offenders, i.e. deterrence.

Block two: individual pathologies

Theories within which offending is viewed as a consequence in some way of biological or psychological abnormalities of an offender; in some way, there is something abnormal or 'wrong' with an individual which causes or facilitates offending. Here, the notion of Positivism (Individual Positivism especially) is used extensively within the literature. Within such accounts, crime must be dealt with through treating or rehabilitating offenders to remove the abnormalities or pathology that has caused the offending. Thus, if for instance offending is seen as being linked to drug addiction/abuse, then drug treatment would be a way forward.

Block three: social pathologies

In the same way that the individual pathologies block presents offending as a consequence of abnormality – something that is 'wrong' or pathological within an individual – this block also presents offending as an outcome of pathology, but this time in the context of processes outside an individual. Pathologies of a community, a culture, or social structures/a society more widely can be considered. The label Positivism is also used within the literature, but this time it is usually termed Social/Sociological Positivism. Thus, individuals are influenced by their wider environments. In responding to crime, broader influences need to be addressed. So, where crime is viewed as a product of economic inequality in society, responses could relate to policies with which to create a fairer society, create jobs, wealth re-distribution through the welfare benefits system, and so on.

Block four: critical approaches

These are theories that present crime in the context of wider social processes, such as inequality, class, power, and marginalisation of some groups. Crime, in such instances, becomes a mechanism for responding or surviving in groups. While, also, processes of criminalisation are highlighted, where, rather than coming at the issue of crime from a position of asking *why do people commit crime*, the crucial question is in instead *who is targeted by law-makers and the criminal justice system, and why?* A social control argument is offered by some of the theories, that is, criminalisation and responses to crime serve to control elements of the population.

Block five: integrated accounts

In this block, theories have combined elements of ideas from the other blocks. This is done because it is believed that a more comprehensive or complete understanding can be offered. So, for example, models might combine aspects of theories to account for both social and biological processes (so called bio-social theories) that influence an individual, or explore aspects of choice and rationality in the context of some form of individual pathology.

2.4 HOW IS THEORY CREATED, AND HOW DOES IT WORK?

Theory does not exist in a vacuum, nor does it come about spontaneously. This means that theory emerges from a series of processes, and theory is inherently related to a series of key intellectual devices, or what might be referred to as a web of knowledge. What this means is that a theory is usually linked to a particular question, or questions shaping enquiry; it is usually rested upon a series of assumptions about the world; it is related to a set of specific concepts, and so on. The following is a detailed account of how it is possible to think about theory and what to keep in mind when thinking about 'theory', where theory comes from, and its purpose: broad issues and concerns of criminology; specific questions; concepts; research activities; evidence; evaluation; and policy. All of these are components of criminological enquiry in the web of knowledge. An explanation of these and their relationship to one another is demonstrated within Figure 2.2, and the accompanying text below.

- Broad issues and concerns of criminology: criminology, as demonstrated in Chapter 1, is centred on a range of key topics and issues, and these drive criminological thinking and research, teaching, and ultimately, policy-making. And so, theories are linked to these in terms of being concerned with specific issues, or in allowing us to better understand those broader issues in some way, for example the 'causes' of crime. Such broad concerns are usually the initial starting points for research and courses of study within criminology. There are many theories (aetiological theories) that offer some specific understanding in relation to that broad issue.
- Specific questions: Honing in from a broader issue or concern, specific questions are then developed or arrived at which capture a specific aspect of the wider issue, and allow for more in-depth thinking and analysis, or a specific application

of theory. Sticking with the example of 'causes' of crime, such a question might be why do individuals engage in criminal behaviour? This could be narrowed down further, for instance, to a particular group in society, and particular form of offending, e.g. why do young men engage in gang-related offences? A pre-existing theory might be used to explain this, and seek to test it in some way. Or instead, a new theory might be developed.

- Concepts: these are mental short cuts in a way, which help to describe or label certain phenomena. Such ideas are not fixed or universal, because understanding of them can vary across space and time. For example, the very idea of crime is itself a concept that describes the phenomena whereby society recognises and reacts to, and formally acts against some behaviours deemed to be problematic. Understanding what is/should be crime, varies across societies, and over time. Concepts are important within this web of knowledge because theories utilise specific concepts within their analyses. Some concepts such as crime might be very common for criminologists, but some concepts are specific to individual types of theories. For example, critical approaches use concepts such as social control – describing a phenomenon whereby groups of people are controlled or coerced by powerful groups in society – whereas other types of theory do not. Continuing with the example related to young men and gangs, an important concept here would be the notion of a gang, to describe a subculture (another concept) or a group who exhibit behaviours and even values outside of the mainstream.
- Research activities: with specific questions in mind, criminologists might then embark on research in order to collect data to inform their thinking and help them to answer the questions they have. Research is dealt with in Chapter 4, but in short, research can be in a variety of different forms, including literature-based work whereby previous academic and other work are brought together to form a new understanding of the data, or it can be empirical whereby new data is collected or generated. Empirical work can itself take many forms, including interviews and questionnaires, observing situations, setting up experiments, and so on. Using the example of young men and gangs, interviewing gang members or observation of them, can generate data, or another strategy could be to explore the backgrounds of gang members using all manner of records and documents.
- Evidence: the data gathered from our research then forms evidence, which is simply information of some form that helps to develop thinking about an issue, or test pre-existing ideas. Taking the example above, this could be statistics or life stories relating to the background of offenders, or information from observations that might shed light on the behaviours of those within gangs.
- Evaluation: using the evidence gathered, the next step is to assess what this means, and what it tells us about the issue/question we are considering. A theory (explanation of some form) might then form from this. Equally, this could also entail using evidence to test a pre-existing theory, and to determine if it 'works'.
- Policy: this is action, a set of practices, or law-making, which is concerned with affecting change, dealing with a problem, or reacting to it in some way, usually

with a hoped-for positive outcome. This is arrived at (or rather, it should be arrived at) from considering the evidence, and the subsequent theory/theories regarding the phenomenon. Taking the above example, if our evidence, and eventual theory, pointed to young men feeling alienated and without legitimate opportunities and role models in society, then policy should seek to address those issues. Policy could then consist of actions that aim to give young men a sense of inclusion and value in society, and open up legitimate employment and training routes for them.

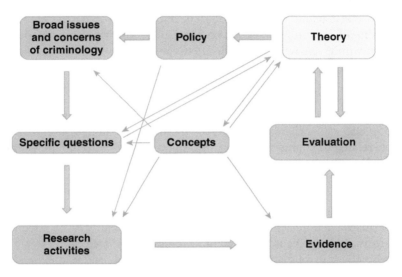

Figure 2.2   The 'criminological web of knowledge'

Within Figure 2.2 it is apparent that theory might be arrived at from starting out with broad issues or concerns of interest, and following this round the web of knowledge. The thinking/focus is narrowed down to specific questions, which then might lead directly to the forming of a theory through an educated guess, or through a more formal process of research which generates evidence, and in turn, leads in to the formation of an explanation or theory. Figure 2.2 is quite complicated because not only does it show the relationships between the various aspects of criminological enquiry, it also demonstrates how in practice, things do not always work in a single direction of influence. For instance, when considering concepts, it is possible to create or use concepts as a consequence of arriving at a particular theory, or the types of concepts we use might lead into forming specific theories, as for example we consider in relation to critical approaches in Chapter 3. Concepts such as class, power and social control derive from a Marxist way of thinking about crime and justice. And if starting out on a research journey thinking about the world in that way, then there is a fair chance that the end product entails arriving at a critical argument to make sense of crime and justice issues.

2.5 SUMMARY AND IMPLICATIONS

This chapter has been concerned with exploring the nature of theory within criminology, pointing to its role and value, and why thinking about theory is important across all areas of criminology. Theory sits within a wider web of knowledge, which includes aspects such as questions, concepts and evidence. Thinking about 'causes' of crime is undoubtedly a key aspect of all this, but it is only one of many possible applications of theory. Though theories within criminology are incredibly diverse, it is possible to bunch them together, albeit in a very crude way, in order to understand general arguments and overarching ways of thinking about crime and justice issues. That approach is offered within this chapter and the text more widely: in relation to aetiological theories of crime. Theories are valuable because they can afford an understanding of crime and justice issues, but they can also be useful in aiding understanding of wider issues, such as human nature, the nature of communities and society, and links between crime and justice and politics, the economy, inequalities, and so on.

RECOMMENDED READING AND FOLLOW-UP MATERIAL

Read

- Tibbetts, S. (2018) *Criminological Theory: The Essentials*. California: SAGE.

  (Reading the entire book is unrealistic, but do have a look at the early chapters that grapple with what theory is and its role.)

Watch

- Channel 4, 'Winning the Battle Against Gang Culture', available at: www.youtube.com/watch?v=pnqylwd3jyQ

  (Watch the short clip and think about how gang membership is explained and, therefore, the responses needed to tackle the problem of gangs. This demonstrates a link between theory and policy.)

CHAPTER REVIEW QUESTIONS

1. What words or phrases can be used instead of using the term 'theory'?
2. What are the five 'blocks' of theory discussed in the chapter, and what are the main features of them which mean that they can be bunched together (individual theories put into broader categories)?
3. What is the relationship between theory and the following: questions, concepts, research and evidence?

REVIEW ACTIVITIES

1. In this chapter, and the next, Karl Marx is discussed as an important author whose ideas have shaped many thinkers within criminology, particularly those described within the 'critical approaches' block. Thinking about the web of knowledge presented to you in this chapter, do some research on Karl Marx using the Internet and other texts you have available to you, and consider some of the aspects of the web of knowledge, including Marx's broad concerns, his explanations, the important concepts he presented, the evidence he based his work upon, and so on. This is a challenging activity, so just do as much as you can, and this will give you a sense for the wider context of his work, and how his analysis of the world came about. When the critical approaches in criminology are explored further in the next chapter, having completed this activity will make it easier to appreciate where some of the arguments have come from, intellectually.
2. Throughout the discussions within the chapter there are lots of concepts and ideas that are in bold. Go back through the chapter and write down all those terms in bold (the same term is repeated sometimes). They are presented in that way because they are important, and they will be encountered throughout the book. Try to define some of them, but do not worry if you cannot. As you move through the book you can come back to them, and add definitions. You can also start to add those terms in bold from other chapters, and end up with a long, but important list of key terms to summarise the content in this book.

CHAPTER CONTENTS

3 CRIMINOLOGICAL THEORY: THE *CAUSES OF CRIME*

Image 3.1

(*Source*: Tony Murphy)

LEARNING OUTCOMES

After reading this chapter you will be able to:

1. recognise and understand a range of 'aetiological theories' of crime that seek to explain crime in some way, the diversity of such theories, and some common features of different theories which link them together;
2. understand and appreciate the application of various theories of crime;
3. recognise and understand the implications that stem from the various theories of crime, in terms of how the nature of society is understood, and how crime should be responded to.

3.1 APPROACHING THEORIES OF CRIME

At the outset, it must be noted that this chapter is in no way an attempt to present or sum-up the entire spectrum of theories of crime within criminology, nor would it be possible to do justice to that in the context of one short chapter. Neither in fact, would this be desirable. The intention, as with this textbook as a whole, is to introduce some of the most important and influential ideas, by way of a foundation in criminology, and at the same time, not to overload readers (and therefore dilute the principle ideas) with too much content at this early stage of study. The emphasis should be on the contemporary use and value of theory, i.e. the relevance of the ideas for the world today. Thus, rather than covering all of the historical background and accounts, the chapter is mainly concerned with setting out briefly that sort of information, before moving on to present the ideas in the present context. This represents a different pedagogical approach (approach to fostering learning) to existing criminology textbooks where heavy detail is usually offered.

This chapter presents key overarching ideas that have shaped how criminologists have sought to explain crime in some way. There is a conscious effort to show how such ways of thinking about crime stem from different ways of thinking about broadly the same events and processes, although some theories are better suited for explaining specific types of crime. It can be helpful to think about the basic concerns and questions there might be in relation to crime, such as *why do people commit crime*? From there, think about the different viewpoints, and indeed common-sense ideas on the matter, and then draw lines to the actual theories within criminology. This is how the theories are introduced. Often, the starting point within such textbooks is the other way around; exploring theories in heavy detail in order to then arrive at the basic argument/s being offered.

When considering specific theories of crime, it is also important to think not only about what the key arguments are in explaining crime, but also the specific concepts drawn on, and broader matters such as the implications for criminal justice or responding to crime, and indeed what the theories suggest about the very nature of society. This is because it is not possible to fully appreciate the various ways of considering the nature of crime without understanding the context within which the various arguments exist. For example, how the nature of governments is understood – *a paternalistic and well-meaning force, versus a force representing the interests of the elites in society* – has an impact on how crime is thought to come about, why people engage in it, and also, what should be done about it.

The key approach within the chapter is using a limited number of blocks of thinking, or broad ways of thinking about crime, to show that despite the plurality of thinking and writing, in many cases there is overlap and connection between different theories whereby, they share overarching basic arguments. Approaching the theories in that way can help to foster an understanding of the most important points, without getting too bogged-down in lots of detail. It is a method for condensing varied and complex ideas into manageable key points. The five blocks presented are:

Block one: choice and decision-making

Block two: individual pathologies

Block three: social pathologies

Block four: critical accounts

Block five: integrated accounts.

3.2 ACCOUNTING FOR CRIME

There is no right or wrong way of approaching the above exercise, but your responses will probably cover in some way aspects of the points covered over the next few pages. From those broad ideas, the links to actual criminological theories can then be established. In terms of broad explanations for offending, common reasons might be:

- Social and economic inequalities that push and pull people towards offending. Perhaps there are no other legitimate routes for people to take to obtain things they want or desire.
- In some communities crime is normalised, and in such communities offending is simply part of life.
- People choose to commit crime out of greed, for their own personal gain, even though other paths are open to them, perhaps influenced by a consumerist society.
- Some people are somehow mentally ill, or even naturally more aggressive or cold than others, which causes them to engage in offending.
- There is an influence of alcohol and drugs, either desensitising people to their own actions, or creating a process whereby crime becomes habitual as part of alcohol or drug use.
- People commit crime because the acts are exciting, and give an offender some sort of 'buzz' or reward that they cannot obtain elsewhere.
- Status and achievement can be obtained through acts of crime, and thus crime is a substitute for mainstream success routes.
- Some people feel a sense of injustice or disrespect, and this compels them towards criminal action in response (protest, terror, etc.).
- Some people are actually criminalised through law-enforcement processes.

Other explanations are possible, but even in the above, it is clear how explanations can be incredibly varied and approach the matter of *why do people commit crime* in entirely different ways: some consider the decisions made by people, some consider individual traits, others social traits or conditions, and others consider matters such as processes of injustice. The next step now involves trying to work out whether certain explanations seem to make more sense in the context of specific types of crime and offending.

3.3 DIFFERENT CRIMES, DIFFERENT EXPLANATIONS?

BOX 3.1 ACTIVITY

At the outset, consider a very basic question: *why do people commit crime?* Spend some time thinking about this, and the following related points:

A. *What might cause **offending**, and how?*
B. *Do different types of offending need different types of explanations?*
C. *Do explanations need to change over time as the nature of society changes and things such as culture, the economy and technology change?*

Jot down a few ideas. Although it is useful to do this before reading the next section of the chapter, do not worry if you can only come up with a few points. The purpose for this is simply to get you thinking about some general explanations.

As described in Chapter 1, there are, broadly speaking, different forms of crime: some are acquisitive in nature, meaning that they result in some form of specific and tangible gain for the offender in the form of money, or an object of value. Or at least a would-be offender has this aim in mind. The other broad label, expressive, relates to events where such a specific and tangible acquisition is not the aim of the action. Instead, the act is a reaction or expression of some sort, usually involving violence or damage of some form, where that violent act is itself the desired outcome. Acquisitive crime can also involve this, but only as a means to an end. Considering this in relation to the discussion above, one argument could be that acquisitive types of offending, such as shoplifting, fraud, theft, robbery, and so on, could be best explained by considering explanations related to greed, or social and economic inequalities, consumerism, or other accounts which present an offender as seeking (perhaps *choosing* in a sense) to engage in crime. This is because of the likely gain they will achieve by doing so. The notion of an offender exercising choice might be considered here, but also arguments where little choice is evident given the lack of legitimate options available to some people/ groups, or the ways in which social environments have shaped their attitudes and outlook on the world.

Expressive forms of offending, such as violent acts, criminal damage, sexual assaults, and so on, could be linked back to processes that result from an individual being unwell in some way, or at least being acted-upon by their state of mind or mental health (even if this is temporary), and this results in the offending.

For example, what might explain an individual who randomly attacks a person in the street, without then taking goods from that person? One explanation could be that the attacker, for one reason or another, is acting out of rage, frustration, or paranoia, which relates to their present state of mind or being unwell in some form. Aspects of the individual's biology or psychology could be responsible.

Also, it is possible to combine some of the arguments, where perhaps the nature of what has happened requires different forms of explanation. Illicit drug use is a good example of this, whereby the use of drugs causes an individual to act in an unlawful way, in terms of taking illegal drugs in the first place, but also then, an addict may need to engage with other unlawful behaviours, such as burglary, in order to fund their drug-taking. This would suggest that on the one hand the individual is unwell in some way and this influences their behaviours, but at the same time, they are also making decisions to engage in acquisitive forms of offending. Equally, an act of robbery could involve the taking of possessions from a victim, and that forms an important outcome for the attack, but additionally, violence meted out in the course of the robbery might also be a welcomed out-come for an offender because of its excitement, the way in which it makes an attacker feel powerful, and so on. Thus, the acquisition gained from the event, and the explanations linked to this, would be relevant, as well as those explana-tions related to expressive types of offending. Here, it is difficult to employ just one explanation in isolation.

What is apparent also is that some of the explanations view individuals as having high levels of choice and freedom in determining their own actions. This can be referred to as agency. Other explanations view individuals as being shaped by forces around them, including social forces and structures, such as the economy and social institutions. Here, the notion of structure is important. Usually, social sciences dis-cuss these two concepts as representing opposite processes; one where individuals can exercise choice and power, the other where individuals' lives are constrained and shaped. In reality, people sit on a point in-between those two, i.e. some have more agency than others, while some have more constraints, but everyone has some form of choice and some form of constraints. Finally, some of the explanations give little attention to the actual role and functioning of the criminal justice system and the State, and so do not challenge the status quo. Others are inherently critical of all that, pointing to processes of criminalisation and control of the poor or specific marginalised groups.

Is there a need for explanations to evolve?

In relation to the final part of the activity above, clearly processes such as techno-logical change must be considered when thinking about the nature of crime. For example, the rise of the Internet and social media technologies have afforded new experiences of offending and victimisation. Also, the changing nature of media and culture cannot be ignored, neither can the nature of the economy and change with this over time, as the economy picks up, or we enter recession, and the impact this has on jobs, living standards and so on. And so the question becomes:

> Must our understanding of why people engage in crime change as the nature of society changes, and the nature of some crimes evolve over time?

Most likely, yes. Specific theories on crime directly explore matters such as the economy and culture, and how this can affect people in terms of offending, and so it is fair to say that such theories have value over different time periods, but also, that they may perhaps need to evolve to keep up with the specific nature of contemporary culture and the economy; while the same might be said of technology, politics and globalisation.

3.4 THE DIFFERENT EXPLANATIONS: INTRODUCING THE FIVE BLOCKS

Early thinking on crime: choice and decision-making

Taking a long-term view, different explanations of crime came into existence at different points in history, related to the nature of society at those points. This will be further explored when considering specific theories later in the chapter. However, initially criminologists approached the matter of understanding crime, and what to do about it, from a legalistic and philosophical position, in the context of society becoming more rational and bureaucratic. This coincides with the period known as the Enlightenment period, and particularly in the eighteenth century onwards. Explanations were focused around decision-making and rationality of actors (offenders), and legitimacy of the criminal justice processes. This is connected to the theoretical position of Classicism. This way of looking at crime has never really gone away, although it has evolved somewhat over time. These key ideas relate to Block one: choice and decision-making.

The influence of 'pathology' on thinking about crime

Next, influenced by the rise of science, criminologists began forwarding explanations based on the difference of, and thus the pathology of offenders; presenting criminals as somehow unwell or even subhuman. Scientific logic and principles around searching for regularity and rules, and applying the tools of scientific method became a prominent feature within criminology. This was particularly significant in the late-nineteenth and early twentieth centuries, but again, this has never fully disappeared. Thinking about crime in this way has remained in some sense, albeit in more sophisticated ways. This broadly relates to Block two: individual pathologies, where Positivism is an important idea ('Individual Positivism' because the focus is personal characteristics).

Then, in the early and mid-twentieth century onwards society, and criminologists, became much more concerned with the influence of social processes upon individuals. From this period onwards, criminologists have considered arguments related to communities and societies (including the economy and culture), such as the influence of social inequalities, disorganisation, and poverty. 'Sociological Positivism' is a common label for this type of approach. Such thinking continues to be very influential and relates to block three: social pathologies.

The rise of critical and integrated thinking

From the 1920s onwards criminologists were influenced by critical outlooks on the world, such as the prominence of Marxist thinking, and began to consider the issues of crime and justice from such critical positions. They began to ask wider questions regarding how society works; to the benefit of whom do the laws and criminal justice agencies work? Class became an important focal point of analysis, but later also, issues of race/ethnicity, immigration, gender, consumerist culture, religion, sexuality and disability. Each might be said to relate to processes of power, inequality, social control and criminalisation. Not all of this has been Marxist in its nature, but critical positions do usually owe something to that earlier analysis of society, where conflict and efforts to control and dominate elements of the population are important ways of viewing society. Such ideas remain very influential. This relates to block four: critical accounts.

Finally, criminologists have sought to combine aspects of those different ways of thinking about crime and justice, as a consequence of understanding the complexity involved, recognition that many of the theories do not fully account for events. Thus, these integrated approaches might view offenders in the context of both social and individual influences at the same time for instance, or combine those issues with a critical view, and so on. This relates to block five: integrated accounts.

3.5 MAPPING OUT THE BLOCKS

The following 'map' is a depiction of the question considered earlier, which is perhaps the most important one within criminology: *why do people commit crime?* Within this, common-sense explanations are fed into the most overarching arguments within each block.

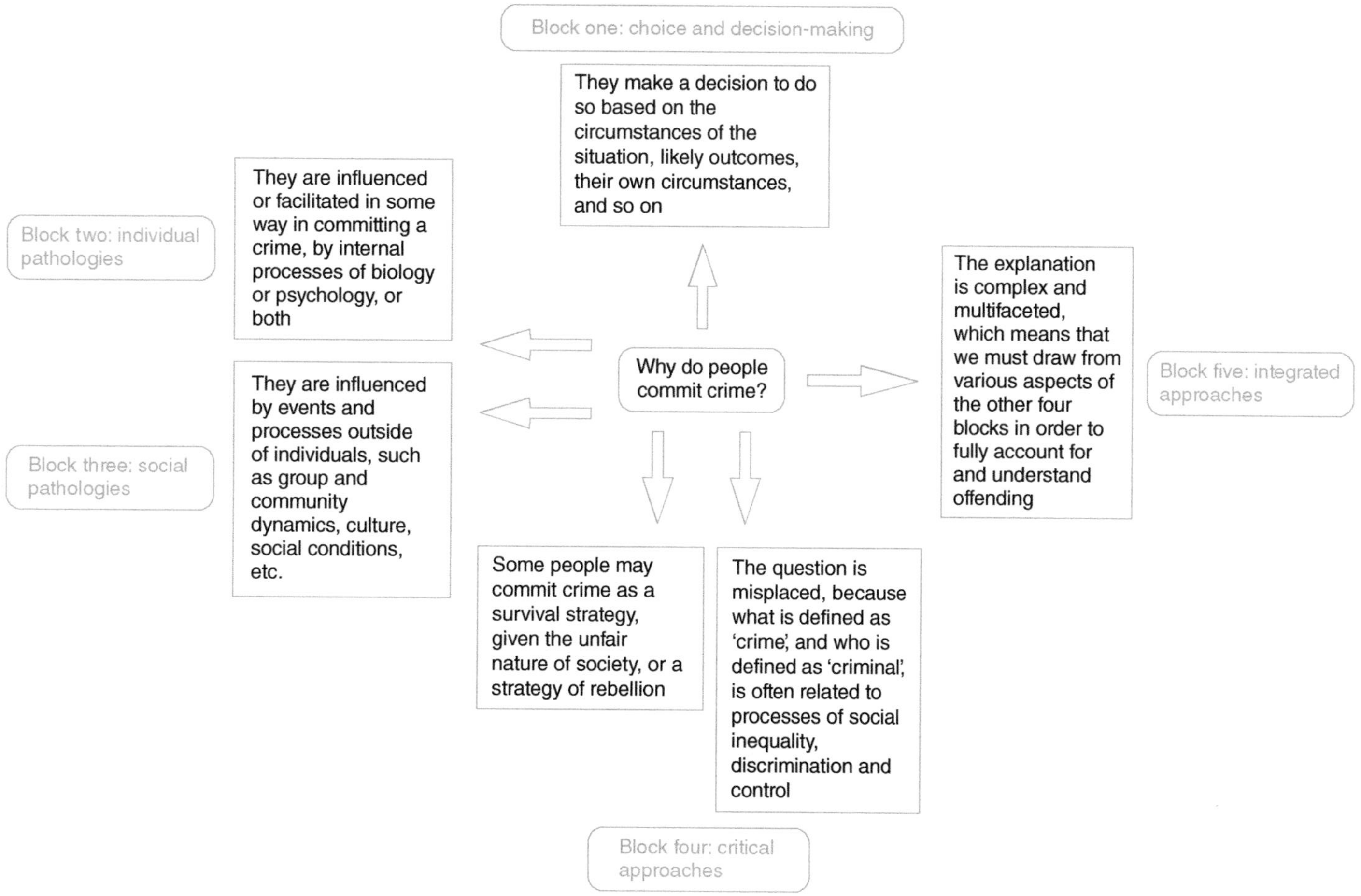

Figure 3.1   Why do people commit crime?

Block five: integrated approaches

The explanation is complex and multifaceted, which means that we must draw from various aspects of the other four blocks in order to fully account for and understand offending

Block one: choice and decision-making

They make a decision to do so based on the circumstances of the situation, likely outcomes, their own circumstances, and so on

Why do people commit crime?

The question is misplaced, because what is defined as 'crime', and who is defined as 'criminal', is often related to processes of social inequality, discrimination and control

Block four: critical approaches

Some people may commit crime as a survival strategy, given the unfair nature of society, or a strategy of rebellion

Block two: individual pathologies

They are influenced or facilitated in some way in committing a crime, by internal processes of biology or psychology, or both

Block three: social pathologies

They are influenced by events and processes outside of individuals, such as group and community dynamics, culture, social conditions, etc.

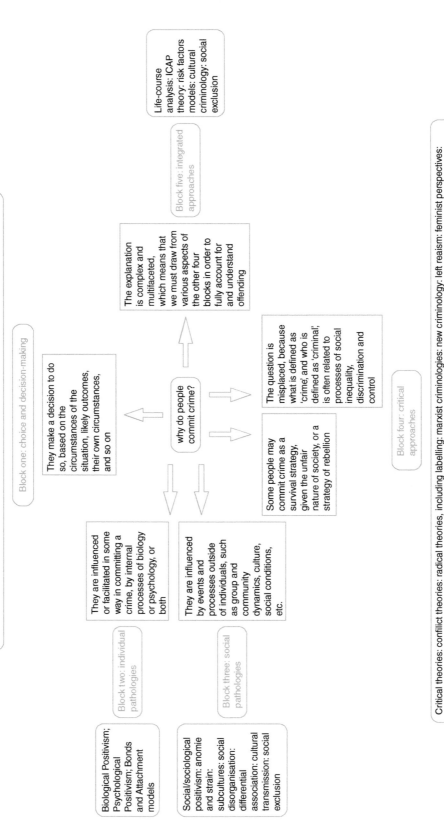

Classicism (traditional and modern); Rational Choice Theory; Routine Activities Theory; Time-Space Analysis

Block one: choice and decision-making

They make a decision to do so, based on the circumstances of the situation, likely outcomes, their own circumstances, and so on

why do people commit crime?

The explanation is complex and multifaceted, which means that we must draw from various aspects of the other four blocks in order to fully account for and understand offending

Block five: integrated approaches

Life-course analysis: ICAP theory: risk factors models: cultural criminology: social exclusion

They are influenced or facilitated in some way in committing a crime, by internal processes of biology or psychology, or both

Block two: individual pathologies

Biological Positivism; Psychological Positivism; Bonds and Attachment models

They are influenced by events and processes outside of individuals, such as group and community dynamics, culture, social conditions, etc.

Block three: social pathologies

Social/sociological positivism: anomie and strain: subcultures: social disorganisation: differential association: cultural transmission: social exclusion

Some people may commit crime as a survival strategy, given the unfair nature of society, or a strategy of rebellion

The question is misplaced, because what is defined as 'crime', and who is defined as 'criminal', is often related to processes of social inequality, discrimination and control

Block four: critical approaches

Critical theories: conflict theories: radical theories, including labelling: marxist criminologies: new criminology: left reaism: feminist perspectives: race/ethnicity focused theories: social exclusion; human right-based perspectives

Figure 3.2   Why do people commit crime (with theories added)?

Looking at Figure 3.1, start from the middle and move out in the various directions to arrive at a different way of explaining crime. The next step is to work out which specific theories fit in each of the five blocks of ideas. After that, the individual blocks, and some individual theories within those blocks can be explored. Again, the aim here is not to cover all theories within criminology, but rather, present some influential examples. In Figure 3.2 the same diagram as before has been expanded with the inclusion of individual theories.

BOX 3.2   ADDITIONAL INFORMATION

Notice how **Social Exclusion** sits within different blocks: block three: social pathologies; block four: critical accounts; and block five: integrated accounts. This is because social exclusion itself is a fluid concept, and has attracted different commentary and perspectives, and it can mean different things to different commentators. In essence, it is a way of describing *multiple forms of deprivations individuals and communities experience at once*. **Ruth Levitas**'s work is useful to consider here (Levitas, 2005), where she presents the different ways of thinking about social exclusion, ranging from viewing it as a result of unfair economic distribution, to viewing it as being connected to attitudes and morals of elements of the poor.

3.6 BLOCK ONE: CHOICE AND DECISION-MAKING

The starting point in terms of thinking about theory within criminology is the model of Classicism: crime is viewed as a consequence of individuals making decisions, and choosing to commit crime. Initially, this might seem like common sense, but until the Enlightenment period, and the subsequent onset of heavy industrialisation in places like Britain, thinking on crime was usually related to irrational, superstitious and often brutal social processes. Punishment was inconsistent and there was lots of discretion built into the system. Offenders were routinely viewed as being evil, or immoral in some way, and punishments were violent, but uncertain and disproportionate. The death penalty or corporal (physical) punishments were the basis of criminal justice.

The Bloody Code in England was a good example of this, whereby a sentence of death was linked to over 200 offences (for example see Emsley, 2010). In practice, most people who were sentenced to death did not have their sentence carried out, because it would have been impractical to do so. Also, the lottery of not knowing your fate even when sentenced to death, and thus the period of waiting to see if a pardon would be granted, was in itself a chief element of the punishment process. Punishment operated in a lottery-type system, whereby some of those who were convicted were chosen to be made an example of, and usually via a public spectacle. Despite this, the role of the death penalty, other violent punishments, and penal transportation, which was prominent until the 1860s, represented something of the ways in which society and the government thought about crime and punishment. Such systems were uncertain, unfair, barbaric, and above all else, ineffective in terms of crime control and lacking in legitimacy.

Writing in that context, Cesare Beccaria, and Jeremy Bentham, wrote about a need for punishment to be more rational and civilised in manner. Their writing corresponded with what many commentators have referred to as a period of history within which places like Britain, and other countries in Europe, became more bureaucratic and centralised in terms of how process of governance worked. Authors such as Norbert Elias (2000) for instance, describe a civilising process, which occurred as society advanced and the sentiments, sensibilities and civic awareness of people increased with this. Thus, we get to a point in history whereby putting people to death publically was no longer seen as acceptable. How we view individuals, and thus the nature of offenders, changed. Similarly, Michel Foucault (1979) also draws on the same direction of travel for punishment, particularly discussing the rise of imprisonment over death and corporal punishments. Foucault's analysis is very critical, in terms of promoting caution around thinking about the changes in terms of 'advancement', drawing on the pervasive disciplinary processes we see via modern imprisonment, and indeed other institutions within society.

BOX 3.3   ADDITIONAL INFORMATION

Although mentioned here, **Elias** and **Foucault** are not 'Classicist' theorists, but their ideas are discussed here in relation to demonstrating the wider context of crime and punishment in the period, within which Classicism developed.

Beccaria's famous publication of 1767 raised some serious questions regarding how offenders were viewed, and the nature of punishment in the period. Beccaria pointed to the ineffectiveness of the death penalty in terms of both dealing with crime, and the lack of legitimacy built into a system whereby punishments were brutal and disproportionate in nature. Beccaria noted that 'as punishments become more cruel, men become more ferocious' (Cockburn, 1994: 155). While thinking specifically about Britain, *The Times* newspaper a decade later captured the concerns of the period in terms of the reliance on death as an instrument of justice: 'a fierceness of temper, a hardness of heart, which places the inhabitants of the most enlightened nation on the earth infinitely below the wildest savage' (Cockburn, 1994: 156).

For Beccaria, law should not be repressive or viewed by society as being overly harsh. Instead, it should seek to be legitimate and *fair* in terms of how people are treated, regardless of who they are. In viewing offenders as rational decision-makers, the law should be clear and offer deterrence to offenders, without being overly brutal; which in itself would take legitimacy from the system (see Lilly et al., 2015 for a good overview).

Beccaria argued that justice should work on the following principles:

- certainty, punishment will follow a crime;
- celerity, punishment is delivered quickly once an offender is found guilty; and
- severity, whereby the actual punishment should be proportionate to the damage or harm caused by the offending.

Through functioning in such a manner, the system would then influence the behaviours of individuals, steering them away from offending. Bentham wrote in a similar vein (for example see Lilly et al., 2015), pointing to the need to understand offenders as rational actors, who engaged in behaviours, including crime, in order to maximise their own outcomes. People are fundamentally selfish according to Bentham, and they will engage in crime if the perceived rewards outweigh the perceived risks and punishment. Anyone can be a criminal, and anyone can commit a crime if the equation is right. In understanding offenders in that way, law should be structured in a manner to deal with this.

This means that a rational system of punishment should be in place, proportionate in how levels of punishment were decided, which people can understand and follow – and ultimately, be deterred by. But Bentham, like Beccaria, was critical of punishment for the sake of punishment, and particularly those which were brutal in nature. He understood imprisonment as a better means of punishment to manage crime. Deterrence is a key theme for such authors; it was better to prevent crime then have to punish people.

Modern Classicism

A Classicist way of thinking about crime and justice, as Bentham and Beccaria's work represent, has been, and continues to be highly influential in terms of legal thinking, and academic work; such ideas are crucial features of modern criminal justice systems. Criminologists in recent times have used the basic principles of Classicist thinking, and added to them to develop their own models of crime and justice. Sometimes labelled as neo-classical or rational choice models, these models have been important. In particular, authors such as Clarke, Cornish, Felson, and Cohen have added to the Classicist tradition. Their work has emphasised that offenders engage in crime in order to advantage themselves in some way. Crime is a consequence of an active decision-making process, whether this is the decision to commit crime at all, or specific choices made in terms of place, time and target of a crime.

Gary Becker, through his claim that people will commit crime if they see the outcomes as likely to be positive, and avoid it if the outcomes are likely to be bad (linked to Bentham's argument), is a starting point for key authors such as Ronald Clarke and Marcus Felson. Importantly, where such recent commentators have shifted the debate forward is through exploring the wider processes of decision-making, linked to individual factors. Thus, decision-making and rationality are then more complex than the early classicist thinking had presented. A good example of this is where Clarke and Cornish (2001) discuss the notion of bounded rationality, to describe how decision-making and an individual's 'rationality' must be understood in relation to their own resources, knowledge and their wider ability to process information.

Clarke (2018: 20) for example declares:

> the dominant model of criminology and crime control should be a neoclassicist, bounded rational choice model, which would introduce situational design and management changes to restrict offenders' choices and modify behavior. That change in orientation would open limitless opportunities for criminologists.

Another important development in the Classicist story can be seen within Cohen and Felson's (1979) routine activity theory (RAT). This, and other models that we might describe as being related to time and space analysis, demonstrate the decision-making and rationality principles in the context of specific crime events. Thus, the principles are applied to understand why crime might occur in a particular place, at a given time (hence time and space analysis), and against a particular target. Although subsequent re-working of the model has been important, famously, at the core of the model it is stated that in order for a crime to occur, there must be:

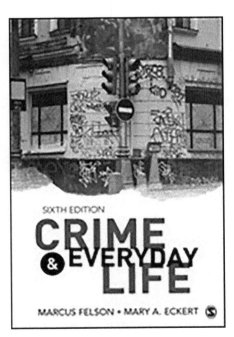

Image 3.2

- a motivated offender: chiefly (but not always) economic motivations for offending;
- a suitable target: a target of value, which can be removed, which has symbolic value, and so on;
- the absence of capable guardianship: the lack of people, processes or physical measures, which would otherwise prevent the offending, or result in the capture of the offender.

Critique

Although Classicist approaches are influential today, a number of issues remain regarding their value in understanding offending. They seem to make sense when thinking about acquisitive crimes, where clearly a tangible reward is on offer, and the complexities of an offence might be understood in relation to time, place and target. But the common critiques often point to ways in which a range of social influences appear to shape peoples' lives, including possibly offending, and classicist models tend to ignore these. The notion of bounded rationality helps in some way to deal with such criticism, but it remains that the Classicist approach is largely ignorant of social processes, such as vast socio-economic inequalities and marginalisation, which are surely important. The premise also that law should view individuals in an equal way, and with respect, is also brought into question when we consider the very unequal nature of many societies, where people are born and live in challenging environments, more conducive to offending. Thus, individuals might be viewed, in principle anyway, as equal before the law, but in reality, individuals in society are very unequal.

3.7 BLOCK TWO: INDIVIDUAL PATHOLOGIES

Subsequent to the writing of Beccaria and Bentham, and coinciding with a set of further shifts in society related to pre-eminence of science, the origins of the second block of thinking emerged. Positivism, which is an incredibly broad label applied to a range of approaches and ideas, emerged as an alternative way of thinking about why people commit crime, and what ought to be done about crime. Crudely speaking, Positivism is often described as a method rather than an actual theory of crime. This is because what joins much of the work together, is an approach of trying to study and understand crime in a similar way to that of the natural sciences. Thus, the approach entails searching for regularities and rules, forming laws, studying people in a discrete and isolated way as one might do with chemicals in a laboratory. The early Positivists, such as Cesare Lombroso, started to research about crime in that wider context.

The other overarching aspects of such models are a result of the very methodological approach adopted. In short, it means that offenders are viewed in a very different manner to the Classicist view; instead of understanding offenders as potentially anyone, given that people choose to commit crime according to Classicists, Positivists present offenders as pathological, meaning that there is something *wrong* with them that makes them offend. Thus, it is therefore possible to look to see who criminals are, and seek to understand their characteristics that make them different to the rest of the population. Offenders are then not rational actors. They are instead influenced by characteristics beyond their own control, initially biological and psychological in nature. The implications of this mean that thinking about deterrence and putting the emphasis on law-making and imprisonment are misguided, given that offenders are not acting rationally, and therefore cannot be deterred. Instead, the pathology must be treated where possible, and where not, the offender incapacitated through isolation, or even death. Thus, treatment or rehabilitation of some sort is required.

Image 3.3

Lombroso *(left)*, the most famous of the positivists, is widely criticised for his arguments and methodology, but the essence of what he presented remains important: linking crime to individual pathology. Lombroso researched via comparing the physical features of convicts with those of soldiers (populations he had available to him), and from this, argued that he could isolate the physical features of criminals. It wasn't that those physical features made people criminals, but rather, those features were outward signs of those individuals being atavistic – evolutionary throwbacks of some sort. Lombroso pointed to the facial features of offenders, allowing us to easily determine who criminals were; the scientific approach is concerned with looking for regularities and forming laws. Other writers, such as Sheldon, Goring, and Kretschmer followed suit in considering the biology of offenders. Sheldon's mid-twentieth century study of body types/shapes was controversial in terms of seeking to demonstrate the link between body shapes and criminality. Studies of twins, and other ways of assessing criminal genes are prominent within the criminological literature. See Lilly et al. (2015) to follow-up on these authors, and others within this tradition.

Throughout the twentieth century, a large number of studies sought to consider the basic claims within a positivist analysis, through looking at both the biological and psychological aspects of offenders, again trying to isolate specific traits of offenders. Those exploring psychological aspects utilised work in other fields, such as from Sigmund Freud and his psychoanalysis, where matters of gender and sexuality are important; Eysenck's biosocial approach linked to personalities; and social learning theory associated not with such as Eric Bandura, and criminologists such as Sutherland (differential association), considered criminal behaviours as being learnt through environments and cognitive variables. Another aspect of this block relates to bonds to society; families and social processes, or lack of them among offenders, linked to prominent writers such as Travis Hirschi. For a comprehensive overview of those ideas, again, see Lilly et al. (2015) and McLaughlin and Muncie (2013).

Despite the seeming complexity of all that, the key message is that in some way, all these arguments about crime/criminals (and indeed many others not mentioned here) are connected through the following:

1. Presenting 'criminals' as different to non-criminals in some way, and the term pathological is important here.
2. Therefore the 'criminal' and 'non-criminal' can be separated, hence differentiation.
3. There are influences on behaviours, beyond the control of offenders, biological and/or psychological in nature, so the term determinism/deterministic is used.
4. In responding to or dealing with crime, treatment, rehabilitation or some other means of dealing with the pathology must be considered.

Critique

Despite a raft of criticism concerning the value of seeing offending in such a deterministic manner, in reality, much of this is considered in the context of how offenders are dealt with by criminal justice systems, whereby assessments are conducted to determine the mental health of offenders, and treatment and rehabilitative programmes are used. Some would argue that such efforts are not emphasised enough within contemporary criminal justice systems. In considering the wider relevance of individual pathologies on thinking within criminology, some recent studies have pointed to their lasting value. For example, Walters (1992) presented a meta-analysis of studies (overall summary of findings), which had looked at the issue of genes and offending, and suggested that there was some link. Although the picture was not entirely clear. While in a study of Finnish prisoners by Tilhonen et al. (2014), it was argued that a significant proportion of violent crimes could be linked to genes. The authors of the study point to both low *monoamine metabolism* and *neuronal membrane dysfunction* as credible links to violent offending behaviours. More recently still, a paper in 2018 by Bondy and colleagues, even makes the link between air pollution and crime, noting the link in particular to less serious acquisitive crimes.

Work in this tradition remains contentious in some respects, because there is often a concern that through seeing people or groups of people as being pre-determined in some way, and different, this opens up the possibility for dangerous policies and attitudes. Such policies and attitudes could be within criminal justice, such as the targeting of groups and even physical interventions, and also more wide-reaching policies. Acts of genocide, eugenics (both related to seeking to eradicate a specific population), and the dehumanisation of groups has been witnessed in recent times, such as genocide in Syria at present, in Rwanda in 1994 and in Bosnia in the early 1990s, as well as earlier genocide and eugenics in Nazi Germany.

3.8 BLOCK THREE: SOCIAL PATHOLOGIES

As was evident in block two, many commentators have approached the matter of understanding crime, and thus, what we should do about it, from the perspective of viewing offenders as somehow being acted upon by biological and psychological processes. Within block three, the same overarching idea holds true, that is, the role of influences on individuals that shape offending behaviours. This time, however, a link is made between the social and the individual. This means behaviours are related to social processes, which could relate to matters such as the immediate environment around individuals, community dynamics, or even economic conditions. This way of thinking about crime and justice is usually labelled Sociological/Social Positivism, but there are a very broad set of accounts which can be included here, included anomie and strain, social disorganisation, and subcultures, masculinities, and so on.

Although the early seeds were sown for connecting social processes to individuals early in the nineteenth century through writers such as Comte and Quetelet, it was Emile Durkheim's (1984 [1893]; 1964 [1895]) work that has proved to be influential within criminology in terms of exploring how the dynamics of a society can shape crime. The concept of anomie was used by Durkheim to describe how individual's normative frameworks, and thus their moral regulation, can disappear as the nature of society changes; Durkheim was interested in the shifting industrial landscape. This may then result in crime. Durkheim viewed certain levels of crime and punishment as healthy aspects of a society.

The work of Robert Merton (1938), who, in the middle of the twentieth century, built on Durkheim's work is perhaps more significant. His formulation of anomie, which is usually referred to as strain theory has since been an enduring feature within criminology. He used the example of the 'American dream' – being able to achieve and obtain success, and the visible demonstration of this through things such as house and car ownership – and considered what happens when such culturally ascribed goals cannot in fact be obtained. One possible outcome is that individuals turn to crime. This can be applied more widely to other societies.

This presents offending as a consequence of individuals not being able to acquire desired products or lifestyles through legitimate means (conventional employment) because of a lack of opportunities, blocked routes to success, cultural attitudes, and so on. For Merton, it is not the case that the lack of a route to success automatically resulted in crime. Rather, in such situations there were a range of possible responses from an individual, and some of these were criminogenic: innovation is the most significant, where individuals seek the desired outcome but

Image 3.4

through innovative means (crime). Other responses, such as rebellion and retreatism could also result in crime, where they lead to actions such as protest and conflict in the first case, and drug use, for example, in the second case. Robert Agnew (*above*) has developed Merton's work. Within his formulation of general strain theory, Agnew (1992) considers other influences on strain beyond economic input, such as negative treatment by others, and the role of emotions such as anger and frustration, which come from strain in shaping offending behaviours. As with Merton, Agnew posits crime as one of several possible outcomes.

Much of that type of thinking is embedded within work on subcultures, and in a related sense, gangs. Subcultures within criminology are groupings of individuals who often adopt their own style and look, but more profoundly, their own values and norms system, which could be criminal in many aspects. Criminologists have debated whether such groups firmly hold on to these different values and norms systems, or whether group members instead drop in and out of them. In the most basic analysis, it is possible to think about the formation of such groups, and their actions, as a collective response to processes of strain they individually or collective might face. For example, work by authors such as Albert Cohen (1955) in the USA was pioneering in this respect.

Cohen sought to account for the formation of such groups among working-class youth. Such groups gave members things they could not achieve within mainstream society: status, respect and achievement. Cohen saw members as rejecting the mainstream values of society. Other authors, such as David Matza (1964), presented a different version of subcultures, arguing that rather than completely rejecting mainstream values, they instead still hold on to them because they drifted in and out of criminal behaviours, and they used techniques of neutralisation (stories they tell themselves to justify what they had done) often to downplay their offending. You can only seek to downplay your offending if you believe that it is wrong. Studies in the UK included work by authors such as David Downes (1966). In modern work, issues of ethnicity, gender, and masculinity are all important in understanding the formation of such groups, their identities and their actions.

Masculinities in particular offer a useful way of understanding violent behaviours of group members. Masculinities, and specifically hegemonic masculinity, describe the nature of being male and the dominant characteristics of 'maleness' within society. As Messerschmidt (2000) notes, this is related to being tough, being dominant, even being violent. Men seeking to live up to ideals of being male can become involved in violence in doing so, especially where individuals and groups do not have legitimate routes to demonstrate their dominance or respect through employment, and where there is a threat by other individuals and groups; e.g. rival gangs.

The Chicago School influence

Much of the above can be linked back to work within the Chicago School, given the intellectual and methodological influences it had. This was a body of researchers engaging in pioneering work around crime from the 1920s onwards, through which much of the work on strain and subcultures emerged. Important ideas around social disorganisation and others also emerged from it. Through adopting new methods within the sphere of criminological work, such as *getting out there* and researching the nature of Chicago in a manner akin to an anthropologist, the researchers were able to point to a number of important processes. They could recognise different parts of a city according to levels of crime, and started to ask questions regarding why that was the case.

Famously, the zonal hypothesis model (see Park et al., 1925) was presented, showing how crime varied according to location within the city. The mistake often made by students is to see the model as a fixed template that they should seek to apply to other cities if it is to be useful; this misses the point. The important part of this is recognising why crime rates are different across the city, and from this, apply the actual mechanisms that are argued to be the causes of this, not the visual template!

Cultural transmission of crime is one of those mechanisms, and in a related way, so too is differential association, linked with Edwin Sutherland (Sutherland and Cressey, 1947). In essence, it was argued that the different value systems evident within heavily urbanised, poor and diverse areas; the poor infrastructures; and the often lack of formal and informal social controls within areas of transient populations, created criminogenic conditions. In that period, these areas in Chicago received many people migrating from other places, and they were the cheapest to settle in. Where crime is concentrated, in the inner city, conditions are poorest and people aspire to move out of such areas, and so they do not emotionally or civically invest in them. Thus, social control processes are weak, and crime occurs.

Further to this, living in such an area, particularly those growing up in such environments ran the risk of having those antisocial and criminal sentiments and value systems, which existed in such places, influence their own attitudes and behaviours. In such an instance, crime becomes a learnt behaviour, but in the first instance, it has come from processes of social disorganisation, where informal and formal social controls are less effective than in other parts of the city.

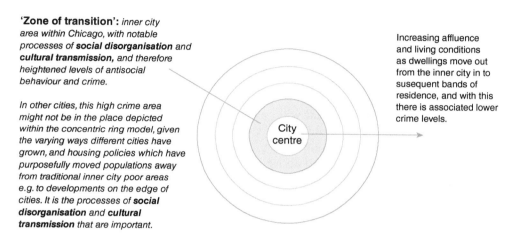

'Zone of transition': *inner city area within Chicago, with notable processes of* **social disorganisation** *and* **cultural transmission,** *and therefore heightened levels of antisocial behaviour and crime.*

In other cities, this high crime area might not be in the place depicted within the concentric ring model, given the varying ways different cities have grown, and housing policies which have purposefully moved populations away from traditional inner city poor areas e.g. to developments on the edge of cities. It is the processes of **social disorganisation** *and* **cultural transmission** *that are important.*

Increasing affluence and living conditions as dwellings move out from the inner city in to susequent bands of residence, and with this there is associated lower crime levels.

City centre

Figure 3.3   Zonal hypothesis model

Critique

More widely, criminologists are interested in economic inequalities and the impact they have on offending; much of that is actually reflected in the early accounts of social pathologies. Discussions of economic recession and social exclusion are common in recent literature, and the mechanism for how those things might influence offending often relate to the ideas presented with earlier social pathologies theories above. Social exclusion as a concept points to multiple forms of disadvantage that people face, and these tend to be connected to one another (see Levitas, 2005). Reviews of backgrounds of prisoner populations in the UK and elsewhere, for example, suggest a link between social exclusion and offending: Houchin (2005) demonstrates this in relation to Scotland; the Irish Penal Reform Trust (2012) shows this in relation to Ireland; and Ramaswamy and Freudenberg (2012) demonstrate this in the context of the USA.

The matter of economic inequality is a key feature within the concept of social exclusion, which appears to drive other types of inequality and deprivation. Although how such inequality comes about and what should be done about it is a moot point, as Levitas (2005) demonstrates in her discussion of the different accounts of social exclusion. Nevertheless, a review by Rufrancos et al. (2013) of the various studies and literature on the links between income inequality and crime concluded that changing levels of income inequality had a strong influence on property crimes, but for violent crimes this was less certain. This publication demonstrates the value in utilising such social-pathology thinking in relation to crime in a modern sense. Another key publication, *The Spirit Level* (Wilkinson and Pickett, 2010), explores the relationship between economic inequality and crime, and indeed a range of other social outcomes. The authors conclude that inequality is linked to all manner of negative social outcomes, including crime. This study also reflects how crime is not necessarily a process in isolation, but part of a wider set of poor outcomes related to economic inequalities (or social pathologies).

If crime is linked to social conditions and inequalities it means, then, responses must be more pervasive than simply the criminal justice system, as is presented in Chapter 10. Instead, policies that will create a fairer society, and reduce the extent to which people feel alienated, disconnected from one another, and in acute financial need should be considered. Yet this way of thinking about crime is not without criticism. Each of the models covered above attracts their own critique, but overall, the ways in which these approaches can suggest determinism of some groups based on socio-economic status or type area, is an issue. Also, why is it that some individuals face such difficult processes, but do not in fact engage in crime? Finally, can a process of rational choice and individuals consciously making choices be ruled out?

3.9 BLOCK FOUR: CRITICAL APPROACHES

What unites the many individual models of crime and justice within a critical approaches block is the fact that they are all *critical* in some sense in terms of challenging the nature of criminal justice processes, the treatment of specific groups within society, and the broader nature of society. Thus, such accounts might be described as being in some way normative in that they come from a positon of highlighting injustices and a lack of fairness. Models within this block may point to processes of economic and social marginalisation of some groups within society, and the need for them to engage in criminal behaviours as a process of survival, and/or perhaps as a process of reaction or protest.

They might also question the very workings and conceptualisation of the criminal justice system, highlighting how processes of criminalisation serve to marginalise or dominate groups within society. Class and socio-economic position more widely are important concepts explored within many of these accounts, and more recently, gender, race/ethnicity, religion, sexuality and other characteristics have also been explored within criminology to highlight differential experiences, treatment and outcomes we see in terms of criminal justice processes. On the matter of gender, a range of feminist positions sit within this block, owing to their highlighting and challenging of male-dominated or patriarchal social processes and institutions, such as the criminal justice system.

The influence of Marxism

The influence of Marxism across many academic disciplines has been profound, and criminology is no exception. Some of Karl Marx's (*pictured*) analysis has proven to be useful, for many writers, in making sense of crime and justice issues. For Marx, *Capitalism* drives the nature of society, creating dominant and subjugated groups. For capitalism to thrive, those at the bottom of society are exploited, kept in their place, and used to create profit for those who own industry and run the economy. The State might then be viewed as either directly a part of this or, at least, complicit in some way. Applying that type of thinking to the issues of crime and justice then results in some profoundly different arguments to those within the other blocks.

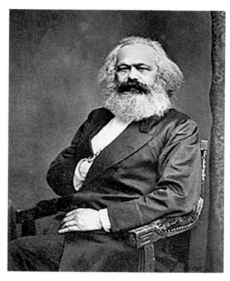

Image 3.5

Not all models within this critical approaches block are Marxist in origin, but they all approach issues from a position that inherently challenges the status quo in some way. The notions of power and inequality are important for all of them. Some of the models can be labelled as conflict, critical and radical theories, others are feminist, or race-focused, post-colonial, and so on. The number of labels used can become a little confusing, particularly because there are overlaps between some of them. For example, there are Marxist feminist models, while some models might be termed as critical or radical depending on what literature you read.

However, in short, such approaches often begin through an initial consideration, as a Marxist analysis does, of the role of social class in determining crime and justice processes. Those at the bottom are targeted by criminal justice processes in order to keep them in their place, and for some accounts, to maintain the functioning of employment and industrial processes, and deal with threats to the social order. All of that is needed for Capitalism to function according to Marxist-inspired arguments on crime. Thus, the law (law-making, the police, the courts, and so on) is used as a weapon within a class war. Laws are created to control the poor, and to serve the interests of the powerful. In such a climate, and the wider ways in which capitalism creates economic precarity for those at the bottom, and greed for all, crime can be both a survival strategy, and an act of individual greed.

There are too many authors to mention here, but it is worth mentioning a few at least. Turk's work, for example, considered class conflict and how this manifested itself within law and order processes (Turk, 1969), while the work of Chambliss was pioneering in terms of pointing to the criminal behaviours of the elite which the system ignored or was not designed to focus on (Chambliss, 1978). The work of Chambliss and others raises questions regarding who the criminal justice system is designed to target, and who it ignores. Others, such as those associated with the New Criminology in Britain (Taylor et al., 1973), clearly set out the links between Capitalism and crime, and criminal justice, including noting how crime was a logical outcome of Capitalist relations, and Capitalism determining the nature of laws, and so on. The New Criminology authors described the approach as more than just a way of explaining crime, but rather, a political project also. Yet, that approach was on the far *left* of critical positions; for example, presenting crime as a political action, and largely dismissing the harms created by crime.

Much of the above thinking, especially that on the extreme *left*, has been challenged for being idealistic in terms of how crime and offending are viewed, where the causes of crime and the outcomes are presented in an overly simplistic manner, e.g. with too much prominence placed on Capitalism, and too little focus on other factors, and indeed the effects of crime. The work within Left Realism (see Lea and Young, 1984) was a response to that critique, by taking a 'realistic' approach to the nature of crime. For example, they closely considered the impacts of crime on the poor, and the role needed for effective criminal justice processes, while still being informed by a critical tradition.

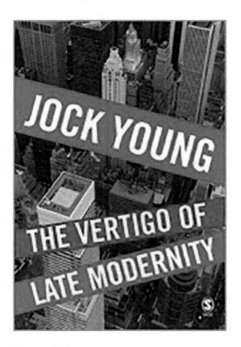

Image 3.6

Later, accounts evolved to move beyond just thinking about 'class' in a traditional sense, to thinking about other lines upon which society is divided and the characteristics that appear to shape lives. Thus, accounts introduced discussions of race/ethnicity and migration, pointing to discriminatory processes, such as racism, which means that black and other minority ethnic groups (BAME) are disproportionately targeted by criminal justice processes, and disproportionately victimised. The fact that prisons in the UK, USA and other advanced economies have greater proportions of BAME prisoners than their overall representation in society is possibly evidence of this. The issue of disproportionate police stop and search practices in relation to BAME individuals, is also often cited as evidence of the targeting of BAME groups. See Bowling and Phillips (2000) for a strong overview of race, racism and criminal justice.

Authors such as Jock Young, whose influential works include *The Vertigo of Late Modernity*, has been a leading critical author within British criminology. Young's work evolved through involvement with both the New Criminology and Left Realism, and beyond this, through later approaches such as cultural criminology (explored in the next section) writing about processes of class, race, power and marginalisation in the context of Capitalism and consumerism.

In parallel to this, feminist writers raised questions concerning the status, experiences and treatment of women within crime and justice processes. Feminism is a diverse area in itself, with many competing models, and it is beyond the scope of this text to grapple with it. However, it can be noted (generally) that it challenges the male-centred analysis within criminology, and points to the importance of thinking about women in terms of offending, victimisation and the workings of criminal justice processes, where their experiences can be very different from those of men. In this body of work, the treatment of women, and outcomes for them, are considered, and one broad argument points to the patriarchal nature of society, which serves to victimise women (see MacKinnon, 1987). Rumgay (2005) reflects aspects of this in her analysis of the close relationship between female offending and victimisation, for instance; most women offenders have suffered a range of victimisation processes, which might be described as being endemic within society.

BOX 3.5   ADDITIONAL INFORMATION

Others have written about gender but from a 'male' perspective, as noted in the previous section in relation to **masculinity**. As was noted, theories of this type consider issues such as culturally defined aspects of being 'male' and how this might create offending behaviours (**Messerschmidt**, 1993). It is equally as valid to place such theories within the critical block, as it is the social pathologies block, because this body of work represents a challenge to present social and cultural representations and processes related to men, especially working-class men. See also Connell (1987).

Labelling

The labelling perspective, associated with Howard Becker, also fits into a wider critical block, by virtue of how it fundamentally challenges understanding of what crime is, and how justice processes work. At its core, is the notion that crime is a product of social processes; reaction to behaviours (deviancy) creates 'crime'. This comes back to what was explored in Chapter 1 regarding the social construction of crime. It is the social reaction that creates the deviant or criminal and, ironically, that can itself create further problematic behaviours through creating a self-fulfilling prophecy whereby an individual takes on the label and lives up to it.

The social reaction can come about through a number of processes, but moral entrepreneurs who have a particular interest or reason for reacting against a particular behaviour can lead and direct the social response. Famously, Becker (1963: 9) noted how:

> Social groups create deviancy by making the rules whose infraction constitutes deviance ... deviance is not a quality of the act the person commits, but rather a consequence of the application by others of rules and sanctions.

Becker used the term 'outsider' to describe the individual who is labelled. Within such an analysis, it is often the poor, the marginal, or the powerless who become criminalised. Useful examples of this in practice include the unequal enforcement of drug laws related to ethnicity (see discussions of this in Chapter 7) and the antisocial behaviour agenda which has served to criminalise elements of the young and the poor (see Fergusson and Muncie, 2008).

Critique

Often, explaining processes such as offending, and the workings of criminal justice in the context of class, or linking injustices and exploitation to the nature of economy (the term *economic reductionist* is used to note how everything is argued to be a consequence of the nature of the economy, i.e. Capitalism), as Marxist analysis does, is often viewed as problematic. The value of talking about 'class' in today's world is debated, while pointing back to the economy appears to be a one-size-fits-all argument. Yet the essence of a critical approach cannot be dismissed, however we might think about class in a contemporary sense, regardless of how important we view the nature of economy to be. Contemporary events such as the investigation into the handling of the 1989 Hillsborough disaster, and subsequent cover-up (see the Hillsborough Independent Panel, 2012 – an exploration of this can be found with Scraton, 2016), throws into the spotlight the ways in which relatively powerless groups are sometimes criminalised and scapegoated for the failings of law enforcement and the State more widely. While more recently still, the Grenfell Tower fire of 2017 demonstrates how class still operates in modern Britain where the poorest can be victimised through State negligence and economic processes. The models related to ethnicity and gender are even more difficult to dismiss in contemporary society.

3.10 BLOCK FIVE: INTEGRATED APPROACHES

Each of the models discussed in the previous four blocks of ideas present particular ways of thinking about crime, but usually they each ignore some important considerations. There are some exceptions; for instance, when considering bounded rationality, there is a sense for how Classicist thinking might start to draw from Positivist work in terms of wider influences of decision-making processes. Yet, that type of synthesis of ideas is limited. This final block relates to thinking about crime where there has been a fundamental fusing together of ideas across blocks in order to offer a more comprehensive understanding of crime. A simple example of this is a paper by Murphy (2019), which considers Routine Activity Theory (RAT) in the context of trafficking and terrorism in South Asia, through reconciling the model with wider social, political and economic factors, which are usually not utilised within that model. Ordinarily, RAT is used to explain specific crime events, but the paper demonstrated the scope for a more expansive application of it, should it be fused with aspects of the social pathologies block. Other examples of such synthesis are much more significant, in terms of fostering new criminological theories. Some important examples are David Farrington's ICAP model; and related life-course analysis; and cultural criminology.

Cultural criminology, associated with Jeff Ferrell, Keith Hayward, Jock Young, and others (see Ferrell et al., 2008; 2015) is distinctive in terms of drawing on ideas in particular from the social pathologies block and the critical approaches block. Ideas related to strain and subcultures, and critical positions on law and order, informs much of the work within the model. This body of work also draws from media and crime analysis (see Chapter 8). Cultural representations of crime and law and order issues more widely are significant, and within it, the ways in which offending can become stylised and also meaningful to actors.

The influence of consumerism is important within this, given that consumerism is a profound aspect of contemporary culture and can result in processes of strain. But also, because crime has been commodified through film, gaming and media more widely, and consumption of such media can influence offending. The thrill and excitement of offending is also considered. Cultural criminology can be described as a form of postmodern criminology, also labelled constitutive criminology, which means that it draws together a range of critical and social explanations of crime, whereby:

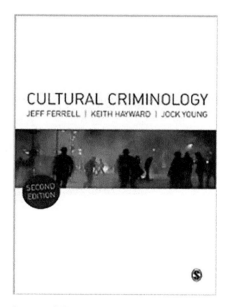

Image 3.7

crime and its control cannot be separated from the totality of the structural and cultural contexts in which it produced, nor can it lose sight of human agents' contribution to those contexts. (Henry and Milovanovic, 2013: 70)

Although seemingly quite complex, cultural criminology is concerned with the ways in which crime and justice issues are mediated (presented/represented), and the interaction of this with issues of power and control in society, and the outcomes of all this. It presents offending and law enforcement in the context of cultural processes, as both cultural products and outcomes. Thus, it can be possible to understand offending, for instance, where it otherwise seems irrational, as being meaningful in the sense of why individuals engage in it and what they are actually getting from it; the *thrill* or *buzz* of transgressing, for instance. However, for some, cultural criminology seeks to do an awful lot, and may run the risk of being too expansive.

The Integrated Cognitive Antisocial Potential (ICAP) theory is another example of an integrated approach seeking to bring together considerations of a range of social background factors, such as family background and economic position, along with personality traits. In effect, the antisocial potential an individual might have; i.e. the greater the number of risk factors of offending they have must then be considered in relation to an individual's cognitive processes in determining whether or not offending is likely.

This was developed from findings from the Cambridge Study in Delinquent Development (e.g. see Farrington, 2005). One potential problem, however, is that the research informing the model has been focused around working-class male offending, and so the potential for a wider application of the model must be explored, while the focus on risk factors also raises possible questions regarding determinism.

Terrie Moffitt's work has also been very influential in this vein. Considering the influence of biological and social factors, Moffitt's life-course persistent/adolescent-limited theory considers why much offending occurs relatively early on in life, but for most individuals, offending stops once they enter adulthood. Moffitt and colleagues' (2011: 55–6) work suggests the following:

- there are differences between how people respond to social drivers of crime, which suggests that there is some form of biological influence;
- some groups appear to be biologically vulnerable to criminogenic environments;
- crime is linked to families, and there are over 100 twin and adoption studies that show genetic influence on offending;
- the important biological drivers seem to be a process of being chronically under-aroused;
- for persistent offenders, brain-imaging research points to 'impaired communications between self-control areas in the brain's frontal lobes and emotional areas in the brain's temporal lobes', and this can result in deficient learning from punishment, lack of empathy and remorse, exaggerated reactions to perceived threats, and weak control over impulses, fear and anger.

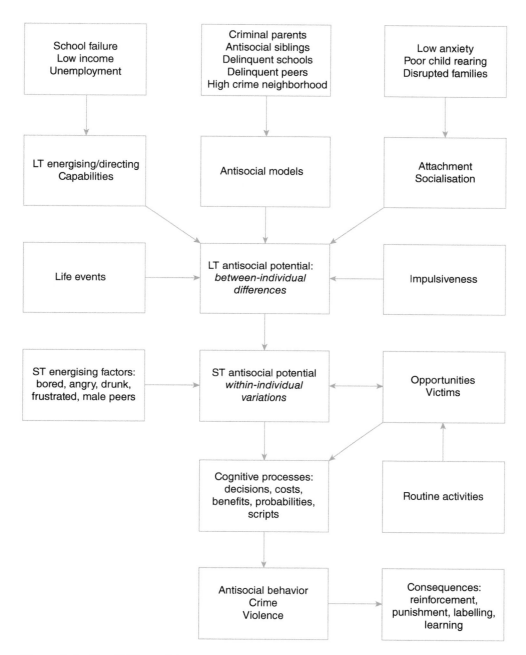

Figure 3.4 The ICAP model

(*Source*: Zara, 2010)

3.11 SUMMARY AND IMPLICATIONS

Understanding the 'causes' of crime is not a simple matter. There are wildly different approaches to the issue, and some explanations appear to be more relevant in the context of specific types of offending, and perhaps, different groups. Nevertheless, each of the five blocks presented within the chapter have been influential, and a range of different authors have considered processes such as rational choice; biological and psychological determinants; social factors; criminalisation and marginalisation; and a combination of those. Various accounts of crime link to the notion of structure, and other aspects link to the notion of agency. These are important ideas within the social sciences more broadly. In the context of this chapter, it means that some accounts of crime link it to individuals shaping their own criminal path in some way, through choosing their actions with a sense of freedom and power. Other accounts link crime to processes that shape the lives of individuals and constrain them in some sense; forces that ultimately remove aspects of choice and power from individuals (structure).

In reality, individuals sit somewhere inbetween those extreme positions in terms of having choices and some freedoms, but these are constrained or influenced to various degrees by internal and external forces. Some explanations of crime are critical of the status quo and the role and functioning of the criminal justice system, and the State, viewing it as a force for domination and control of the poorest and most marginal groups. While recent theories of crime have combined aspects of pre-existing models to offer a more comprehensive or integrative analysis, ultimately, how crime is understood, impacts on who is viewed as 'criminal', and what is determined as an appropriate response to crime; whether this is via the criminal justice system (Chapter 10), or more expansively through other institutions of society (as Chapter 11 suggests).

RECOMMENDED READING AND FOLLOW-UP MATERIAL

Read

- McLaughlin, E. and Muncie, J. (2013) *The SAGE Dictionary of Criminology* (3rd edn). London: SAGE.

(Use this to look up some of the key theories and concepts mentioned in this chapter – those written in bold. The more you can look up the better in terms of developing an understanding, but do not worry about completely understanding everything at this stage because it can get fairly complicated in places.)

Watch

- Robert Agnew's SAGE Knowledge video, 'An overview of general strain theory' available at: http://sk.sagepub.com/video/an-overview-of-general-strain-theory?seq=1? fromsearch=true

  (This presents a modern application/development of strain theory.)

- Dr Wanda Wyporska's video lecture on 'Inequality is not inevitable', available at: www.equalitytrust.org.uk/dr-wanda-wyporska-inequality-not-inevitable

CHAPTER REVIEW QUESTIONS

1. What are the different ways of explaining the existence of crime?
2. Why have the integrated approaches to understanding crime emerged? What do they seek to do?
3. Which ways of thinking about crime appear to be relevant today, and why?
4. Are different explanations needed for different types of crime, and perhaps for different types of people engaging in crime?

REVIEW ACTIVITIES

1. Create a map for one or more of the blocks of theory presented in this chapter. Start by writing the name of the block in the middle of the page and around this write out the overarching ideas that unite the various theories within the block. Finally, draw lines out to individual theories, the key points, and authors. As you learn more about some of the specific theories and models, you can then go back and add additional details.

2. Think about the types of policies that might help to deal with the problem of crime from the social pathologies perspective, including the issues of social/economic inequalities? What would they look like in practice? Do some research around current welfare benefits policies, and other social policies, and think about how well (or not) policies address inequalities, and poverty more generally. Here are some places to start your research:

The Department for Work and Pensions: www.gov.uk/government/organisations/department-for-work-pensions

The Joseph Rowntree Foundation: www.jrf.org.uk/

LSE's Centre for Analysis of Social Exclusion: http://sticerd.lse.ac.uk/case/

3. Consider the example of the English riots in 2011, which caught the public imagination and was covered by the national press over a period of time. From this it is possible to get a sense of how the same events can be considered from different perspectives. The then Prime Minister, David Cameron, and others, put it down to feral youth, and an antisocial culture among some groups, while prominent studies have pointed to processes of disenfranchisement and marginalisation of some groups. Others have described it as purely wanton criminality. Research the events of the riots further and, importantly, the arguments made in relation to the offending. Consider that there were different types of offending which took place, by different types of groups, and so consider this within your research. Start by looking at the following sources:

- **David Cameron's speech on the riots, delivered on 15 August 2011:** www.gov.uk/government/speeches/pms-speech-on-the-fightback-after-the-riots

- **The Guardian and LSE study 'Reading the riots':** http://eprints.lse.ac.uk/46297/1/Reading%20the%20riots(published).pdf

- **Joe Sim's paper: 'Shock and awe: judicial responses to the riots'**, available at: www.tandfonline.com/doi/abs/10.1080/09627251.2012.721974

CHAPTER CONTENTS

4 DOING CRIMINOLOGICAL RESEARCH

Image 4.1

(*Source*: ACMD, 2018)

LEARNING OUTCOMES

After reading this chapter, you will be able to:

1. understand the types of issues and aspects of crime and justice processes that criminologists might want to know more about, and why;
2. understand some of the approaches that can be taken to research around such crime and justice issues;
3. recognise the distinction between qualitative and quantitative data, and analysis and uses of each;
4. recognise and understand some key concepts and terms used in relation to the research process, and in researching crime and justice issues.

4.1 INTRODUCING RESEARCH WITHIN CRIMINOLOGY

BOX 4.1 ACTIVITY

At the outset, ask yourself the following questions:

1. Why do we want to know about/research around law and order issues?
2. What exactly might we want to know?

Doing criminological research is crucial in terms of being able to find out about crime and justice issues, and importantly, to effect change in some way. Chapter 2, which focused on the nature of theory, demonstrated how research was a key component within the criminological web of knowledge, and indeed, this is true for the social sciences more broadly. Academics, professional researchers and policy-makers of all sorts, engage with research, but as a student you might also be tasked with doing this at some point, whether this is small project work as part of a unit of study, a dissertation project, or even a research-based postgraduate course, such as a Ph.D. In fact, it is almost certain that you will. In short, through research activities, we can gather information about issues, better understand them, and potentially, impact change in some way. Revisit the web of knowledge set out in Chapter 2, and think about where theories and policies come from.

Students can often approach the issue of doing research with trepidation, and it can be overwhelming when confronted with the heaps of research methods in university library books and on course reading lists; not to mention the vast array of complicated-sounding terms and jargon used. But it need not be a scary process. In fact, doing research can be very enjoyable and rewarding. And just as described in the context of theory and, indeed, starting out on your journey through criminology more broadly, understanding the basic ideas and appreciating some of the differences of approach possible, is a perfectly adequate starting point. As with other topics in criminology, there is a tendency for authors to over-complicate things. To that end, this chapter seeks to offer a brief and accessible entry into the process of doing research, and within it there are signposts to more comprehensive texts dealing with *doing* criminological research, which you are urged to consult. See the reading listed at the end of the chapter.

This chapter is closely linked to the next chapter, which specifically deals with the matter of counting crime: *how do we know how much crime there is; who is committing it; who are the victims; what are the consequences*; and so on. That process of 'counting crime' is one of many different strands of research within criminology. Consider the table in section 1.4 of Chapter 1, which sets out different areas of focus within criminology and thus where research might take place;

ranging from the processes through which people stop offending (desistance research), to the nature of victimisation. When exploring the various examples and case studies presented throughout the book, think about how the issues might have been researched.

4.2 DOING RESEARCH: THE RESEARCH PROCESS

On starting out with research it is important to be clear in terms of:

- the what;
- the why; and
- the how of the research.

What is meant by this is that there needs to be a clear understanding of what exactly you are seeking to do – so this might be the specific aims of the research and the questions you want to address. Then demonstrate: *Exactly why are you doing this? How does this fit within the wider work in your area of research? Why it is that what you are doing is significant or relevant?* Finally, show how exactly you are doing this, in terms of both the broad approach to be taken, as well as detail of how the approach will unfold, including design, method, sample, analysis, adherence to ethical considerations, and so on. In general, the more of this you can clearly set out at the start the better.

All of that is important in terms of presenting work to others; for example, for your tutor, or for reviewers and editors for publication. Strong projects have clarity of purpose and approach, and they have some significance or value to the field. It is also important for your own sake, in terms of helping you to articulate your thoughts, to ensure the project has been given enough thought, and to ensure that the project stays on track. Arguably, the difficult part of doing research is often the initial brainwork required to determine the nature of the research and to plan it out in detail.

In terms of the way in which a research project can/should be approached, having in mind what the research process entails is incredibly important. Research in practice can be more complicated and 'messy' than initially imagined when starting out, but there is a general process that can be followed. In reality, how this plays out will be dependent on the broader approach and theoretical influences (for example, an inductive versus a deductive approach, or interpretivist versus positivist in terms of epistemology, and so on – don't worry, this is all set out later in the chapter). Yet it is possible to point to a general process that transcends this, as in Figure 4.1.

The diagram shows a sequence or order of activities, but there may be a need to revisit elements of this sequence as the research unfolds. A good example of where that might happen is when collecting data; a researcher may recognise that too few research participants may have been included, and then go back to collect more data using more participants. Thus, re-sampling could occur. Another example could be a situation where as data is gathered, there is a realisation that additional questions around a particular theme might have been asked, and so there is a need to re-design the interview or questionnaire tool being used.

Elements of the process set out in Figure 4.1 are explained within the chapter, including some of the terms used, but for now consider the text and arrows on the left; this comes back to what was noted about the research process often being more complicated than anticipated, and the need sometimes to go back a step, or a few. The term reiterative simply means back and forth.

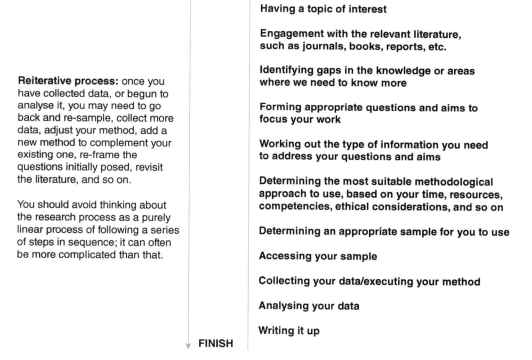

START

Having a topic of interest

Engagement with the relevant literature, such as journals, books, reports, etc.

Identifying gaps in the knowledge or areas where we need to know more

Forming appropriate questions and aims to focus your work

Working out the type of information you need to address your questions and aims

Determining the most suitable methodological approach to use, based on your time, resources, competencies, ethical considerations, and so on

Determining an appropriate sample for you to use

Accessing your sample

Collecting your data/executing your method

Analysing your data

Writing it up

FINISH

Reiterative process: once you have collected data, or begun to analyse it, you may need to go back and re-sample, collect more data, adjust your method, add a new method to complement your existing one, re-frame the questions initially posed, revisit the literature, and so on.

You should avoid thinking about the research process as a purely linear process of following a series of steps in sequence; it can often be more complicated than that.

Figure 4.1   The research process

At this point, it is worth defining a few of the terms used in the figure, and used elsewhere; they tend to be terms used fairly universally across the field when approaching research. These are purposefully limited in number here to avoid overwhelming you. These are arranged in order of the research process. Later in the chapter, in Table 4.2, the different methods and approaches are set out and additional terms are presented there within a much bigger list.

Literature: writing and commentary on a topic or issue, including academic journals, books, reports, blogs, experiments, legislations, and so on. This relates to the main ideas, theories, studies and issues in relation to a topic. It is important to engage with as much of this as possible when setting out on research.	Gaps in knowledge: where the literature on a topic is limited or has not explored specific aspects of a topic. As a researcher, you want to find and address gaps in knowledge through research; hence the importance of engaging thoroughly with the literature at the outset.	Question/s: the overall thing shaping research in terms of what is being addressed. This relates to a gap in the present knowledge on a topic. Sub-questions might also be used, which help to address the overarching research question.
Aims/objectives: a series of specific milestones to be reached within research, in order to be able to address the overall question. Usually, these are specific steps to go through to get to a point where the sum-total allows for the question to be fully answered/addressed.	Methodological approach and method: the actual strategy and tool used to collect data. For instance, the method could be interviews, and the approach could be doing them over a period of time, at different points in time with the same interviewees (**longitudinal design**: see Table 4.2).	Triangulation: the process of using several methods or collecting several forms of data in order to develop a fuller or more convincing set of results. If results from the different methods, or data, point in the same direction, then there can be greater confidence regarding the accuracy of findings.
Ethics: On the most basic level, ethical considerations can be thought about as a range of things to consider in terms of the safety, rights and respect of those involved with or connected to research in some way. In short, it is your responsibility to safeguard those things: for your participants, yourself, your university or organisation, the wider public, and the field of criminology itself.	Sampling: the process of determining who, or what you include within research, with some form of justification for their inclusion/exclusion in your work.	Sampling frame: the population, body of information, or database from which a sample is taken. This could be telephone directory, a list of social media users, etc. This can be **probability** or **non-probability** in nature.
Sample: the actual group of participants, cases, or elements of the literature used with research. This can be a **probability** or **non-probability** sample; and **representative** of a wider population, or not.	Case: an individual participant or item within a sample.	Data: the information collected within research. This can be both **qualitative** and **quantitative** in nature, and can be in the form of words/text, numerical information, images, sounds, emotions, etc.
Analysis: the process of looking at data, and trying to understand it and determine the key points within it. Qualitative and quantitative data often entail different data analysis processes. This can be done manually, or using specialised software, especially for quantitative data analysis.	Coding: a process used to help analyse qualitative data, whereby you move through text, images or sounds, and indicate common features, emergent ideas, and so on, within the data.	Themes: key findings from the data that seem to emerge from it through analysis, perhaps through using coding. These are the few key points that come out from the data. Usually, this is linked to qualitative data analysis, but can also relate to quantitative analysis.

Variable: a factor or dynamic within research, which is measured in some way. For example, participants' age, gender, class, ethnicity, etc. would be variables, so too would things such as levels of offending, levels of victimisation, attitudes towards the police, etc.	Independent variable: when research entails measuring the impact of one factor or 'variable' on another, this is the variable which is stable, i.e. thought to be doing the influencing. For example, exploring the impact of 'poverty' on offending rates, the variable of 'poverty' would be the independent variable.	Dependent variable: when research entails measuring the impact of one factor or 'variable' on another, this is the variable that is being affected, i.e. thought to be influenced by the other. For example, exploring the impact of 'poverty' on offending rates, the variable of offending rates would be the dependent variable.
Validity: this comes in several different forms, but in short, it relates to the extent to which the research process, data, and analysis of it, are accurate and represent what you set out to do. (See section 4.8)	Writing-up: the process of writing out work, and findings, and putting it all together, usually in a defined sequence or order, similar to the **research process**.	Publication: the process of research being made available to others through channels such as academic journals, books, blogs, and so on. Research then actively contributes to the **literature** on a subject.

Table 4.1   Key terms related to the research process

Finding a focus for your work

Good research projects are framed around good questions and a clear set of aims. The questions being posed can make or break a project in terms of its value and relevance, and in guiding the work forward. Similarly, setting out a few clear aims (or objectives) is important in terms of there being a few discrete steps to follow and achieve in order to be able to answer the wider research question. For sure, the nature of research questions can change or evolve over the course of the research, but identifying something suitable to guide work from the outset is important. Identifying something that is topical, novel, of contemporary importance, linked to ongoing issues or concerns, builds on the current state of knowledge around an issue, and so on, should be the starting point for work.

How to determine what is a suitable topic, and how to determine good questions to frame the research. Knowledge and understanding of a topic, an appreciation of the current state of knowledge, builds through engagement with the literature; the more time spent studying criminology and becoming familiar with the literature – the specific topics, ideas and issues – the better. That is especially true if engaging with the most recent literature, which tends to outline aspects of the current state of knowledge.

Reading the published literature is crucial, including academic journals, for example the *British Journal of Criminology*, books from module reading lists, and academic blogs, such as the LSE's *British Politics and Policy* blog. It is also important to keep abreast of government policy, reports produced by government and other organisations, such as the *Howard League*, which are related to your area of interest.

This will become more familiar as your engagement with the field increases, but module/course reading lists are usually the best place to begin, and consult your tutors for further suggestions. This is all about understanding the specific aspects of a topic you are researching around, and identifying the gaps in the knowledge that you can address.

4.3 ETHICS AND RESEARCH

Whether a student or professional researcher, research must be guided by an understanding and application of ethical principles. In fact, a university department will not allow research to be undertaken unless a consideration of ethical concerns is clearly demonstrated, and it is shown how a range of ethics issues are to be dealt with. Much of the research that students might want to undertake would be discouraged, and even forbidden; students wanting to engage with highly vulnerable groups, or research criminal behaviours at first-hand, are unlikely to be granted permission.

Also, as a researcher, and particularly in a field such as criminology, values are increasingly important as a source of guidance. We might think about values as principles that we hold to be important, and the standards that we want to uphold within research. This comes into research in terms of the purpose for conducting research; *why do it, and for whose benefit?* Also, this comes through within the aims and intentions for those to be included within the research, in relation to a wider sense of social justice and equality, empowering participants, and so on. As noted in Chapter 1, increasingly some criminologists view themselves as activists of some kind. Much of this is embedded within ethical principles and the values that shape their research; in a sense, where they are *coming from.*

Within the history of research in the social sciences, some notable examples demonstrate why thinking about ethics is so important, as they represented unacceptable levels of harm to those participating in research. Research ethics are crucial now, but this has not always been the case. One of the most prominent examples of that, with dire consequences, is that of the infamous Stanford Prison Experiment.

BOX 4.2 CASE STUDY

Stanford Prison Experiment

In 1971 researchers Zimbardo, Haney and Banks conducted a controversial psychological experiment to explore the behaviours of individuals placed within a negative

---

or coercive environment. The issue of how people responded to authority, and how power affected them, were important aspects of this. The basement of Stanford University's psychology labs was transformed into a prison and student participants were randomly assigned to be either a 'prisoner' or 'guard'. As the experiment unfolded, the 'guards', and those running the experiment, allowed things to get out of control, and prisoners were subjected to processes of punishment and abuse. Those participating (both prisoners and guards) began to become affected by the process and suffer psychological harm.

You can find out more about the study via: www.youtube.com/watch?v=760lwYmpXbc

A modern re-making of the experiment is available via: http://www.bbcprisonstudy.org/index.php?p=9

Compare that scenario of the Stanford Prison Experiment with the need now for every undergraduate student to produce a lengthy ethical considerations document in advance of their student research projects, regardless of how mundane the work might seem. And for professional researchers, the onus on ethics is greater, with a demand for them to spend even longer satisfying the various considerations around ethics before a department or funders allow them to undertake research. There are various Codes of Ethics that researchers use to guide their work, and students must also consider one of these within project work. Each field tends to have their own framework, and in criminology, the British Society of Criminology (BSC) Code of Ethics is the most likely one to be used. The British Psychological Society (BPS) and British Sociological Society (BSA) would also be of relevance, given the overlaps that exist between criminology and those areas. Regardless of the 'code' followed, the principles are essentially the same, insomuch as raising the same issues, and urging researchers to adopt the same sorts of safeguards. Usually, there are common-sense and humanitarian elements apparent.

On reading through those codes of ethics, and reading around the issue of ethical concerns more widely within the wider texts focused on research methods, it becomes evident that the key issues relate to:

- A researcher's competencies and development: as a researcher you have a responsibility to be prepared and able to conduct the work you set out to do. This means that you should seek the appropriate guidance, training and support throughout. You should be competent to use the methods you want to use, and if not, develop your competencies (through training, guidance and support), or adopt an alternative approach.

- Informed consent: those participating within your research should have a voice in actively choosing to take part. This means that they would normally sign a document, or give some other form of permission. Crucially, being informed means that participants should know what the research is about; what it entails; the consequences of it, etc. In practice, there are questions in relation to this, particularly when wanting to conduct work around illicit behaviours; doing observations in busy environments; where informing people what you are doing might influence their actions (e.g. in experimental work); etc. Sometimes, informed consent might be sought after the event. It can also be problematic to gain informed consent where younger or troubled participants are required, in terms of determining an individuals' capacity to fully understand.

- Right to withdraw: it is the right that people should have to pull out of the research at any point, even if they have already agreed to participate. This might happen for a number of reasons, but participants should not be pressured to continue in their participation if they do not want to, and you should make it clear to participants that they have this option.

- Confidentiality and anonymity: the requirement that the participants are treated with privacy and that they are not named in research; making it impossible to trace the research back to them in some way. This is important always, but especially so when dealing with sensitive topics. This connects to another safeguard, that of the secure storage and management of data you collect. This is important because in order to ensure confidentiality and anonymity, you need to make sure that any information you collect is securely stored, with appropriate strategies for managing who can access it.

- Storage and management of data: for instance, storing paper questionnaires in a locked cupboard in your tutor's office, or storing electronic items on a secure server or hard drive could be good strategies. This also relates to another feature of ethics, around not adversely impacting on the lives of participants in some way through your work, and/or the publication of findings. This not only relates to individuals you include in your work, but also to groups and communities who you focus your work on. You have a duty of care towards those you involve.

- Not adversely impacting on the lives of participants: this could be through intrusion in peoples' lives, or impacting negatively on them as a result of the research process, or publication of findings.

- Harm: of your participants (as witnessed within the Standard Prison experiment), to the wider public and to researchers, must be avoided. Harm comes in many different forms; including physical, psychological, emotional, social, and so on, but you need to anticipate the likely consequences of your work and do everything you can to avoid harm. In the end, your plans should not be carried out if harm is likely to occur.

- Criminal/illegal behaviours: your research should not entail you engaging in criminal activities and you also have an obligation to report criminal activities you might witness to the appropriate authorities. This is why research that entails you coming into contact with gang activities, organised crime, and so on, is particularly problematic.

- Giving false hope to participants: not promising to change participants' lives or have some form of positive impact that is unrealistic, and thus offering them false hope around the nature of your work and what it will achieve.
- The importance of giving something back to participants: whether this is updating participants with your findings, perhaps signposting them to support services related to the issues you are researching, or even creating pathways for their personal development and moving forward with their lives.
- Professionalism, integrity and respect: it is your responsibility to conduct yourself with the highest possible standards of behaviour, which includes being respectful of others and trustworthy.
- The reputation of your institution and field of study: you are the public face of your department, university, and field of subject, and that comes with obligations to behave in a proper manner and follow the rules and etiquette set out.

A good example of a project seeking to give something back to participants is that of the *Right Turn Veterans Recovery Project*, conducted by researchers at Sheffield Hallam University (Albertson et al., 2017). Within that project, the research team evaluated a drugs and alcohol recovery programme, in collaboration with related charities, designed specifically for armed forces veterans. Within this, researchers sought to both empower those who participated, and encourage positivity among the veterans. This also entailed treating participants as *experts*, who had the knowledge, experiences and the means for turning their lives around.

In revisiting the Stanford Prison Experiment, it is possible to recognise how safeguards such as getting full informed consent, offering the right of withdrawal, preventing harm to those participating, and so on, were clearly disregarded within that study.

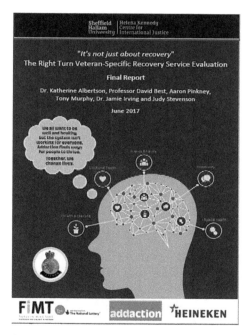

Image 4.2

4.4 EPISTEMOLOGY AND ONTOLOGY

The distinction between qualitative and quantitative approaches to research is an important one. As noted in Figure 4.1, data we gather through research can be either qualitative or quantitative in nature, or it is possible to collect both at the same time. On a very basic level, the distinction here relates to the nature of the form of data obtained; however, it can be more fundamental than that. You are urged at this point to consult the research methods texts listed at the end of the chapter to explore this in more detail. But in short, the way the two approaches look in practice might be distinguished by noting that qualitative work tends to be relatively small-scale in terms of the number of participants involved, and usually entails some form of detailed data collection, such as gathering lots of text or recorded discussion. And this data may not necessarily be representative of, or generalisable to a wider population. On the other hand, quantitative work tends to involve a larger scale, so more participants, but the level of data collected is usually less detailed or expansive, instead numerical in nature, but this is more likely to be designed to be representative of, and generalisable to a wider population because of the size of a sample and an expressed aim of being representative. These are crude generalisations.

Not only that, but this distinction also relates to the concepts of ontology, and epistemology. Ontology relates to what is the nature of *reality*, and what we can know, and thus how we can then find out about it through research. Whereas, epistemology relates more to what constitutes valid knowledge, and how we might actually go about accessing knowledge itself; so it is related to the actual knowledge-gathering process. Both dictate the type of research undertaken, and the methods employed. Thus, to study crime and justice issues, on the one hand it might be determined that it is important to approach matters from a position of seeking to understand experiences and interactions at an individual level, where it is not possible to understand phenomena without that level of detail. This corresponds with interpretivist and constructivist epistemological approaches. According to such positions, there is no one single reality as such, but multiple-*realities* exist. To get at them (to research topics and understand them), qualitative methods are needed, given their ability to obtain the experiences and insight of individuals, and provide rich accounts.

Or, it might be determined that it is important to explore issues by looking for trends, patterns and regularities, and thinking about processes above the level of individual rich experiences and accounts. And it might be argued that it is possible to be value-free within the research approach. This corresponds with a positivistic epistemological approach. Within a positivistic approach, a single *reality* is considered, and to get at this (to research it) quantitative methods are employed, which are designed to collect structured numerical data, on a representative and generalisable scale. There are of course other approaches, such as a pragmatic approach and a critical approach. All of this relates to what is described in Table 4.2 around inductive, deductive and abductive research designs. Generally speaking, quantitative approaches are more likely to be positivistic in nature and foster a deductive research design, and a qualitative approach is more likely to be interpretivist, constructivist or critical in nature, and foster an inductive approach.

4.5 CHOOSING A RESEARCH APPROACH/METHOD

When approaching doing research in criminology, it is necessary to approach this from the attitude of seeking to employ the research method or instrument best suited to the specific nature of project in question. Depending on what it is the research is focused on, and the aspects of it to be explored, specific types of information or data are sought. That specific type of information or data can be obtained through specific methods, and therefore it is necessary to use the relevant method/s. There might be more than one method that can offer the information required, and in that instance, the most practical or achievable method should be chosen, based on the available resources, expertise and experiences, consideration of ethics, and so on. It might be the case that several methods can be employed together to develop a stronger evidence-base, and to provide mutual support for the methods employed. Triangulation is a term often used whereby different methods, or different data types, can be collected with the aim of building a more comprehensive and convincing evidence-base.

Within Figure 4.2, a range of different methods (not exhaustive) are presented. Startling from left to right, there is media analysis work drawing on news-media outputs, and also social media posts/data; analysis of existing datasets; literature-based work drawing on published work, including a literature synthesis approach, or discourse analysis; experimental work of some form; interviews and survey work (questionnaires), both structured and loosely structured; focus groups, bringing together a range of people together at one time to explore issues; observation work of some form, whereby phenomena are observed, from the outside, or through being

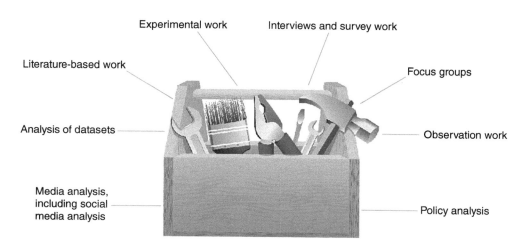

Figure 4.2   The methodological 'toolbox'

actively engaged within the phenomena, and this also links to the wider approach of ethnographic work; and policy analysis, whereby the outcomes or effects of specific policies are assessed. These tend to be the common types of methods used in criminological research.

Researchers may often favour specific methods or approaches, and they become experts within that. But when setting out as a student, knowing how to do different types of research, and employ different methods, is important, and this helps to safeguard against the research undertaken being shaped simply on the basis of starting out with wanting to employ a particular method. Ideally:

> Start from the research questions and aims, and from there work out the type of data required to address them, and therefore go to the actual method/s best suited to those ends.

Table 4.2 below is a brief overview of different research methods and approaches available within criminology; in which contexts you might want to think about using them; and their strengths and limitations. This is not exhaustive, but it covers most of the methods within published work, and most of the methods of relevance within student project work. Use this information in tandem with the suggested research methods texts listed at the end of the chapter. Be aware that some of the entries will overlap, that is, a particular approach, such as an inductive approach can be taken, and this might entail using a specific method to achieve it, for instance, interview work, and this could for instance, be a snapshot design.

It is common for studies to adopt more than one method, in order to collect more than one type of data. This could be to address different aims within the same study for instance. A recent study which reflects this is that carried out by Lorraine Gelsthorpe and colleagues (Gelsthorpe et al., 2012; Philips et al., 2017; *image right*). This aimed to explore the prevalence of deaths following release from State custody, used two main methods. The first was quantitative analysis of data collected and collated by the government. The data were analysed in order to identify the main risks that are correlated with dying after release from prison or police detention. The second method of data collection was interviews with key stakeholders.

the Howard League for **Penal Reform**

Deaths on probation

An analysis of data regarding people dying under probation supervision

Image 4.3

Method	Details	When to use	Strengths	Possible issues
Interview work	Can be **structured** to varying degrees, meaning that it can be as rigid or loose as desired in terms of the questions asked and the process followed – with varying outcomes.	Used extensively across most topics. Useful particularly when getting at the attitudes, knowledge and experiences of people or groups on specific issues.	Direct way of getting at the attitudes, knowledge and experiences of your target group.	Possible difficulty of accessing your target group; how the interview unfolds can affect the results; asking the *right* questions is key.
Survey/ questionnaire	*As above.* The term 'survey' simply means accessing many participants to get a broad coverage of a population. Usually short interviews or self-completion forms. They can be administered in person, online, through the post.	*As above*	Can include many more participants than through standard interview work. They can be done remotely so participants might be more willing to divulge sensitive information.	*As above.* There is less time per participant, and participants cannot always be aided to complete. Completion rate can be low. Hard to develop **rapport** to aid information flow.
Focus group	Usually a group discussion format, whereby specific questions or issues trigger discussions. Can be rigid or loose in format.	*As above.* Usually where circumstances, time, resources, do not allow for engaging with people individually.	Include several people's voices quickly, and gather lots of data in one hit. Nervous participants might engage if they are with peers.	Potential **social desirability effect:** people might be less likely to be honest in front of others. Group dynamics might lead to a few dominant voices.
Media analysis	Obtaining and analysing data from media platforms, such as newspapers. **Content analysis** is an example of this.	Exploring news-media coverage of crime and justice issues; the way specific events and groups are represented.	Only way of accessing some types of information, e.g. media accounts. Databases exist to aid you.	Which news-media elements, and time period? The importance of the search terms used to search databases.
Social media analysis	Obtaining and analysing data from social media platforms, such as Twitter and Facebook. **'Scraping'** is a specific method.	Attitudes towards specific events and groups; exploring illicit activities online; hate crime, etc.	Accessing hidden views. The spread of social media means it is a tool for accessing many participants.	Problems of taking comments as truthful; accessing non-public discussions; and informed consent.
Literature review/ synthesis	Drawing together the range of published accounts, studies and ideas on an issue: physical print items and online materials.	When wanting to know the state of knowledge on a subject, and the overall findings from the research available.	Fairly straightforward, without the need to actively collect data. Safer approach (ethics) for sensitive topics.	Dependent upon the necessary information having been collected. What to include, and to exclude?
Secondary data analysis	Analysing a bunch of data (a data-set) that has been previously created, normally by someone else. For example, analysing data from the CSEW.	Exploring trends and patterns where collecting enough data yourself would be difficult. Exploring links between crime and various variables; fear of crime; victimisation, and so on.	Allowing analysis that is otherwise impossible given the scale/numbers involved. Fewer ethical issues.	You have not collected the data, so does it reflect what you wanted to find out, or is it a compromise? Technical competencies required.

(Continued)

Table 4.2 (Continued)

Method	Details	When to use	Strengths	Possible issues
Experimental work	Where the researcher makes some form of intervention, in order to measure the effects of this. The intervention could be made to an individual or an environment/situation.	Understanding impacts of situations on behaviours, often using a **control group**. Useful when exploring norms/reactions to situations, e.g. Stanford Prison Experiment.	Gives opportunity to directly test or measure impacts of events, situations or a stimulus on how people behave; not just taking their word on it.	Risk of ethical dilemmas; measuring artificial results because you have manipulated events (they are not natural); practical difficulties.
Natural experiment	Utilising changing events, such as new laws, which create the opportunity to consider impact on outcomes such as crime given the 'before' and 'after' situations which have been naturally created.	Considering the effect of changes to law, policy-making and social circumstances, on things such as crime rates, sentencing practices, offender outcomes, etc.	Experimental conditions created without you having had to intervene in some way. Can be large scale 'experiments' to utilise, such as new laws.	Measuring the effects of the changes might be difficult, with lag times, unintended consequences/outcomes which are not considered, etc.
Observation	Watching or observing situations or groups. Can be observational only or involve **participation**; engaging with the group/behaviours being studied. Can also be **overt** or **covert**. Links to **ethnographic** work.	Where there is a need to actually watch a group or phenomenon, in order to understand them/their behaviours. Useful for work on subcultures, gangs, criminal justice institutions, etc.	Some processes might only be explored through watching, listening and taking in the atmosphere. It would otherwise be difficult to explain, describe, or properly capture the full data.	Ethical issues, especially for covert work; danger of shaping behaviours via your presence, and impacting on a group more generally; witnessing illegal behaviours.
Ethnographic work	Methods can be 'ethnographic' if they involve sustained and deep engagement with a research subject, e.g. being in an environment you are researching over a period of time, taking in what you see, hear, feel, etc.; extended interviewing.	Where there is a need to spend time within a setting in order to properly understand, and for the group to be comfortable enough for you to view them in a more **natural** state. Useful for work on gangs, subcultures, institutions, etc.	As above. Understanding certain behaviours lends itself less to interview/survey work than others might. Getting at the lived experiences and feelings, and gathering very detailed data.	As above, especially in relation to ethics. Time-heavy; difficulty in negotiating access/prolonged participation of those being researched.
Policy analysis/evaluation	Exploring the nature of specific policies, their context, aims, processes and outcomes. Can be a literature-based process where pre-existing information exists, or, entail generating new data.	To assess specific policies or areas of policy in relation to punishment, law enforcement processes, effects of social policies on crime, etc.	A way of determining the success of CJS and broader policies on a wider scale. Frameworks for analysis are available.	Which points are you evaluating on the basis of? Possible lag time for the full effects of policies to be witnessed. Is the information you need available for you to be able to evaluate?

Method	Details	When to use	Strengths	Possible issues
Comparative work	Seeking to compare the situation in different places or amongst different groups.	Topics such as comparing patterns of offending, punishment, and attitudes, the wider social and cultural contexts in different countries, etc.	Offers scope for determining wider trends and patterns beyond a single country or situation.	Determining your choice of cases for comparison. Availability of the same information for each case; comparability of measures?
Longitudinal design	Research focused on looking at events over time, such as social attitudes, or crimes rates. Measurements are taken from different points in time.	To consider change over time, or follow a group over a period of time, e.g. on changing social attitudes; desistance from offending, etc.	The only way of looking at changes over time, and gives scope for considering patterns and trends.	Ensuring direct comparisons, i.e. using the same measures or the same at each point in time; sometimes 'proxies' have to be used.
Snapshot/cross-sectional design	Focusing research on one moment in time, to consider things at that point.	Most topics in criminology where understanding processes at just one point in time is adequate.	Relatively straightforward to do.	What is the significance of the point in time chosen; is it 'normal' or atypical?
Inductive approach	Setting out to **create new knowledge**, without (in theory) letting pre-existing theories shape your work. Linked often to **qualitative** methods, and an **interpretivist** or **constructivist** approach.	When seeking to create new explanations. Starting the research process with the aim of collecting data to then inform the development of an explanation or theory. Linked to **grounded theory**.	Meant to prevent pre-existing ideas determining the findings; the ideas emerge from the data itself.	How possible is it to be completely devoid of intellectual influence? The questions asked, topics covered, etc. are all surely *leading*, to some extent, what we do, and thus find?
Deductive approach	Setting out to test **existing knowledge** from an existing theory or explanation. Linked to **quantitative** methods, and a **positivistic** approach.	When starting research with a theory or model in mind to be tested or developed. Often involving a hypothesis.	Ability to test theories or ideas, perhaps in a new context, in a new period of history, etc.	The danger of bias because work has been actively shaped by the ideas at the start, perhaps omitting other ideas.
Abductive approach	This is a comprised version of inductive and deductive approaches, which is a more **pragmatic** approach.	Starting with data or information regarding phenomena, and then moving to the creation of a new, most likely, hypothesis or explanation to further guide the research.	Can potentially deal with the weaknesses of inductive and deductive approaches.	Difficult to actively distinguish and employ this approach in practice.

Table 4.2 Approaches and methods in criminological research

The researchers interviewed a range of experts in the field including prison officers, coroners, and police custody sergeants in order to identify the main practice and policy issues surrounding these deaths. The data shed light on how practitioners can and cannot work to reduce such deaths. The study is also a good example of how the process of dealing with ethics can work in practice. For example, the study needed approval by the HMPPS national research committee, which ensured all ethical concerns had been dealt with. These issues were mainly around re-traumatising practitioners who had worked with people who had subsequently died, and because of the small sample involved there was a risk of identifying participants or deceased people.

BOX 4.3   ACTIVITY

Access the report from Gelsthorpe et al. (2012) published via the Howard League for Penal Reform https://howardleague.org/wp-content/uploads/2016/05/Deaths-on-probation.pdf

Think about how the researchers set out the *what*, the *why*, and the *how*, in relation to their study.

4.6 SAMPLING

Regardless of the method employed, or the broader methodological approach taken, sampling is always a crucial feature. In short, this is related to choosing what or who is needed to include within the work, and then having a strategy for getting it/them. Often, the term access is used to label the process undertaken to get to the research participants or elements. For example, access to groups of people could be achieved, depending on who you think you need to include, through a range of different processes; using telephone or voting registers, or social media user lists; approaching people in a particular place at a particular time, such as on a high street; through putting out requests for participation, including your information or access to the research tool (such as a URL link to a questionnaire) on a public noticeboard, on forums etc.; or through library search engines and databases in the instance of literature-based projects.

The sampling frame is very important because this is the list or collection of possible participants or elements for a study, from which specific cases are chosen. This needs to be carefully chosen, and so too, is how exactly participants will be accessed; this ultimately influences what the data will eventually look like. If doing survey work, access to lots of people is required, and ideally, a sample that is as representative of the broader population as is possible in order that findings can be generalised to the wider population. Conversely, if doing in-depth interview work, fewer participants are required, and although some diversity within a sample might be sought related to dynamics such as gender, ethnicity and age, there is usually less concern for a representative sample and generalisable results.

Access to a sample can be fairly straightforward where open-access lists and contact details exist, or where simply stopping people in the street is sufficient. But generally, the more specific research becomes, and the more sensitive or serious the issues become, then the more problematic it is. The participants required might be accessible through specific organisations, or a lead contact, sometimes known as a gate-keeper, who can aid access to participants, or block this. Also, as an undergraduate student, it is more than likely that access to people in secure environments, such as prisons, or to access vulnerable groups, such as victims of serious crimes, will be unfeasible.

There is a range of different sampling strategies, but crudely, these can be split between probability- and non-probability-based sampling. The first is where the cases within a sampling frame have a defined probability of being selected, e.g. every person in a list has a one in ten chance of inclusion, and an effective strategy for picking each case based upon that is employed – such as jumbling all names up in a hat and drawing out names until you have enough. Thus, selection is done on the basis of random selection (random in terms of not biasing the selection). In the instance of non-probability sampling, picking is done haphazardly or at will, or through using a convenience method, such as stopping people in the street, or using people who you have direct access to already. Or, a more systematic process can be used, e.g. picking every tenth person from a list, whereby not every case then has the same chance of being picked because it depends from which point you start picking and the interval used.

The distinction between random and non-random sampling is important. Within a random sample, the possibility of inclusion is random in the sense that the likelihood of inclusion is not biased. Stopping people in the street is not truly random, because you have limited who can be included by choice of location and time. Ideally, every relevant possible case for the sample will have a known probability of inclusion. In practice this can be very difficult to achieve because of the range of influences and variables at work; true random sampling is, arguably, almost impossible. Thus in practice, stratified sampling can be used, whereby effort is made to at least randomly sample within the different segments of a population to ensure that there is some appropriate diversity within a sample. Or, cluster sampling can be used, where similarly, some form of random sampling is attempted but only within some specific defined clusters, or specific groups deemed to be important to include.

Non-probability, and thus, non-random sampling, might instead be used. Typically within this, the approach of quota sampling could be used, whereby it is worked out from the total sample size, how many of a particular group need to be included within the research in order to at least try to offer inclusion of an important subgroup, or sub-groups. The process of getting them is not a random one. Alternatively, a less rigid form of sampling, that of purposive sampling, could be used, typically seeking to include a specific sub-section of a population deemed to be relevant to your study, and targeting them specifically. Convenience sampling is the least rigid of all, which simply relates to picking who you can. A good example might be stopping who you can on a high street, and who is willing to participate, or using students in your university who you have easy access to. Finally, snowball sampling is another option, whereby one participant leads to another, such as interviewing one person, who then suggests a contact who also has experience of the same issue being researched. That can be useful when researching very specific issues, taboo subjects, illicit networks, and so on.

4.7 RESEARCH VALIDITY

On the most basic level, research validity is related to the extent to which the research process, data, and analysis of it, are accurate and represent what you set out to do. Sometimes, the terms faithfulness or truthfulness are used within the literature around this. There are a number of aspects related to validity, or different forms of validity. At this point in your studies it is easy to get bogged-down with the array of specialised jargon, but there are a number of forms of validity to be aware of; it is not vital that you commit these to memory, but recognise that validity relates to the different aspects of the research process. The following are useful as a point of refer-ence, and they can be followed-up on in more specialised texts (e.g. Jupp, 2014). The forms include: external validity; internal validity; criterion validity; content validity; construct validity; concurrent validity; and face validity. Some of these are more explicitly relevant to quantitative approaches.

The notion of reliability is one of the more important aspects of validity that you do need to commit to memory. This is the extent to which the work can be replicated or repeated and yield the same results. If that happens then it is likely that the research process was successful in properly measuring what you set out to do, if not, then perhaps the results obtained are a consequence of the way the research was implemented; and this contaminated the outcomes in some way.

4.8 SUMMARY AND IMPLICATIONS

Although knowledge on crime and justice issues can sometimes be taken for granted, this in fact comes from a process of researching that can be complicated in nature, and fraught with all manner of difficulties and ethical dilemmas. Developing crimi-nological knowledge usually means that we must employ a series of research tools, chosen to suit the job in question, to get at the information needed, in order to make sense of issues. But as researchers, there are constraints of factors such as ethics, the practicalities of doing research, employing the research process effectively, and accessing the type of sources or participants that might be needed.

But through doing this important work, we are able to continually add to our understanding of issues, and evolve criminology forward. The following points have been covered in some way, and if you can recognise them from your reading of the chapter and can understand why they are important, then you will have a good grasp of what is a crucial aspect of criminology:

- We research in criminology across many issues and topics.
- Often, this is linked to affecting change in some way; for instance, through shaping theories and policy-making.
- There are many different methods that might be used, but it is important to choose the method best suited to the requirements of the research, i.e. suited to producing the type of data required.
- An array of specialised terminology exists. You do not need to commit it all to memory at this point, but merely recognise and understand some aspects of this.
- The research process is useful to keep in mind, but in practice research can be 'messy'.
- Qualitative and quantitative approaches exist, and there are implications for adopting either over the other.
- Ethical considerations, sampling and validity are important to bear in mind when approaching research.

RECOMMENDED READING AND FOLLOW-UP MATERIAL

Read

- Francis, P. and Davies, P. (2018) *Doing Criminological Research* (3rd edn). London: SAGE.

  (This offers some great examples of criminological research in practice, showing the breadth of research within the field, and the methods employed.)

- Jupp, V. (2014) *SAGE Dictionary of Social Research Methods*. London: SAGE.

  (This gives short coverage of key terms and concepts related to this research, many of which are mentioned at some point in the chapter.)

- Field, A. (2016) *An Adventure in Statistics: The Reality Enigma*. London: SAGE.

(This presents a strong and accessible guide for doing **quantitatively**-focused research, which is an area where students are more likely to struggle when setting out in their studies.)

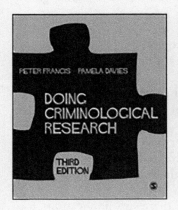  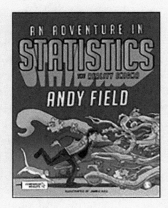

Watch

- James Treadwell's SAGE Knowledge video, 'An Ethnographic Study of the 2011 England Riots', available at: http://sk.sagepub.com/video/an-ethnographic-study-of-the-2011-england-riots

CHAPTER REVIEW QUESTIONS

1. What are some of the different types of research methods and approaches used by criminologists?
2. What should you consider when determining which method to employ within your own research?
3. Consider the various ethical considerations within research outlined in this chapter. Are some of these more important than others? If so, could you put them into order of importance?

1. Revisit Chapter 3, and think about how we, as criminologists, have arrived at those various theories for explaining crime. Choose some of the theories, and consider what research those ideas are based upon – what have been the approaches and specific methods used, the type of data collected, and so on. You might find this difficult to do because little is noted of research approach in that chapter, but think about what the authors have argued, and the type of research and data needed to present such an argument. Also, through doing some wider reading around those specific authors mentioned you will find this easier to do.

2. Access and explore the Right Turn project via: www.fim-trust.org/wp-content/uploads/2017/06/Albertson-et-al-Right-Turn-evaluation-final-report-June-2017-p.pdf. Look through the project details; in particular, look at the methodological approach used, and the ethical considerations in place.

3. Draw up a glossary or list of key terms and ideas related to researching crime and justice, as covered in this chapter. Start with the short list presented in Table 4.1, and those in Table 4.2. You might also want to add other terms to this, which were mentioned elsewhere in the chapter. Please ensure that you understand what the terms mean, and why they are important.

4. Think about the three research scenarios listed below, and consider:

    i.   What exactly the study is about.
    ii.   Why this might be important.
    iii. How exactly might the study be carried out?

    It is not expected that you will be able to come up with concrete answers here, but rather, it is meant to get you thinking about the matter of approaching research in different ways.

    Scenario one: for a student research project, as part of your course, you have been asked to find out about public attitudes towards imprisonment. In particular, your tutor wants you to explore whether people think imprisonment is a good solution for tackling crime, what they think about the outcomes of imprisonment, and whether imprisonment is better suited for some types of offences, and some types of offenders.

    Scenario two: you are a professional researcher working in a university, and you have received funding from government to undertake research around the use of social media and racism. In particular, there is a worry that racist incidents, such as abuse, use of derogatory language, and threats, are becoming increasingly common online. The government want to determine how much of this type of thing is happening, why people are engaging with such behaviours via social media platforms, and what the effects of this are on victims.

Scenario three: as a member of a research team based at Amnesty International, you are tasked with exploring the human rights situation within a war-torn country. In particular, it is important that you find out whether or not human rights are being respected, and if they are being violated, how common is this, who is being victimised, and who is it that is violating human rights.

CHAPTER CONTENTS

5 COUNTING CRIME

Image 5.1

LEARNING OUTCOMES

After reading this chapter you will be able to:

1.   understand what we might seek to measure in relation to counting crime and why, including numbers of crime, but also aspects such as offending and victimisation, place and time of crime, trends and patterns, and fear of crime;
2.   understand how we can collect data on crime, including the role of official data-collection processes, victimisation surveys, self-report surveys, and wider data collection from other bodies;
3.   recognise the strengths, limits, and specific uses of those various mechanisms for measuring aspects of crime and justice.

5.1 COUNTING CRIME: WHAT TO COUNT?

As Chapter 1 demonstrated, defining crime is not as straightforward as we might imagine. The implications of this are profound: how crime is defined impacts on what exactly is measured, and how. In other words, if there are different ways of defining what crime is, this means that the actual behaviours determined to be criminal, or harmful (in relation to the harm perspective), can vary, and therefore, seeking to count how much of that activity is taking place, leads to different outcomes. Behaviours are only included within counts of crime if they are determined to meet our criteria regarding crime (or harm).

Thus, the matter of counting *crime*, including harms, becomes a subjective process. For instance, accidents, deaths and unreasonable working conditions within a workplace will have largely been absent from conventional measures on crime for most of the period in which we have counted crime in an organised manner. Over a long period of time various activities of employers and responsibilities have eventually been added in to legislations. Authors such as Steve Tombs and David Whyte have generally questioned the lack of attention on such behaviours, and the dearth of actions for dealing with employers and organisations that have, in effect, harmed employees through their negligence, disregard, and sometimes outright dangerous practices.

Also, much of those events have been hidden or not properly recorded because of record-keeping processes of agencies such as the Health and Safety Executive (HSE) (see Tombs and Whyte, 2008, 2013). Figure 5.1 presents the HSE's estimate for the number of workers who had fatal injuries in the period of a year, and then the changes over time related to this. The long-term downward trend would suggest that attitudes are changing and the issue of safety is now being taken more seriously than it was in the past. However, as Tombs and Whyte (2008) have noted, this data is most likely an underestimate.

That noted, there are a number of now long-established mechanisms for counting crime that have existed in places such as the UK for decades, and in the instance of official data, since the first half of the nineteenth century. These measures have tended to follow the legal definition of crime in determining, and thus including, behaviours and events within their totals. But even within this, the picture is further complicated by the fact that if we take a single counting mechanism, the official recorded data, then the actual processes employed to count crime have changed over time. That is, there have been different criteria used; different categories of crime created; the inclusion and exclusion of different behaviours as a result in the changing of law over time; and the priorities and competencies of the police in detecting and responding to specific behaviours have changed over time.

BOX 5.1   ACTIVITY

Go online and visit the HSE's website, specifically their timeline of key events via www.hse.gov.uk/aboutus/timeline/index.htm

Read about the various pieces of legislation and tragedies that have contributed to the current role and responsibilities of the HSE. This shows how over time greater focus has been placed on different aspects of working conditions and processes, and how additional behaviours have become regulated. Yet as Tombs and others demonstrate in their work, there is still some way to go with all this.

147
Workers killed in 2018/19 (RIDDOR)

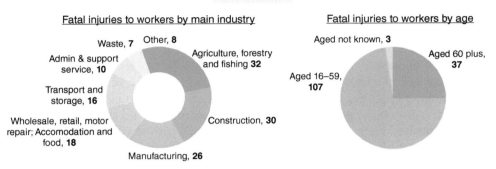

Fatal injuries to workers by main industry

Waste, **7**   Other, **8**
Admin & support service, **10**
Agriculture, forestry and fishing **32**
Transport and storage, **16**
Wholesale, retail, motor repair; Accomodation and food, **18**
Construction, **30**
Manufacturing, **26**

Fatal injuries to workers by age

Aged not known, **3**
Aged 60 plus, **37**
Aged 16–59, **107**

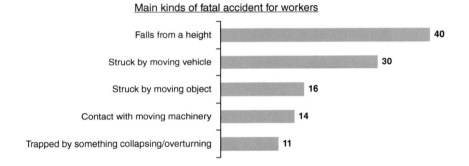

Main kinds of fatal accident for workers

Falls from a height — **40**
Struck by moving vehicle — **30**
Struck by moving object — **16**
Contact with moving machinery — **14**
Trapped by something collapsing/overturning — **11**

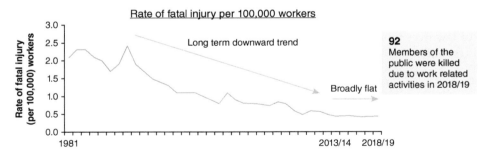

Rate of fatal injury per 100,000 workers

Rate of fatal injury (per 100,000) workers

Long term downward trend

Broadly flat

1981   2013/14   2018/19

92
Members of the public were killed due to work related activities in 2018/19

Figure 5.1   **Deaths at work**

(*Source*: adapted from HSE, 2019)

It is not just about counting crime in the sense of actual numbers of different crimes committed, although that is very important. Criminologists are also interested in issues such as who is committing them; who is the victim; when did it take place; where did it take place; what are the changes over time, and so on. Some of this information then allows for processes such as crime-mapping, whereby the police can plot incidents against geographic areas and times, to determine hot-spot areas, and thus direct resources accordingly in order to tackle crime. Such practical applications of crime data are important. Yet as the chapter demonstrates, the different methods used for counting crime vary in relation to how they work and the accuracy with which they paint a picture of reality. Each way of measuring crime can be of particular value in some contexts, but limited in relation to others.

5.2 HOW DO WE COUNT CRIME?

The conventional wisdom regarding how to count crime, that is, what is expressed in most books that explore the issue, is that there are two main measures, and a third which is less significant in terms of time and resources invested in it, but still nevertheless important. Those two main measures are official crime data from agencies who have some direct involvement in dealing with law and order issues (traditionally called official statistics, or police recorded data, even though it is not just the police who collect this information); and information taken from victimisation survey work, the main one in England and Wales is the Crime Survey for England and Wales (CSEW). The CSEW was called the British Crime Survey (BCS) until 2012, so there are references made to that within texts printed before 2012. That important victimisation survey started in 1981, but the methodology used has evolved a great deal since then. There are other such surveys in other countries, such as the National Crime Victimisation Survey in the USA, which began in 1973. Both official crime statistics and the CSEW are taxpayer funded, but they adopt very different approaches to the issue of counting crime. The methodologies employed for both have evolved over time.

The third measure of crime comes at the issue from a different angle. The official statistics relate to data from known incidents reported or dealt with (which are thus recorded), and the victimisation survey data entails asking a representative sample of people if they have been a victim of crime in the past 12 months, and the national picture is then extrapolated from the findings among the sample. Think about how this relates to what was covered in Chapter 4, concerning sampling, representativeness, and validity. The third method for counting instead is centred around the question *have you committed a crime in the past 12 months?*

Thus, so-called self-report surveys are the third category. As might be imagined, approaching counting crime from that angle could produce different findings; one obvious outcome of this is that you can include many crimes otherwise not counted because they were not reported, or not recognised by a victim, or perhaps even, they are victimless crimes. One of the most notable examples of such a survey in this country has been conducted as part of the Cambridge Study in Delinquent Development; explored in Chapter 3 in relation to the ICAP model within the integrated approaches block of theories. This research forms part of that work.

It is possible to add a fourth type of measurement to the list: data from nongovernmental organisations and investigative journalism. There might possibly be more. The fourth measure is significant in terms of informing us about specific types of crimes. This might be in the same way as those three other measures, but arguably, this fourth measure of counting includes aspects of crime and justice that those others cannot. This might be in relation to revealing information to us regarding offences that are more difficult to track, those that may be more underground in nature, more emergent, or international and transnational in scope, which makes it more difficult for individual countries to keep track of, and broad large-scale surveys to track.

Data from non-governmental organisations and investigative journalism, including the United Nations, Human Rights Watch, Amnesty International, Channel 4 News, the BBC, Sky News and many others, can provide a better sense of what is happening in relation to events such as the sex trade, slavery, human rights violations, war crimes, and so on, than is possible within those other measures. Indeed, some of these things are not actively covered in any form within those other measures. The United Nations for example, have dedicated teams researching issues such as the illegal trades in animal parts, weapons, drugs, and so on, on an international level. Similarly, considering recent conflicts in the Middle East, it has been organisations such as Amnesty International, Human Rights Watch and news-media who have been on the ground determining the nature of crimes committed and the harms done, such as in relation to war crimes, human rights violations, sexual violence, and so on.

5.3 OFFICIAL RECORDED DATA ON CRIME

Official data on crime is routinely recorded by the police and courts, and published twice each year for England and Wales. Usually, the publication of figures is accompanied by close media coverage, scrutinising the nature of the present *crime problem*. This links to the focus of the next chapter, the politics of law and order, as well as Chapter 8, media and crime. This data can be accessed quite easily, and freely, which in itself is an advantage in using such data in your own work. The Office for National Statistics (ONS) available at www.ons.gov.uk/peoplepopulationandcommunity/ crimeandjustice holds all such data for this country. It also holds data from the main victimisation survey data, which is described in the next section. Datasets for several years can be explored, and within each dataset, there is a high level of detail, as well as visual summaries of the data in tables, charts and graphs.

Not only does this data relate to information on crimes themselves (the type of crime, how many), but also a range of other related details. On the face of it, this then appears to be a reasonably effective and accurate source of collecting information on crime, because it is a record of events that have taken place. Thinking back to discussions of methodology within Chapter 4, then we might see this process of listing such events, or to be precise, notifiable offences, to be free from issues such as sampling, ethics, the need to create a relevant data collection survey or other instrument, and so on.

BOX 5.3   ADDITIONAL INFORMATION

'Police recorded crime figures are supplied to us via the Home Office (HO), from the 43 territorial police forces of England and Wales, plus the British Transport Police. The coverage of police recorded crime statistics is defined by the Notifiable Offence List, which includes a broad range of offences, from murder to minor criminal damage, theft and public order offences. In January 2014, a UK Statistics Authority review found that statistics based on police recorded crime data did not meet the required standard for designation as National Statistics.' (ONS, 2016: 1)

Also, other countries collect similar forms of data, in similar ways. For example in the USA, the Uniform Crime Reports present information gathered from the various local police departments. In theory then, it should be possible to compare levels of crime, offenders, victims, time and place of crime, trends over time, and so on, across different countries. But caution is required. How crime is collected, how it is defined in the first place, the categories used for offences, and indeed, the thresholds used, can and do vary across different countries. This then makes direct comparison internationally, difficult in practice; see the example of *Japan's Secret Shame* later in this chapter.

Looking at the general pattern of crime, according to the police-recorded data, then in the long term, from the Second World War, and particularly from the mid 1950s up to the mid 1990s, recorded crime numbers increased significantly. The bulk of the rise has been linked to property crimes. However, the ways in which crime has been reported and recorded, and indeed, the classification of offences as crimes, social circumstances, and so on, have all changed significantly, and so the stark rise witnessed does not automatically indicate that society has become more dangerous. Rather, we live in a different type of society, and we have a very different criminal justice system. A more useful time period to consider would be the past 30 years or so.

Looking then at the past few decades, the total volume of crime seems to have fluctuated somewhat; that is, the numbers have moved up and down. In the most recent few years, a rise in crime has been witnessed and, of concern, this is particularly linked with violent offences. This is against the trend witnessed for the preceding 15 to 20 years. The reasons for this might be linked to explanations for offending, as Chapter 3 sought to do – for example, pointing to processes of economic downturn causing more property crimes. It is interesting to consider Figure 5.2, and try to account for those changes over time in a similar way. However, it also becomes apparent that some of the changes in crime numbers witnessed have been a result of the different approaches taken by the police to the counting and recording of crimes, as Figure 5.2 describes. Thus, caution is required when interpreting the data, especially when accounting for significant dips and falls over a short period.

The figure only reflects overall crime numbers, and so it is also important to look at individual types of crime to determine trends, and attempt to account for them in some way; Chapter 3 considered how different explanations of crime might be best suited to specific types of crime.

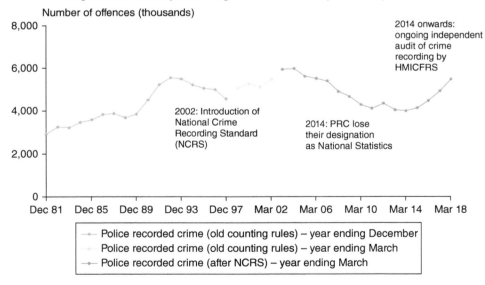

Figure 5.2 The recent trend in recorded crime in England and Wales

(*Source*: ONS, 2018a)

Other forms of official statistics

There are also statistics routinely recorded related to other aspects of the criminal justice process, all of which are invaluable to criminologists. Statistics related to sentencing outcomes, imprisonment and probation for example are very important. Here, we can find out about who is being sentenced, or imprisoned, for instance, outcomes of probation work, and so on. Each of these gives scope for considering matters such as trends over time. For example, are more people being sentenced to imprisonment than previously? This becomes even more interesting when considered in conjunction with other statistics, for instance, comparing how many people are sent to prison, alongside what the data notes regarding actual levels of crime. Indeed, one of the worrying trends witnessed in punishment in countries such as the UK in the past twenty years or so, is the steady rise of people being imprisoned, corresponding with generally falling crimes rates.

It could be assumed that crime levels have generally been falling (but they now appear to be creeping back up again) over the recent past because more people are being sent to prison, and are thus unable to commit crime. Many criminologists, however, are quick to point to other processes at work, in terms of falling crime corresponding with factors such as economic and social conditions (think back to Chapter 3), and the use of imprisonment in some sense being linked to the politics of law and order. This is associated with authors such as David Garland and Loic Wacquant, and this is explored further in Chapters 6 and 9. David Garland for example, in his culture of control thesis has pointed to the increasing use of imprisonment in the context of a tougher outlook on crime and offenders in recent times, which has seen the public and policy-makers advocating tougher measures on crime (Garland, 2001).

Measuring the outcomes of punishment is one interesting use of statistics in this area. Notably, exploring reoffending rates is one such application. Levels of recidivism, which is the label used for reoffending, varies according to the different types of sentences imposed. The notion of recidivism is officially defined by the Ministry of Justice:

> a **proven reoffence** is defined as any offence committed in a one year follow-up period that resulted in a court conviction, or caution in the one year follow-up or a further six month waiting period (to allow time for cases to progress through the courts). (2017a: 5)

How young offenders are dealt with is particularly problematic in this context, in terms of responses to offending actually fostering proven reoffending, especially in relation to the use of custody, i.e. being locked up in some form. For example, reoffending for this group was at about 75 per cent in 2004 and although down a little in 2015, it was still approaching 70 per cent (MoJ, 2017b: 7). Imprisonment generally, especially short-term imprisonment, seems to be problematic. For example, the reoffending rates for adults, on release from prison after serving 12 months or less, has been hovering just under 60 per cent throughout the period of 2004 to 2015. This is much higher than for longer sentences, and indeed, much higher than for community-based sentences (MoJ, 2017b: 6). This is considered further in Chapter 9.

Critique of official statistics on crime

The official recorded data on crime is subject to criticism on a number of levels. Some of this has already been outlined in the preceding sections of this chapter. The most obvious criticism is that the data is a product of a series of processes which eventually end in the listing of events which have taken place (notifiable offences), and along the way, data is lost. How? The processes of recognising, reporting, and recording are all important. This means that in order for a crime event to end up in the data, it has to have gone through those three stages, and at each point, there is a chance that the event is lost from the eventual total.

The notion of the dark figure of unrecorded crime is one that features frequently in literature. This refers to the volume of crime that is in the shadows (not recorded) owing to being lost from the final count for whatever reason. Authors such as Coleman (1996) have taken this further through the analogy of an iceberg. Within the analogy, only the part above the water is visible (recorded incidents of crime), and not the remainder lurking below (unrecorded crimes), which is likely to be numerically greater, and perhaps even different in its characteristics.

Another useful analogy for thinking about official data on crime is that of steeple-chase horse racing (Figure 5.3), whereby horses race over a course with lots of jump obstacles, which serve to slow horses down, but eventually, also, whittle down the number of horses who finish the race. It is common for horses to fall or pull-up at the obstacles. Within such an analogy, lots of horses arrive at the start line, i.e. lots of crimes take place in a given period of time. On reaching the first hurdle, that of recognition – the need for a crime to be recognised as having taken place, or recognition of the behaviours which has occurred being illegal in the first instance – some horses pull-up or fall. That is, some of the total numbers of crimes that have taken place do not make it over the hurdle.

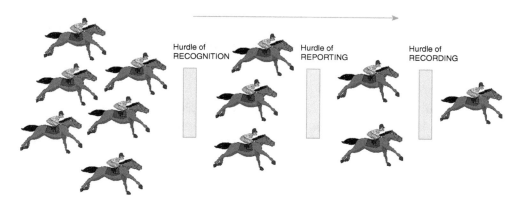

Figure 5.3   Attrition of crime numbers

There are lots of reasons why people might not notice their victimisation, such as the triviality of the event, or them not properly keeping track of their possessions or finances. And victimless crime, too, must be considered. Next, the remaining runners hit the next hurdle, that of reporting. Not all crimes that are recognised are reported: victims might distrust the police; they might want to deal with matters themself; they may think it too trivial; they might have been engaged in embarrassing or illegal activities when they became victimised; they might be fearful of reprisal, and so on. And so, more of the horses are lost; more of the total amount of crime is lost.

Finally, the remaining runners hit the hurdle of recording, where again, various reasons dictate that many crimes are not formally recorded (more horses pull-up or fall). Here, there might not be enough evidence of an offence; the police might distrust a reporter; the police might not want to include an offence in a particular category, where there is scope for discretion because of priorities or targets they have, and so on. At the end of the race then, only a portion of the horses finish, i.e. only a fraction of the total amount of crime that we think has taken place ends up within the recorded crime statistics. The term attrition can be used here, which relates to a process whereby more and more of the total is lost over time, through the various stages. The level of attrition can vary over time, and between different policing jurisdictions and bodies.

A poignant real-world example to think about in terms of the possible flaws in official data is that of the definition of, and reaction towards, sexual violence within Japan (and, indeed, within other societies). In the 2018 BBC documentary, *Japan's Secret Shame*, it was shown how the victimisation of young women within Japanese society is often ignored, or in many cases, determined to be the fault of the victim; this is a product of history, culture and the workings of the legal system within Japan. This example not only points to the ways in which crime might be viewed through a social constructionist lens (as considered in Chapter 1), but also, how that then impacts on the actual ways in which crimes are counted, or not, as the case tends to be. Also, how the police handle cases, and their cultural and social *baggage* within this matters in terms of how events are determined to be a criminal offence or not.

The historical context in Japan has seemingly had an important impact on how certain actions are understood and reacted to. As is described within the documentary, being a victim of sexual violence has often been understood as simply part of being female in Japanese society. Also, the make-up of the police in terms of representation of both men and women matters within this example, in terms of this impacting on how such events are responded to. Clearly this has a bearing on how events are understood, and reacted to. The official statistics in Japan suggest that rape is much rarer than it is in the UK, for example, but there is good reason to doubt the accuracy of such data. Linking this back to discussions of official data on crime, those missing episodes of sexual violence from the crime statistics in Japan, ties in to all of the three 'Rs': recognition in the sense that sexual violence has often not been viewed as a criminal action; reporting in the sense that the taboo nature of the topic in Japan, the shame on victims, and also the lack of support for victims, means that victims are reluctant to come forward; and recording, in terms of how cases might not be taken forward by the police for a number of reasons, such as the male-centred policing culture, and victim-blaming.

Another useful example to consider, closer to home, is that of domestic abuse against both men and women. Usually presumed to be a predominantly female-centred form of victimisation, the issue of men being assaulted or abused by partners, whether female or male, has increasingly been a feature of campaigning by groups such as Mankind. For both men and women, domestic abuse can be a taboo issue, and a difficult issue to report, and so the official statistics on this are a small reflection of the total prevalence of the issue. For example, within an ONS statistical bulletin in 2017, it was estimated that there were close to two million victims of domestic violence aged 16 to 59, but closer to 1.1 million cases were actually recorded by the police (ONS, 2018a). Furthermore, an individual victim is likely to have been victimised several times, thus, the actual recording rate is low. Further added to this, is that people can be victimised outside of the noted age range, meaning that the total number of victims will be even higher than noted.

There is a close link from the matter of counting crime to that at the centre of the next chapter: the politics of law and order. In addition to the various critiques of officially recorded data on crime already outlined, the effects of political decision-making on what the crime statistics look like are also notable. This is explored in Chapter 6 but, for example, it is possible to identify examples of where policing priorities and practice (dictated by government, local pressures, etc.) have resulted in significant changes in crime numbers being recorded. Recent examples include the heightened focus on dealing with hate crimes, sexual violence, and abuse, whereby increasing public, media and campaign-group pressure has resulted in the toughening-up of the legislative and policing landscape around those issues. Thus, more of those types of offences appear in the recent statistics than in the past. Similarly, the reverse is true in relation to issues such as abortion, homosexuality, and so on.

5.4 VICTIMISATION SURVEYS

As noted earlier, on the ONS website official recorded data on crime sits side-by-side with victimisation survey data. That is to say, the government, in recognising some of the difficulties in interpreting the official recorded statistics, also present findings from a notable victimisation survey, the Crime Survey for England and Wales (CSEW), in order to better demonstrate the nature of the *crime problem*. In fact, the CSEW is government funded. Neither type of data is perfect, but utilising both might offer a more accurate picture of what is happening. Other such surveys are available, both domestically and internationally. For instance, the Commercial Victimisation Survey (CVS) in this country, and the National Crime Victimisation Survey in the USA. The former is a relatively new data-collection instrument, exploring victimisation of businesses. The latter example has been running since 1973, and in its present form, includes a sample of around 135,000 households (about 225,000 people are included) and collects data *'on the frequency, characteristics, and consequences of criminal victimization'* (BJS, 2018).

Considering discussions of methodology within Chapter 3, the approach taken within such victimisation surveys is an attempt to produce a generalisable set of findings, based on a complicated representative sample of respondents: complicated insomuch as trying to account for the various types of diversity within society; the sample size for the CSEW for example, is approximately 40,000 people at present. For the CSEW, participants complete a questionnaire in the presence of a researcher, who visits their home. That researcher is both able to aid the completion of the questionnaire and clarify questions. This represents a fundamental difference from the approach of the official data: asking people about their experiences of victimisation in the past 12 months, rather than counting recorded events. The questionnaire, in the main, is focused around that, but it also captures information on the background of participants, as well as issues such as fear of crime, and attitudes towards the police. Thus, its wider value is significant in terms of exploring links between crime levels, victimisation, and confidence in policing.

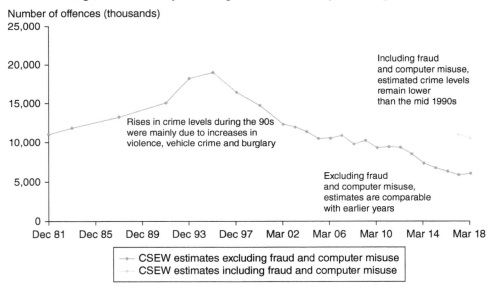

England and Wales, year ending December 1981 to year ending March 2018

Figure 5.4   Crime numbers according to the CSEW/BSC

(*Source*: ONS, 2018a)

By examining results of the CSEW (and the British Crime Survey (BCS) up to 2012) a different set of figures on crime are apparent from that of the official count. In fact, it suggests that there are many more offences, although in recent times the two measures are converging. Figure 5.4 shows the broad trend, but again, it would also be useful to look at specific types of crime to get a better picture of what is happening. Which data is correct: the official count, or the victimisation survey data? The crime survey data probably gives us a closer picture to the actual numbers of crimes we think exist, because many of the events not reported to the police, and some of those reported but not recorded, are likely to be included here. But both measures have obvious strengths and weaknesses, as Figure 5.4 shows. Perhaps it is relevant to note, then, that where both measures show a rise or fall at the same time, then there can be more confidence regarding what is happening in relation to crime, even if the actual numbers presented are different.

One key issue flagged-up is the comparability of data over time; that is, the extent to which the results for one year can be directly compared with those from another. Mostly, that form of comparison is possible, but changes to police-recording practices in the instance of official recorded data, and changes such as the inclusion of new types of crimes and young victims in the instance for BCS/CSEW, means that directly comparing like for like from year to year is not possible. See the individual points within Table 5.1. Also, for the CSEW, there are issues around the accuracy of memories, truthfulness of answers; this comes back to the discussion of social desirability in Chapter 4. Also, the recognition element of the '3Rs' is a flaw within the victimisation data.

Crime Survey for England and Wales	Police recorded crime
Strengths	**Strengths**
Large nationally representative sample survey that provides a good measure of long-term crime trends for the offences and the population it covers (that is, those resident in households)	Has wider offence Coverage and population coverage than the CSEW
Consistent-methodology over time	Good measure of offences that are well-reported to and well-recorded by the police
Covers crimes not reported to the police and is not affected by changes in police recording practice; therefore, is a reliable measure of long-term tends	Primary source of local crime statistics and for lower-volume crimes (for example. homicide)
Coverage of survey extended in 2009 to include children aged 10 to 15 years resident in households	Provides whole counts (rather than estimates that are subject to sampling variation)
Independent collection of crime figures	Time lag between occurrence of crime and reporting results tends to be short, providing an indication of emerging trends
Limitations	**Limitations**
Survey is subject to error associated with sampling and respondents recalling past events	Excludes offences that are not reported to, or not recorded by, the police and does not include less serious offences dealt with by magistrates' courts (for example, motoring offences)

(Continued)

Table 5.1   (Continued)

Crime Survey for England and Wales	Police recorded crime
Potential time lag between occurrence of crime and survey data collections means that the survey is not a good measure of emerging trends	Trends can be influenced by changes in recording practices or police activity as well as public reporting of crime
Excludes crimes against businesses and those not resident in households (for example, residents of institutions and visitors)	Not possible to make long-term comparisons due to fundamental changes in recording practice introduced in 1998 and the year ending March 2003
Headline estimates exclude offences that are difficult to estimate robustly (such as sexual offences) or that have no victim who can be interviewed (for example, homicides and drug offences)	There are concerns about the quality of recording — crimes may not be recorded consistently across police forces and so the true level of recorded crime may be understated
Previously excluded fraud and cybercrime	

Table 5.1   Comparing police recorded crime with the CSEW

(*Source*: ONS, 2018b)

5.5 OTHER DATA SOURCES ON CRIME

Self-report surveys

Just as the victimisation surveys approach the matter of counting crime from a different perspective from that of the official recording process – that is, being victim-focused in asking about victimisation – self-report surveys do something similar, albeit with an offender-focused approach. Simply, the focus is on peoples' experiences of offending in a given time period. Thus, a survey approach can be taken to ask people about their involvement with crime. *Why do this*? Keeping in mind what was noted of official data, through going *straight to the horse's mouth*, so to speak, and asking people directly about offending, crimes can be included that are ordinarily lost to the recognition and reporting hurdles, and perhaps even the recording hurdle.

Possible distortions within the data must be considered, whereby the accuracy of peoples' accounts are important, including, again, the issue of social desirability, and the possibility that people can exaggerate to 'big-up' themselves. Furthermore, a completely true picture of offending still may not be arrived at unless the survey is representative in nature – in reality, the sample sizes are usually smaller then victimisation survey samples – and inclusive of all types of crimes. And again, the extent to which people recognise the illegality of behaviours also matters. It is quite feasible that respondents will not report some crimes because they do not understand their actions as criminal.

A notable example of such a survey in this country is that used within longitudinal research at the University of Cambridge, associated with Anthony Bottoms and

David Farrington, as part of the Cambridge study in Delinquent Development. That longitudinal approach is a common one within this type of data collection, whereby collecting data from people at different points in their life, and thus taking a life-course approach is seen as necessary. Elsewhere, the National Youth Survey in the USA (from 1970 onwards) is a notable example, which has been better placed at offering a representative sample given the sample size and sampling methodology used. Krohn et al. (2010) offer a useful overview of the development, use and issues around such self-report instruments.

NGOs and journalism

Often overlooked, a range of other sources of data on crime have proven to be highly valuable to criminologists and society more widely. These can be described as the activities of NGOs and investigative journalism. *Why*? Although the various measures outlined so far undoubtedly offer an effective window into the *crime problem*, it might be argued that those measures have a tendency to focus on activities that have a particularly local or national context or basis, and which more readily lend themselves to formal legal conceptualisations of crime and established issues. Increasingly within criminology, there is concern for issues that are international in terms of how they play out; emergent in terms of issues being new or until recently not receiving adequate attention; and underground or hidden from the gaze of the formal criminal justice system.

Some forms of Internet crimes; offending facilitated by social media; human rights violations; war crimes; modern-day slavery; and the illicit arms trade are just a few of many types of offences that have traditionally been omitted from the usual data-collection processes, and they are quite often better captured by alternative sources on crime. Here specifically, it is possible to highlight the work of non-governmental organisations, such as the United Nations (UN), Amnesty International, Human Rights Watch, and so on, and the investigative journalism of media bodies such as Channel 4 News, Sky News and the BBC.

It is helpful here to explore a few examples of how the activities of such organisations can shed light on events and processes where this is not normally afforded through the other sources on crime. Initially, the example of BBC investigative journalism can be considered. For instance, a documentary for BBC3 in 2017 presented by Stacey Dooley focused on the use of social media apps for drug dealing. Here it was shown, although with a limited sample and scale, the ways in which such illicit behaviours can be facilitated by social media platforms. The presenter and research team demonstrated the relative ease with which dealers could operate via this medium, and the term digital dealers was used to describe this emergent issue. But notably also, through research conducted for that documentary, some sense of the nature and size of the problem was offered (BBC, 2017).

Looking to the role of NGOs, the role of the United Nations (UN) in shedding light on all manner of issues, including slavery and illicit trades, is clear. The UN is among the most important sources of data on crime. The work of Human Rights Watch is also a strong example to explore here. Their work is researching and reporting on all manner of human rights and social justice issues, some which clearly demonstrate breaches in law, or processes of social harm, and generate data on issues often not covered within the other data collection/reporting instruments. For example, a report in 2018, which had drawn from interviews with people affected by pesticide drift in Brazil, in farming communities, indigenous communities, and in schools, shed light on an issue seemingly disregarded elsewhere, despite the clear harms meted out to the victims. As the report noted, there are often no laws protecting people from such harm, and government data on this is widely inaccurate (HRW, 2018).

Similarly, the work of Amnesty International must be recognised, whose research on a range of issues, across armed conflict, the use of the death penalty, freedom of expression and political imprisoning, and so on, is one of our chief sources of information on a range of critical issues. This is typified by a 2018 report, which was built on research Amnesty International had conducted over a decade on Sierra Leone, and included field work in 2017 and 2018 (including interviews), analysis of court documents, video and photographic evidence, and media analysis and medical records.

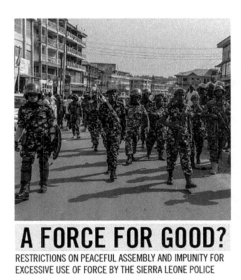

Figure 5.5   Amnesty International report on Sierra Leone

Within the report, it is demonstrated that peaceful protesting has often been prevented from taking place, particularly protest from rival political parties and activists. Further to this, criminal sanctions have been dished out to some for seeking to exercise their rights of free speech, and thus, abuses of power were evident (Amnesty International, 2018). It is that type of work on the ground, through dedicated research teams in place, which can help to better inform us about crime and justice issues.

5.6 REVISITING THE ICEBERG ANALOGY

Having now explored the different means of collecting data on crime, beyond the officially recorded count, it is worth thinking about how those other means of counting crime relate to that official count. Coming back to the analogy of an iceberg is useful here. As noted earlier, in the instance of an iceberg, and as we think is also the case with recorded crime data, most of the mass is hidden from sight under the surface. A revised version of the iceberg analogy is presented in Figure 5.6. Here, the analogy is developed further, by showing that not only is the bulk of the mass under the water, but this can be divided into different elements according to the recognition, reporting, and recording of crime.

Further still, it is shown how those other crime data collection processes might fill in some of the gaps. As Coleman (1996) has suggested, not only might that hidden bulk of crime be numerically bigger, it might also be different in nature. Therefore, there could be certain types of offences systemically missing from the official count; sexual violence against women in Japan would be a good example of this. But also, things such as low-level driving offences would commonly not feature in the data owing to the low chances of them being reported and recorded. Similarly, we can also think about illicit drug-taking.

5.7 SUMMARY AND IMPLICATIONS

As demonstrated within the previous chapter on researching crime and justice issues, the specific issue of counting crime is perhaps more complicated than one might first imagine. The information often taken for granted, is in fact the consequence of various processes, which, in some way add a level of uncertainty or scope for error within the crime numbers arrived at. Official recorded data on crime is a good example of this, but that type of data is of course only one part of a much bigger story on counting crime. Taking together the various means we have of collecting information on crime, we arrive at a much more informed position on the matter, even though each measure of crime comes with a series of 'health warnings'.

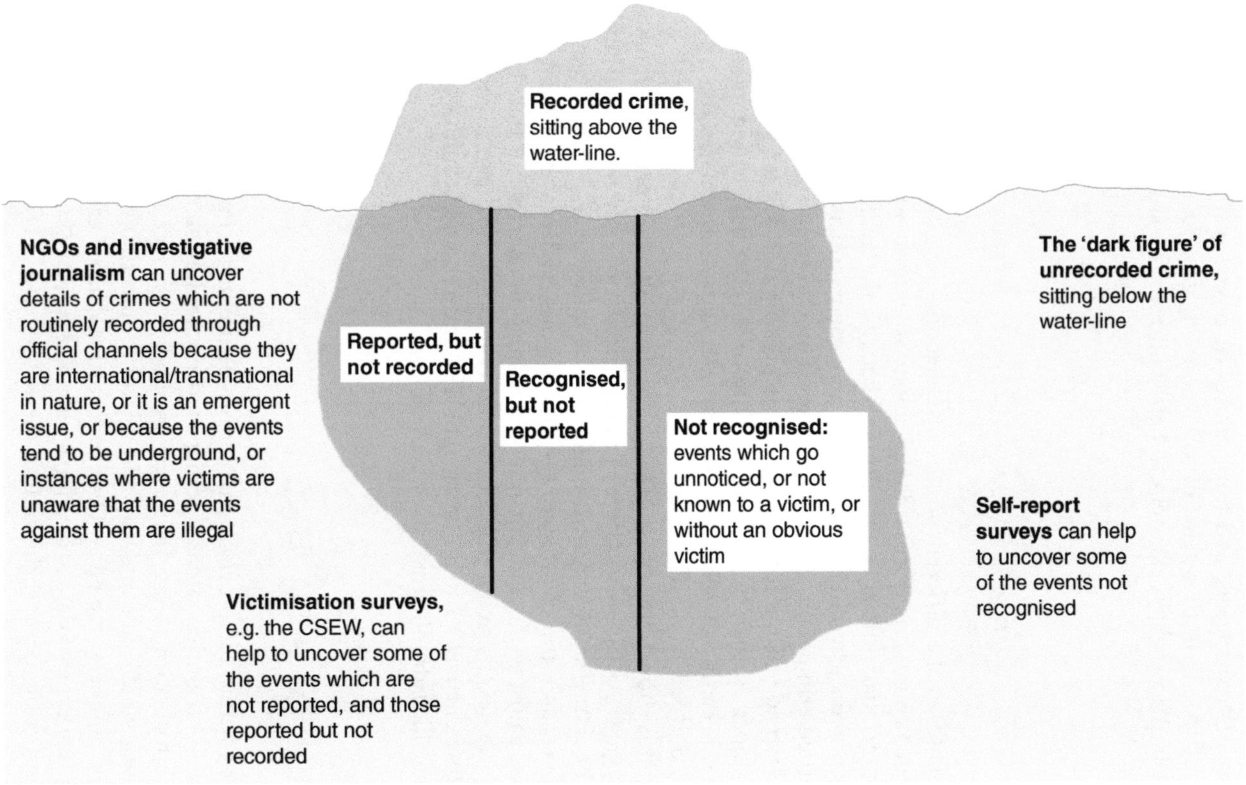

Recorded crime, sitting above the water-line.

Reported, but not recorded

Recognised, but not reported

Not recognised: events which go unnoticed, or not known to a victim, or without an obvious victim

The 'dark figure' of unrecorded crime, sitting below the water-line

Self-report surveys can help to uncover some of the events not recognised

NGOs and investigative journalism can uncover details of crimes which are not routinely recorded through official channels because they are international/transnational in nature, or it is an emergent issue, or because the events tend to be underground, or instances where victims are unaware that the events against them are illegal

Victimisation surveys, e.g. the CSEW, can help to uncover some of the events which are not reported, and those reported but not recorded

Figure 5.6   Revisiting the 'iceberg' analogy of unrecorded crime

The following points have been covered within the chapter, and so you should be able to recognise them, and understand their significance:

- There are different ways of collecting data on crime.
- Information collected through the course of policing, sentencing and imprisonment, are examples of this.
- So too is data collected through specially designed data-collection tools, such as surveys.
- The role of NGOs and investigative journalism should also be considered.
- Each way of collecting crime data comes with strengths and limitations.
- Generally, it is thought that crime numbers have increased significantly since the Second World War.
- In the past 30 years, crime numbers appear to have risen steadily until the mid-1990s, and then dropped significantly, before rising again since about 2014/15.
- However, we must look at individual crime types, and consider the trends within them, if we are to better understand what is happening.

RECOMMENDED READING AND FOLLOW-UP MATERIAL

Read

- Maguire, M. and McVie, S. (2017) 'Crime data and criminal statistics: a critical reflection', in Liebling, A., Maruna, S. and McAra, L. (eds), *The Oxford Handbook of Criminology* (6th edn). Oxford: Oxford University Press.

  (This is a good overall text to explore the topic as a whole, and it is also very recent.)

- Office for National Statistics (2018c) 'User guide to crime statistics for England and Wales' (July 2018), available at: www.ons.gov.uk/peoplepopulationandcommunity/crimeandjustice/methodologies/userguidetocrimestatisticsforenglandandwales

  (This is a lengthy document, so it might not be feasible to read it all, but have a look at some of the early sections to get a sense of how the statistics are constructed, and changes over time in terms of how they are collected. This is also useful in terms of linking this and Chapter 4 together.)

Watch

- The Human Rights Watch video, 'Torture in Somali Region Prison in Ethiopia', available at: www.hrw.org/video-photos/video/2018/07/04/video-torture-somali-region-prison-ethiopia

  (When watching this, pay particular attention to the actual processes of data collection used/described.)

- BBC (2018) *Japan's Secret Shame*, via BBC IPlayer.

  (Consider how the example links to what has been explored in the chapter related to the problems of measuring crime, and the inaccuracies within official counting processes.)

CHAPTER REVIEW QUESTIONS

1. What are the different ways in which crime is counted, and what are the basic processes involved?
2. What are the consequences of the different ways in which crime might be counted?
3. In which contexts are each of the four crime-counting mechanisms outlined, especially useful or insightful in comparison with the others?

REVIEW ACTIVITIES

1. Spend some time thinking about how this chapter builds on the previous chapter, which focused on researching in the context of crime and justice. Jot down a few points to demonstrate how this chapter links to, or has built on, the previous one.
2. Visit the United Nations (UN) website, and in particular this part of the site: www.unodc.org/unodc/en/data-and-analysis/index.html?ref=menuside

Here you will see the range of crime- and justice-related areas that the UN has concern with and, crucially, actively engages with, in terms of collecting data on crime (both primary collection on the ground, and bringing together pre-existing data across different countries). Explore some of those coloured boxes and have a look at some of the activities the UN engages with.

3. Visit Human Rights Watch online (www.hrw.org/publications) and similarly as with the UN, consider the sorts of research activities Human Rights Watch are engaged with, and the type of data on crime and harm they produce.

4. Think about, and jot down some answers to the questions below. You will need to go online and find statistics via the Office for National Statistics for UK crime data (https://www.ons.gov.uk/peoplepopulationandcommunity/crimeandjustice), and the UN's International Labour Organization for question 4, at: www.ilo.org/global/topics/forced-labour/definition/lang--en/index.htm

   i.   Which type of crime measure tells us that there is more crime in a given year, police-recorded data, or victimisation survey data? Why? (You will find both types of data on the ONS website.)
   ii.   To the nearest 100,000, how many property crimes were recorded in England and Wales according to the latest available dataset?
   iii. What are the trends for both violent crimes and property crimes since the early 1990s? For example, has there been a steady rise in one, or both, a decline in one or both, movement up and down, etc?
   iv.   How many people are currently thought to be in forced labour, globally, and who are the victims?

PART 2

SOCIAL DIVISIONS AND CRIME

CHAPTER CONTENTS

6 THE *POLITICS* OF LAW AND ORDER

Image 6.1

(*Source:* @realDonaldTrump (2018))

6.1 POLITICS AND LAW AND ORDER: CRIME POLICY AS *CURRENCY AND BAGGAGE*

Thinking about politics in the widest sense, in terms of the activities of the State and other actors within the governance of a country, specific place or even international regions, and the interactions and debates related to that, it becomes apparent that many social and public policies have deeply political currency or baggage attached to them. What this means is that that they can somehow have value for those creating and implementing them, where policies are popular or seemingly relevant, or conversely, they can act like heavy weights pulling down policy-makers and even stopping them in their tracks, where policies are unpopular or perceived to be ineffective.

For example, the issue of immigration is a deeply charged one, and politicians must tread carefully in terms of how they approach the issue. Controversially, the UK government has set immigration target numbers in recent years in an effort to reduce numbers of migrants coming into the UK, and adopted other tough measures such as the use of much-criticised detention centres. All of this has occurred within the context of public anxieties on the subject of immigration. Indeed a 2018 poll by Deltapoll reported overwhelming support by the UK public for less immigration into the country (Gerdziunas, 2018).

Immigration was one of the main issues leading to the UK's vote to leave the EU in 2016. The political cartoon in Figure 6.1 captures something of this, alluding to a migration 'crisis', which is overwhelming the EU member states. The UK's decision to leave the EU via the Brexit vote was in no small part a consequence of public anxieties around immigration. Campaign groups latched onto this to sway voters towards a leave vote, and there was also a broader anti-establishment movement (Hobolt, 2016). Such sentiments have also been witnessed elsewhere in Europe where similar concerns over immigration exist (Hobolt, 2016).

Figure 6.1   The EU migrant crisis

(*Source:* Faye, 2015)

Although the issue of immigration might be seen as being separate to the matter of law and order, they do in fact deeply intersect with one another because of the ways in which immigration policies and processes can serve to criminalise or victimise specific groups, and because of how they reflect processes such as social inequalities, power and class ('class' in a broad sense). A useful example to consider here is that of the spate of migrant-related crimes in Germany, following the arrival of large numbers of asylum seekers in 2015 and 2016. Sexual assaults against women were particularly noteworthy within the press over the period, including the infamous New Year's Eve 2015/16 spate of rapes and other sexual assaults that took place on the same evening. Data collected by Zurich University of Applied Sciences does appear to support a link between heightened offending among the migrant asylum-seeker population (Bershidsky, 2018), yet regardless of this, the discussion around immigration and crime in Germany has become toxic. Chancellor Angela Merkel had publically backed the mass movement of people fleeing conflict into Germany in the face of other countries opting to do the opposite. This proved to be politically damaging once cases of migrant offending started to be reported. The issue created a media and public backlash and, in part, contributed to a resurgent far-right movement in the country.

Similar processes can be recognised within the example of welfare benefit policies, whereby some government decisions can be unpopular, or conversely, populist in nature. Recent policy decisions related to the so-called 'bedroom' tax and the transition into Universal Credit received heavy media coverage and sparked public interest. Partly, this has been a result of adverse outcomes for those in receipt of welfare benefits because of those policy decisions, such as entering into acute financial difficulties (Power et al., 2014 for example). Notably, it is often the poorest areas that suffer the most from such reforms (Beatty and Fothergill, 2016), a theme picked up on in the next chapter on victimisation. In particular, there have been concerns regarding the impacts of reforms for those with a disability, as the protesting in Figure 6.2 reflects.

But interestingly, the issue has become a polarising one, with the political left (and associated media platforms) seizing upon this to highlight social injustices, while the political right (and their associated media platforms) frame this in the sense of common-sense reform to crack down wasteful benefits processes and 'fiddling' of the benefits system. In fact some might claim that such reforms do not go far enough.

There is a clear link here to the harm perspective in terms of how such reforms adversely impact people and communities. Much of this is explored within subsequent chapters: Chapter 7 in relation to victimisation, and class, power, and marginalisation, and Chapter 10 in relation to linking criminology to social policy. Within Chapter 10 specifically, the 'entanglements' between crime and welfare policies are considered; that is, the ways in which these policy areas overlap and impact on each other. Law and order issues are similarly as politically loaded as the issues of migration and welfare benefits. That is, crime and what is to be done about it attracts a great deal of political commentary, public interest and news coverage. Not only

Figure 6.2   Protesting against stringent and unfair disability eligibility tests

(*Source:* Worthington, 2018)

that, the interest shown in relation to this has some profound implications in terms of shaping what happens on the ground. Thus, not only do such policies have currency and/or baggage, but because of this, policies are often a consequence of such. Some examples of this are considered later in the chapter.

In trying to summarise the importance of politics to the matters of law and order, the following outline is a useful starting point, and aspects of this are developed as the chapter progresses:

> Crime and criminal justice issues become increasingly politicised. That is, policy-making, law-making, practice and political discussions around crime, and indeed other aspects of law and order, have become increasingly determined by public opinion and reaction, news-media, political positioning, and the need for policy-makers/government to be seen to be doing something and be on the side of the people; which generally means being tough. This may, or often may not, be linked to what experts think will 'work' in terms of dealing with the law and order issues themselves.

Thus, the political dynamics of law and order issues can shape the ways in which crime and justice are talked about, and the nature of responses to crime and justice matters. The notion of currency and baggage is a useful way of framing this:

- Currency means that something has value, and owning that thing gives the owner some form of worth or merit, and even status. This can be witnessed in relation to the politics of law and order, whereby being seen to be actively tackling crime and effectively dealing with offenders creates public trust and approval, even if what you are doing might in fact be creating further problems. For example, the general academic consensus is that our approach of sending record numbers of people to prison in recent times is counter-productive. This links to the notion of penal populism, associated with authors such as Anthony Bottoms, and relates to ways in which law and order issues have political currency in terms of politicians and policy-makers using law and order issues for their own electoral or wider political gain; seeking to appease the public who are assumed to be punitive in outlook; and tough on crime/offenders.

BOX 6.1   ADDITIONAL INFORMATION

Prisons 'crisis': Over recent years, the state of prisons in England and Wales has come under extreme scrutiny. A rise in the numbers of assaults on prisoners and staff, self-harming, staffing shortages and over-crowding have exacerbated prison conditions. This has done little towards creating rehabilitative pathways for prisoners. The **Howard League for Penal Reform** and others have been tracking this. For instance, a Howard League report in 2018 demonstrated that additional sentencing in 2017 (equivalent to almost 1,000 years) helped to fuel the present crisis (Howard League, 2018). A series of prison riots took place in recent years owing to prison conditions, such as those at HMP Oakwood in January 2014 and at HMP Birmingham in December 2016. In 2018, the running of HMP Birmingham, a private prison, was taken over by the government.

- Baggage is the opposite of the above. The politics of law and order dictate that dealing with the crime problem comes with responsibilities; pressures; and in many ways, an impossible balancing act between implementing the policies and practices which might genuinely create positive change, versus the need to please the public and media, and demonstrate a tough stance on law and order issues. Here, for example, adopting a tough stance does not always mean that the issue is being dealt with in the best possible way. Again we need only to consider the present crisis with the English and Welsh prison system, and the political damage this has had on ministers. The notion of baggage is something that is carried around, which is often heavy, cumbersome, and restricts the freedom of movement. It is something that might adversely shape law and order policies and practices.

The wider 'political' influences

Law and order issues do not exist in a vacuum. How crime issues are defined and reacted to does not happen spontaneously, or without influence. Instead, a range of factors shape this. An obvious starting point here might be research and data collection on crime issues, linked to what was covered in Chapters 4 and 5, which highlight genuine law and order challenges, and issues that can be tackled. However, the need to please the public, who are generally viewed as being punitive, and the media (Chapter 8) are significant. This is where the notion of penal populism becomes important. Other influences, such as processes of political rhetoric, and the ideology that political parties or individual politicians, policy-makers, and media outlets might hold on issues can also be significant. Unfortunately then, what the evidence conveys regarding the law and order threats faced, and what might be done about them, can lose some of its influence in the midst of those wider factors.

What is recognisable then, is how the political dynamics of law and order issues can shape the following:

1. What is deemed to be problematic, in terms of the threats, the events and the issues of note and concern.
2. Who is deemed to be the problem, in terms of who is to blame, who is the threat, who are the criminals, and so on (this links to Chapter 7, which is concerned with 'offenders' and 'victims').
3. What ought to be done about it, in terms of the types of laws, policies and practices seen.

6.2 THE ROLE OF THE MEDIA

The media play an important role within this wider discussion of politics and law and order. This is because of the ways in which the media report on specific issues, and the effect this can have on the public and policy-makers alike. This is explored in detail in Chapter 8, but it is difficult to separate out the relationship between crime, politics and the workings of the media (the news-media especially). In short, the media can both *reflect* and also *fan* public worries and anxieties about law and order issues, and the media may influence political discussions and responses to law and order issues. The concept of moral panic is particularly useful here (see Cohen, 1972), and it captures a core element of the chapter as a whole: public and government reactions to law and order threats can be fuelled by the media.

Through media coverage of crime issues, public understanding of the nature of crime events can be distorted, through the focus on atypical crimes and circumstances. Steve Chibnall's work (Chibnall, 1977) demonstrates how and why some events become popular inclusions for the news-media, while other events receive less attention (see Chapter 8). Public fears and anxieties regarding law and order issues can be exacerbated, or even created, through the heavy focus on specific issues and 'risky' groups. This can link to reactionary campaigns within elements of the newsmedia, for instance, as seen in relation to child abuse, and this can then lead to further anxieties and put pressure on politicians for legislative or policy change. Political discussions of law and order issues can ensue which emerge from heavy media coverage of some crime events, and their campaigning on issues. Reactionary policies can then develop to deal with those perceived threats to law.

BOX 6.2   ADDITIONAL INFORMATION

The News of the World (NOTW) campaign, on behalf of Sarah's family, following the murder of Sarah Payne by known paedophile Roy Whiting in 2000, eventually led to the implementation of *Sarah's Law* in 2008. This allowed parents to access information from the sex offenders register. A similar event and law had been earlier witnessed in the USA: *Megan's Law.*

Figure 6.3   The NOTW campaign for 'Sarah's law'

(*Source:* Mailonline, 2011)

Political tough talk and the need to mitigate public anxieties are, then, important. Populist responses can emerge, even if they may be counter-productive and result in disorder and alienation of some groups. The image of Sarah Payne (left), now iconic, appeared on the front of newspapers, and caught the public's imagination. The policy reaction here might be viewed by some as a very positive change, whereas others might see it as being a slippery road to head down. In other countries too, similar processes have been evident. In the USA for instance, Pennsylvania changed its law on clemency for inmates serving life sentences following the media frenzy in response to the high-profile murders carried out by Reginald McFadden in 1995. McFadden was paroled at the time of the murders; as one source has described: McFadden became Pennsylvania politicians' poster boy for what could happen when an unreformed convict goes free (DiFilippo, 2016).

Within such instances, the media are said to play a pivotal role in terms of framing the nature of the threat posed to society's moral fabric. They frame the individuals or groups involved within this, whether victims or offenders, and, crucially, help to define the nature of the response required. Sarah's Law is a classic example of where a wide-reaching response (eventually) emerged in light of a perceived threat of stranger danger. Such policies and rhetoric can target and marginalise some groups, through processes of labelling. Often this is connected to ethnicity, class and age; where ethnic minority groups, migrants, the poor, and the young become defined as threats to society and thus legitimate targets for policy intervention. Classic studies in criminology, both old and new, reflect this, such as the seminal *Policing the Crisis* by Stuart Hall et al. (1978/2013), and research following the 2011 riots in England. *Policing the Crisis* demonstrated this in relation to ethnicity and policing practices, especially stop and search, whereas research into the 2011 riots demonstrated it in relation to age and social background (e.g. Lewis et al. (2011). What is interesting, is how following the riots of 2011 and the extensive media coverage of the events, research suggests that public sentiments towards disorder became more punitive (Hohl et al., 2013).

6.3 THE IMPACTS OF POLITICAL INFLUENCE ON LAW AND ORDER PROCESSES

It is possible to recognise the influences of politics in a number of ways. One such way is how the various aspects of criminal justice are impacted; for example, how policing or sentencing practices appear to have been shaped in some way. Here are some aspects of the criminal justice where an influence might be considered:

- Policing priorities: tackling terrorism; gang activities; burglary and robberies in student areas, and so on, are examples of how anxieties might shape the allocation and focus of policing resources (and rightly so in many instances). This is influenced by both local and national priorities. The creation of Police and Crime Commissioners from 2012 onwards, who are able to influence policing through setting priorities in line with public concerns, is a good example of how this might work in practice. The appointment of such Commissioners is a deeply political exercise, linked to public reassurance and making the police accountable to the communities they serve (see APCC, 2018). The signal for the creation of the Commissioners came amidst the 2010 General Election, with calls to make policing more accountable.

- Policing practices: e.g. heightened stop and search activities and scrutiny of specific areas and communities. For example, Hall et al. (1978/2013) linked stereotyping and marginalisation of black youths within the press and political popular discourse, to police targeting of such groups. Even today, tensions between some communities and the police stem from (at least in part) present and historical policing practices, which have resulted in damaging the relationship between some communities and the police. The shooting of Mark Duggan, and reactions to this from the local community in North London, which preceded the 2011 riots, is a clear example of this. There, relationships were fractious to begin with, and the police handling of the case pushed those relationships to breaking point. That was the trigger for the riots, even if then other motivations took over once the riots spread. Some authors have linked the subsequent events to inequality and marginalisation within society. See, for example, Lea and Hallsworth (2012).
- Law-making itself: e.g. 'Sarah's Law' and 'Megan's Law' are clear examples, and so too are a range of other reactive laws, and indeed, others that appear to be deeply ideological in nature, often driven by neo-liberal principles. See Garside (2015) for a good overview of such matters, across different areas of the UK criminal justice system.
- Sentencing practices: e.g. following the English riots of 2011, tough sentencing practices were witnessed as a means of appeasing the public, and as a form of deterrent (Baird, 2011). Crucially, also, the over-use of imprisonment in places such as the UK and USA can be considered here because of its popularity among the public. David Garland's (2001) thesis is useful in making the link between public anxieties and such sentencing practices, and this is explored in the final section of the chapter.
- The role of the victim within the justice process: e.g. victim impact statements are now an important fixture within court proceedings in the UK, USA, Australia and elsewhere. This is in line with a wider movement for giving victims a voice within the justice process. Studying this sits within a wider field of victimology; an important element within the broader field of criminology. See Daigle (2013) for a comprehensive discussion of this field.
- The collection and use of statistics on crime and justice matters: linking closely to what was covered in Chapter 5, there are notable examples in the UK, USA and elsewhere, of how crime statistics can be ceased upon by political actors to serve their own interests. In the UK, the now famous exchange between Michael Howard and Tony Blair in the 1990s reflects this, whereby competing measures on crime were cited by both to serve their own political argument. Reiner (2007: Chapter 3) offers a strong overview of the political dynamics of crime statistics.

- The governance and organisation of criminal justice services: privatisation of aspects of criminal justice is a notable example of this, whereby the ideological position of governments in the UK, and elsewhere (a neo-liberalist ideology), has led to private firms managing and delivering services. For example, the probation system in England and Wales became part-privatised from 2014 onward, while by 2018, there were 14 private prisons operating in the UK (HM Prison Service, 2018). Private sector involvement in both probation and prisons, and other CJS functions also, has attracted strong criticism. For example, in 2018, the running of HMP Birmingham was taken over by the State from the private contractor G4S, because the management of the prison and its conditions were deemed to be unacceptable following inspection. There had been a major riot at the prison just two years earlier. Similarly, the use of contractors within probation has led to questions regarding the ethos of probation and its effectiveness. See Bean (2018) for a good overview.
- The imposition of one nation's criminal justice philosophy onto another: in essence, this relates to the ability of one nation to dictate to another, aspects of criminal justice policy because of the relative power-difference of those states, and the political ramifications of a weaker state refusing to cooperate. This could relate to processes such as extradition of suspects to contexts where it is known that they will face treatment that is outlawed in their country, or facilitating such investigations. For example, in 2018, there were calls for a judicial review after it was claimed that UK Home Secretary Sajid Javid cooperated in the investigations of terror suspects El Shafee Elsheikh and Alexanda Kotey, knowing that they could face the death penalty. This deviated from the UK government's anti-death penalty position. This was said to be a political decision; as Edward Fitzgerald QC remarked: 'This country should not facilitate the imposition in another country of a punishment we ourselves recognise as inhuman and unlawful … He took those steps in large part because of the anticipated outrage of certain political appointees in the Trump administration if the UK insisted on death penalty assurances' (Dearden, 2018).

6.4 THE FOCUS ON DRUGS

Thinking about responses to illicit drugs is a useful focal point for this wider discussion around the politics of law and order. It is possible to recognise how the same act of consuming a drug such as cannabis, takes on different qualities depending on the national context. For example, the drug is illegal in some countries and actively policed; illegal in some countries but not actively policed; legal in some countries for specific uses; and legal in entirety in others. The same substance, but different political and cultural contexts shape responses towards it. There is a good link back to the discussions in Chapter 1, concerning the socially constructed nature of crime. The political climate around such a drug has been pivotal in shaping the nature of the responses.

In 2004, after several years of planning, the UK government decided to reduce the classification of cannabis on the basis of expert guidance, and the difficulties faced in policing it. By doing so, they reduced the severity of response from the criminal justice response to users and those in possession, and this would enable the police to concentrate on more serious drug use. Cannabis was downgraded from a 'class B' drug to a 'class C'. However, by 2009, this had been reversed, in the context of a changing political landscape, and some media and public concerns regarding the message it sent out. This was despite advice from the Advisory Council on the Misuse of Drugs. This is an example of how the politics of law and order can work in practice, with the government changing policy despite the advice of experts on the matter.

In recent years the debate on cannabis in the UK resurfaced in a significant way, with the legalisation of cannabis for medicinal purposes now underway. In July 2018, the Advisory Council recommended that cannabis-derived products should be available through prescription (ACMD, 2018). In 2018, Canada decriminalised the recreational use of cannabis possession of (less than 30 grams), following the decriminalisation of it for medicinal purposes in 2001. Uruguay was the first country to decriminalise cannabis for recreational use in 2013, many other countries have also softened their approach, permitting it for medicinal or recreational use. Such changes have usually followed shifting social and cultural landscapes.

The USA is another interesting example to consider. The famous war on drugs – crack cocaine being a key focus of this, but it extended to illicit drugs more widely – is an important example, with a series of Presidents finding that a tough approach to law and order, especially on drugs, brought political success. This included Richard Nixon and, notably, Ronald Reagan, who called for a 'national crusade' against drugs. This came in the context of rising crime, and links made between this and drug use. Notably, this took on a racialised dimension, and proved to be highly controversial because it often resulted in the targeting of black citizens. And not least because the swell in the prisoner count in US prisons over the past few decades could be attributed in some way to the *crusade* on drugs. It was the inner-city black population who faced the brunt of policing and sentencing (see Carroll, 2016, for a useful overview). The present situation in the USA is somewhat different, with many states now adopting a more pragmatic approach, involving a softening of attitude towards *softer* drugs, e.g. cannabis.

The issue of cannabis consumption is all the more interesting when considering the work of Weissenborn and Nutt (2012), who have demonstrated that the consequences and, indeed, harms associated with the use of common intoxicant drugs such as alcohol and cannabis have generally not been properly reflected within the policy decisions witnessed in recent decades in the UK. Alcohol, for example, which was described by the authors as being more than twice as harmful as cannabis to users, and five times more harmful to other people, has not received the regulatory responses (including criminal justice sanctions) as cannabis has within the UK. They claim that the reaction to cannabis resulted in needless criminalisation of young people.

Seemingly, the context around the use of cannabis is a good example of where the evidence produced by the experts, such as David Nutt and others, appears to have been compromised because of entrenched public attitudes towards drug use, and political ideologies. Yet within current reforms in the UK to allow consumption in some circumstances (for medicinal use), there seems to be a softening of attitudes, as there has been in other countries. The discussion around cannabis links not only to the issue of politics, but also the very idea of defining crime, whereby social attitudes at a given time can inform what is seen as being criminal, and indeed again, the socially constructed nature of crime: one harmful behaviour is criminalised in many countries, while arguably a more harmful behaviour, e.g. some forms of alcohol consumption, are not.

Clearly, there is also relevance here in thinking about the harm perspective. Also, there is a link to discussions in earlier chapters on the matter of what exactly *counts* within the crime statistics, with definitions of crime determining what ends up in the statistics. There are, then, two very clear sets of links to Chapter 1 and Chapter 5, which demonstrates the often fluid and connected nature of many topics within criminology, and why students should be alert to these connections.

6.5 PRESIDENT DONALD TRUMP: PENAL POPULIST *PAR EXCELLENCE*?

In the USA there are a number of recent, high-profile instances of where the politics of law and order are clear in practice, operating under the presidency of Donald Trump. For example, President Trump pardoned a prisoner, Alice Marie Johnson, in 2018 after publically meeting with mega-celebrity Kim Kardashian West. This had followed campaigning by Kardashian-West. Johnson had been sentenced to life without parole in 1996 following a first offence linked to a drugs conspiracy. This example points to the sometimes populist and political nature of crime and justice policies: a serving President publically engaging with a famous television personality over the issues of law and order, and then pardoning a prisoner as a result. It is difficult not to see this in the context of popularity and public relations work. Even though, many might agree with the actual decision to pardon based on correcting an apparent injustice.

Another ongoing example has been the proposal to build a large border wall between America and Mexico in order to keep 'gang members', 'murderers', and 'rapists' from flooding in to America; as the President described (see Gitlin, 2017:16). Gitlin's text, *The Border Wall with Mexico* (Gitlin, 2017) offers an interesting overview of this. Whether the President actually believes the logic of this or not, the fact remains that Trump was elected into office on the wave of populist politics, which included a strong focus on law and order among other things, and such rhetoric about crime and immigration struck a note with some American voters. Trump's route to the White House involved playing the law and order ticket heavily. His rhetoric on crime, immigration and the supposed corruption and incompetence of those in power, seemed to both reflect and channel the anxieties and fears of many voters.

Ultimately, it was Trump's focus on some deeply controversial, yet topical issues which got him into power. He was savvy to the political nature of law and order issues, and it could be argued that he has been a master of understanding and wielding penal populism.

Figure 6.4   President Donald Trump with Kim Kardashian West

(*Source:* @realDonaldTrump, 2018)

6.6 POLITICS OF LAW AND ORDER WITHIN A WIDER CONTEXT

A number of influential authors have sought to make sense of the broader nature of law and order policies, and have pointed to patterns and trends that can seemingly sit across individual nation states. That is, there appears to be a similar policy direction, or directions, which many countries are pursuing/have pursued in recent years, seemingly, as part of a wider trend. Within such accounts, this direction of travel is depicted, mainly, as being a more punitive one than that of the past, and often this is said to be influenced by neo-liberal principles. David Garland's account (Garland, 2001) for example, is perhaps the most well-known attempt to do this.

Within Garland's thesis, the **Culture of Control,** he highlights a series of 'indices of change' that point to a broader, shifting policy landscape in places such as the USA and the UK. Among those indices (or indicators), Garland signals the rapid rise in prison populations as a marker of a more punitive outlook on law and order matters. For Garland, it is not just that policy-makers are becoming tougher on crime and offenders in recent decades, but so are public attitudes and sentiments. In fact, it is those wider attitudes and sentiments that help to fuel policy-making as it becomes a reaction to them. All this, in some way linked to the progression of neo-liberalism over that period of time. Garland presents this as the shift from a welfarist outlook on offenders, to a more punitive one, hence the notion of a punitive shift towards a culture of control.

Thus for Garland (2001), and indeed others such as Loic Wacquant (2005), and John Pratt (2007), the ways in which punishment is conceptualised and put into practice has become increasingly connected to wider anxieties and concerns for managing disorder and offenders, and not necessarily just about dealing with the reality of the *crime problem*. This means that punishment and, specifically here, harsher attitudes towards punishment and tougher punishment practices, have become common-place in countries such as the UK and the USA. For Wacquant (2005), there is a heavy emphasis on 'race', and how African Americans are treated as being *dangerous* within the politics and policy-making processes.

Wacquant links the status of black communities to the changing economic conditions in the USA which brought about declining job markets and social marginalisation for African Americans. Rather than dealing with this in a welfarist or social security context, there has instead been a desire to manage disorder and the perceived threat to law and order that such groups represent through tougher crime control measures (Cochrane and Talbot, 2008: 14–15). This then warrants their close handling by and their drawing into the criminal justice system. This all then ties back to the onslaught of neo-liberalism. Thus, in a similar way to Garland, the changes have been moving societies away from welfarism in the context of neo-liberalism, and the impacts have been profound. Pratt's (2007) work here is interesting in pointing to Scandinavia as an exception in the context of an 'era of penal excess'. That is, such countries have been less influenced by neo-liberal forces and, as a result, a more welfarist approach to punishment can be witnessed, one less politically driven.

6.7 SUMMARY AND IMPLICATIONS

Understanding the political nature of law and order issues is a crucial aspect within modern-day criminology. It is possible to recognise how law and order issues are often deeply connected to wider influences, such as needing to please the public and respond to media and social anxieties, and indeed careerism. And this can also link to wider policy areas, where issues of crime and justice, immigration, and welfare benefits appear to intersect. The politics of law and order can influence the nature of the issues deemed to be problematic, who is deemed to be the problem and what ought to be done about it all. Key criminological concepts such as penal populism and moral panic are relevant here in terms of making sense of much of the topic, but on the most common-sense level, it can be noted that the influence of research evidence and expert commentary on law and order issues, is, at best, locked in competition with a range of other influences working to shape the law and order policy landscape.

RECOMMENDED READING AND FOLLOW-UP MATERIAL

Read

- Garside, R. (2015) 'Criminal justice since 2010: what has happened and why?', *Criminal Justice Matters*, 100(1). Available at: https://www.crimeandjustice.org.uk/publications/cjm/article/criminal-justice-2010-what-happened-and-why

  (This provides a good sense of the changing nature of criminal justice in recent times, and the wider context / influences)

- Reiner, R. (2007) *Law and Order: An Honest Person's Guide to Crime and Control*, Cambridge: Polity Press.

  (Look at Chapters 1 and 5 to get an overall sense of the topic, and thus, the present context of law and order policies in the UK.)

Watch

- Nancy Marion's SAGE Knowledge video, 'The Politics of Criminal Justice', available at: http://sk.sagepub.com/video/the-politics-of-criminal-justice

- Ronald Reagan's speech on drugs from 4 August 1986. This is available at: www.c-span.org/video/?150381-1/presidential-drug-speech

  (Here, the President sets out his plans for a national crusade against drugs.)

CHAPTER REVIEW QUESTIONS

1. What is meant by the term the 'politics of law and order'?
2. What is meant by 'penal populism', and 'moral panic', and why are they important for understanding aspects of the topic?
3. Should policies on law and order issues be influenced by public anxieties and media campaigning, for example, as was witnessed with 'Megan's law' in the USA and 'Sarah's law' in the UK? What are the pros and cons of this?

REVIEW ACTIVITIES

1. Using a large piece of paper, do a mind-map for this topic, covering key issues, examples, authors and links to other topics covered within this text. As you learn more about some of the issues at hand, such as the ways in which offenders and victims are defined/presented (Chapter 7); the role of the media in reporting on law and order issues (Chapter 8); the broad nature of responding to crime (Chapters 9 and 10) you can come back to the map and add to it given the clear connections between the topics.
2. Follow up on the case study of illicit drugs in relation to the politics of law and order. Using the Internet to search, draw up a list of countries where cannabis is illegal in all forms; a list of countries where recreational use is criminalised but not medical use; and finally, a list of countries where recreational use of cannabis is legal. If possible, think about the contexts within each of those countries. Do we see patterns in terms of the types of countries or contexts within which decriminalisation has occurred? For instance, where some form of decriminalisation has occurred, are those governments more politically liberal than those where decriminalisation has not occurred? Are there other common features among the various countries on your various list, such as social/cultural attitudes, the nature of the economies, and so on?

CHAPTER CONTENTS

7 OFFENDERS AND VICTIMS

Image 7.1

(*Source:* Worthington, 2018)

7.1 DEFINING 'VICTIM' AND 'OFFENDER'

Thinking about victims of crime and offenders is perhaps more complicated than we might initially assume. In a similar way to how what is seen as being a crime is a product of social, cultural and historic forces, as Chapter 1 demonstrated, and indeed Chapter 3 (in terms of criminalisation of groups), so it is that who is defined as a victim or an offender is a product of complex processes. In the most basic sense, a person or group who have been offended against in some sense by an illegal behaviour or action can be viewed as a victim. Conversely, those who are responsible for the action or behaviours are the offenders.

That holds true in a common-sense way. However, it has to be remembered that the very process of defining specific actions or behaviours as being criminal, potentially means that some groups are included within this process, while others are not. How we define what is criminal also then determines who can be a victim; you cannot be a victim of crime for example, if the event which occurred has not been criminalised: rape within marriage is a good example of this, given how it was only relatively recently (1991) made an offence in England and Wales (see Chapter 1). This is one of the reasons why using the notion of harm as an alternative to crime offers great value to criminologists.

Furthermore, seeing the categories of victim and offender as being separate is also problematic. That is, it is possible to recognise where the boundary between offending and victimisation is blurred, where an offender might also be a victim, and vice versa. This is important to note because there is a tendency to see these two categories as mutually exclusive; a victim as someone who is devoid of blame, while an offender is someone who does not deserve sympathy. Nils Christie's conceptualisation of an ideal victim (Christie, 1986) stems from this, specifically, in relation to how the media present worthy victims, and thus, conversely, offenders. A useful example of where this distinction breaks down is that of sex work; those illegally selling their bodies are all too often victims of robbery, assault, rape and abuse through the course of their work (Phoenix, 2018; 27).

It is also important to keep in mind how what is presented within data on offending and victimisation, and indeed, data relating to harms also, such as the Health and Safety Executive (HSE), reflect how it is usually the poorest or working poor who disproportionately feature in that data. Concepts such as class, power, inequality, and community, which are linked to the critical approaches block of theory, offer some value in terms of understanding influences on who commits crime and who becomes a victim. But also more generally, which groups tend to be disproportionately drawn into the criminal justice system based on who they are. Finally, it is also crucial to keep in mind the international dimensions of offending and victimisation; processes of class, power, inequality and community also operate internationally, and so their effects can be seen in relation to examples such as people trafficking and corporate crimes. Chapter 11 develops this idea further in the context of global justice, so this chapter should be read in close relationship with that later chapter.

Beyond a legal construction

Within the context of national legal frameworks, a victim can be viewed as someone who has suffered some form of injury, loss or disadvantage as a result of another person's actions, whereby such actions have been formally outlawed. Thus, an offender is therefore the person (or group) who perpetrated the act, and normally, there has to be some form of intent on the part of the perpetrator. Coming back to Chapter 1, victims and offenders in a legal sense, are determined by a restricted understanding of the notion of 'crime', and whether or not the specific act has been formally acted against within law in that place at that time. A fairly expansive definition of victimisation is offered within the United Nations Declaration of Basic Principles of Justice for Victims of Crime and Abuse of Power:

> 'Victims' means persons who, individually or collectively, have suffered harm, including physical or mental injury, emotional suffering, economic loss or substantial impairment of their fundamental rights, through acts or omissions that are in violation of criminal laws … The term 'victim' also includes, where appropriate, the immediate family or dependants of the direct victim. (cited in Goodey, 2005: 10)

Such a definition is still closely linked to the idea of formal criminal laws, but nevertheless it is possible from this to think about victimisation and offending in a broader way, one more in line with a harms-based approach given the type of language used within the statement. Within such an approach, the notion of 'victim' can relate to people or groups who have suffered unfairly in some way, even if the event or process is not criminalised, and therefore, an offender is someone who has directly or indirectly led to the suffering.

The wider issue of victimisation is in itself a sub-discipline of criminology, called victimology. This has burgeoned into the study of the nature, prevalence, causes and experiences of victimisation, and the consequences of this, as well as consideration of the various actors who are involved in some way shaping or responding to victimisation. For example, Paul Rock (2002) has argued the need for a dynamic understanding of the 'victim' identity, which recognises the victim's experience and the social construction of 'victim' by different actors in different contexts:

> 'Victim', in other words is an identity, a social artefact dependent … on an alleged transgression and transgressor and then, directly or indirectly, on an array of witnesses, police, prosecutors, defence counsel, jurors, the mass media and others who may not deal with the individual case but who will nevertheless shape the larger interpretive environment in which it is lodged. (cited in Goodey, 2005: 10)

From this, there is a clear sense that a category such as 'victim', and therefore 'offender' also, is actually quite complicated; there also appears to be an interplay between individuals who suffer harm and those who are responsible for the harm, the law, criminal justice actors, and indeed wider society. This becomes more complicated yet, when considering that there may be different types of victims, and different types of offenders. For example, there are individuals or groups who are victimised once, versus those who are repeatedly or continually victimised (repeat victimisation). Are the experiences of these comparable? Also, victimisation in relation to different types of crimes might entail a different type of experience and social reaction. It could be considered that there are different types of offender/offending, and whether or not these constitute the same categorisation, experiences and explanations:

- the 'serious' versus the 'low-level' offender;
- the 'persistent' or 'career' criminal versus the one time offender;
- the 'mundane' versus the 'exceptional';
- the local, the national, the international;
- the opportune offender versus the offender who goes out of his/her way to offend.

7.2 THE DATA ON VICTIMS AND OFFENDERS

Closely linking back to Chapter 5, it is possible to access data on who offenders are, and who victims are through official recorded data (mainly from the police), victimisation survey data (such as the Crime Survey for England and Wales, CSEW), self-report offender surveys, and from other sources, such as NGOs, regulatory bodies (e.g. HSE) and even investigative journalism investigations. From this, it is possible to build up a picture of whom a 'typical' offender might be; in an overall sense, or in relation to different forms of crime. And conversely, who a 'typical' victim is. The data tends to point to some fairly clear patterns. However, it is important to be aware that different sets of data can give different patterns of offenders and victims. For example, self-report data on drug use paints a very different picture of reality from that of official data relating to sentencing and prison population; the first suggests little differences in offending in relation to ethnicity, while the former suggests a significant difference based on ethnicity.

Yet, there are seemingly some evident patterns that can be pointed to. For example, patterns relating to gender and offending type: males are generally more likely to commit a violent crime, but also be a victim of such crime; whereas women are more likely to be victims of sexual violence. Age also plays a role: younger people are at heightened risks of violence (offending and victimisation) for instance. It is also possible to consider the dynamics of class or socio-economic status; ethnicity; geography; type of residence, and so on. All of these, and indeed other factors, can seemingly relate to the likelihood of being an offender or a victim of crime.

Thinking about gender specifically, the following is taken from the most recent Ministry of Justice report on women within criminal justice processes (MoJ, 2016: 10):

- In general, females appear to have been substantially under-represented as offenders throughout the CJS compared with males. This is particularly true in relation to the most serious offence types and sentences, though patterns by sex vary between individual offences.
- Females were also typically under-represented among practitioners in the CJS and among victims of violent crime, although they were more likely than males to have been a victim of intimate violence or child abuse.
- Trends over time for each sex often mirror overall trends, though this is not always the case.
- Less than a quarter of those given a penalty notice for disorder (22%) or caution (24%) were female. Women were under-represented to an even greater extent among those arrested (16%), who are typically being dealt with for more serious offences than those dealt with out of court.
- For both out of court disposals and arrests, females were particularly likely to have been dealt with for theft offences.

Recent data on victimisation, specifically CSEW data for the year up to March 2018, reports that men age 17 to 24 had the highest risk of victimisation against all crime as a whole: 22.4 per cent of them were victimised for that year, while the lowest risk was for men 75+ years, closely followed by women 75+ years – at 5.5 per cent and 5.7 per cent (ONS, 2018c). Considering the factor of geography, and related socio-economic position, those within the '20% most deprived Output Areas' had a rate of victimisation at 17.2 per cent (all crime as a whole) in the year, versus 11.1 per cent for the '20% least deprived Output Areas' (ONS, 2018c). Focusing on a specific type of crime, for example, crimes against the person, disability was a factor, with 20.1 per cent of those with a long-standing disability being victimised within the year, versus 8.1 per cent of those without a long-standing disability (ONS, 2018c).

More generally, the CSEW and academic research:

> ... consistently report that single parents ... youths, the unemployed, those on low incomes ... and people born abroad experience the highest levels of victimisation ... crime victimisation surveys reveal that people from lower classes with lower levels of education attainment and those from minority ethnic groups experience higher levels of victimisation. (Bows, 2018: 58)

The CSEW thus shows in general that factors of age, employment status, gender, disability and ethnicity can all relate to increased probabilities of becoming a victim of crime (Bows, 2018: 59). All of that is based on statistical calculation from the version of reality determined through the various means of collecting data on crime. For some of the patterns, the data can be compelling, but it is important to keep in mind how such patterns are overviews, and they do not constitute laws of behaviours. There are always exceptions to the trends presented within the data, as the Vanessa George example below shows. Crucially important also, is avoiding understanding specific groups in an overly deterministic way, i.e. seeing a particular group as being criminogenic because they feature heavily within statistics on offending.

BOX 7.1   CASE STUDY

Vanessa George, an unlikely criminal

In December 2009, Vanessa George was given an indeterminate prison sentence following her involvement with a paedophile ring. Vanessa worked at 'Little Ted's' nursery in Bristol, and used her access to children to abuse them, and to take indecent pictures on her phone, which were then sent on to a male member of the ring, Colin Blanchard (She had met Blanchard online in 2008.) The ring also included other women, including Tracy Lyons, who had briefly been a voluntary nursery worker in Portsmouth, and Angela Allen.

Vanessa's offending was the main focal point of the news coverage of the episode. Her offending, and the case more widely, is particularly interesting given the nature of the offence, and her occupation, as well as the involvement of other women. These were seemingly at odds with common-sense understandings of that offence and the likely offenders, which tend to be backed up by the data at an aggregate level. This was also enhanced by the fact that Vanessa's primary job function (and to a lesser extent that of Tracy) was to care for vulnerable children.

Not only is it important to keep in mind how the statistics are social constructs of one form or another, and processes of law-making, policing, sentencing and punishment can draw-in some groups, but also when thinking at an individual level, the aggregate-level trends cannot be assumed to hold true. Also, there are significant dangers of labelling and criminalisation, as Chapter 3 set out. Chapter 6 and 8 also consider this in relation to how politics and media can create offender stereotypes. For example, Stuart Hall et al. (1978/2013) explore the myth of the *black mugger* in the 1970s, this still perpetuates to the present day, which was a creation of the media and the political and social climate of the period. Such a myth, and a wider myth of the *black criminal*, contributed, and indeed it still does contribute, to disproportionate policing and imprisonment of the black population in the UK and elsewhere. Figure 7.1 reflects that point. Reflected within trends on offending and victimisation are various decisions and processes, which eventually lead to the recording of an incidence of crime/victimisation. The critique of official recorded data on offending in Chapter 5 clearly demonstrates this. To develop this idea further, consider the example of ethnicity within the criminal justice system, specifically the interaction of minority groups with the CJS in the USA, in relation to drug offences:

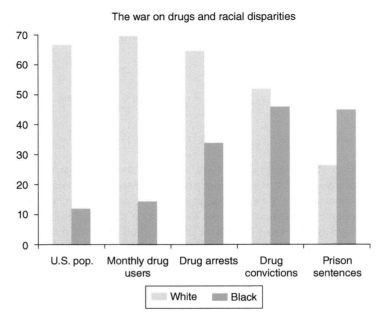

The war on drugs and racial disparities

Figure 7.1 **Ethnicity and drugs offences**

(*Source:* adapted from Bennett, 2018)

Figure 7.1 demonstrates how the criminal justice interaction of suspects based on ethnicity is disproportionate to the general population, but also, how that inequity appears to get worse at each stage of the criminal justice process. Thus, in terms of incarceration for drugs-related offences, the proportion of 'black' prisoners is dramatically at odds with not only their make-up of the general population, but also, data (self-report data) on regular drug use. All of this can be interpreted in a number of ways, but the existence of a racial bias within law and enforcement processes must be considered; the black community is viewed as being 'risky'. This links back to the myth of the *black criminal*, which exists in the USA, UK, and elsewhere. Furthermore, this figure also raises issues regarding the influence of the politics of law and order on who ends up being drawn into the criminal justice system. The war on drugs was considered in Chapter 6, and this has had an ugly racialised element to it. Considering the over-representation of black and minority ethnic groups within prison populations more generally, the per centage of the white population within US federal and State prisons in 2016 was only 30.2 per cent, meaning that minority groups accounted for nearly 70 per cent of the prison population (The Sentencing Project, 2018: 5). A similar pattern, albeit less extreme, is evident within prisons in England and Wales: 26 per cent of inmates are black or minority ethnic (BAME), while black men specifically are 26 per cent more likely to be remanded in custody, and are more likely to be held in segregation (Prison Reform Trust, 2017: 24–5).

7.3 CONCEPTUALISATIONS OF OFFENDER AND VICTIM

The offender

The label of offender, as demonstrated in Chapter 3, can be dependent upon the laws in place, and the application of them; criminalising certain behaviours, and enforcing laws specifically against certain groups. Theories on crime each often note something regarding who an offender might be. Yet within this, there is the issue of whether different types of offending and crime might warrant different ideas regarding who an offender might be. The theories within the choice and decision-making block (e.g. Classicism) present an offender as potentially anyone in the context of circumstances, through rational thinking determining the decision to commit a crime. Those within the individual pathologies block present offenders as different people from non-offenders, based upon biological or psychological differences. Within the social pathologies block offenders are presented as products of their environment.

Within the critical approaches block, who is labelled as an offender can be a consequence of criminalisation through laws and policing, the application of power, and marginalisation of specific communities. But on some level, the poorest might be viewed as more likely to be offenders of survival and protest-type crimes, while the wealthy are more likely to be offenders of crimes of domination, corruption and greed. The integrated approaches block on the other hand, points to a number of different dynamics of an offender, across social and biological processes. Terrie Moffitt presents a distinction between most offenders who offend in adolescence and those who persist well into adulthood. In her work, Moffitt depicts offending trajectories with age using a bell-shaped curve, whereby most offending appears to take place during adolescence and early adulthood, labelled as adolescent limited. Yet some offending persists well into adulthood, albeit a much smaller amount of crime. It is this life-course persistent offending that is related to entrenched offending careers.

Moffitt's work considers the influence of biology in terms of making some groups more vulnerable to criminogenic environments, and raises the possibility that for life-course persistent offenders there is a genetic influence (Moffitt et al., 2011: 55–6). For adolescence-limited offending, lifestyle factors and environmental conditions may play a role, and for those who persist beyond adolescence, a biological element must be considered. This pattern of offending appears to be supported with official data in the USA across different crime groups:

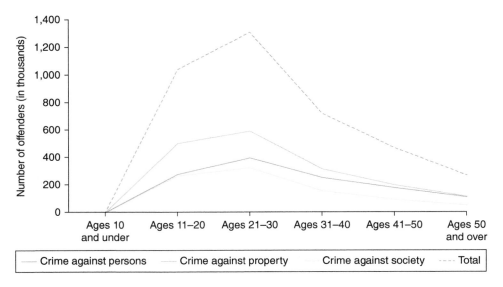

Number of Offenders in the United States, by Age and Offense Category, 2012

More than 60 per cent of known criminal offenders are under the age of 30, with individuals ages 11 to 20 constituting roughly 27 per cent of offenders, and individual ages 21 to 30 making up an additional 34 per cent.

Figure 7.2 Offenders by age and offence category

(*Source:* adapted from Mississippi NAACP, 2018; original source DOJ, 2012)

The victim

The label of victim is often an unappealing term, with negative connotations, and linked to negative imagery. Some crimes are referred to as victimless (Chapter 5), but in the main, an incidence of crime usually has some tangible impact on a victim or victims. Yet, some victims are viewed as more worthy than others. A classic exploration of this is Nils Christie's conceptualisation of ideal victim (Christie, 1986): an ideal victim is weak, is generally a good person, blameless for their involvement and engaged in normal behaviours when victimised. This is in contrast to victims who are somehow responsible for their victimisation, or are of questionable character. Furthermore, the issue of victim blaming can be apparent, whereby victims themselves are responsibilised, or even actively blamed for what has happened to them. In a related sense, victim typologies have been presented, which in some way help differentiate between different types of victims, often based upon their own involvement or level of culpability for their victimisation.

This is linked to the notion of victim precipitation, that is, the extent of a victim's own involvement or encouragement of their victimisation. Examples of such typologies include those from Mendelsohn; Hentig; Schaffer; and Sparks. Sparks' typology (1982) consists of factors that in some way relate to vulnerability and likelihood of victimisation. Among the factors are precipitation, and other factors such as the vulnerability characteristics or attributes that can increase the chances of becoming a victim; attractiveness of a target; and facilitation, in terms of putting yourself or your property in harm's way.

There are also other factors that link to worthiness or full status as a victim of crime. As Greer notes, the determination of who may legitimately claim victim status is influenced by social divisions, including class, race, ethnicity, gender, age and sexuality (Greer, 2007: 33, cited in Bows, 2018: 61). Seemingly, those who sit towards the bottom of social hierarchies are more likely to be viewed as being culpable in some way for their own victimisation. It is possible to recognise links to Chapter 8 within discussions of representations of victims within media.

The issue of secondary victimisation (and even 'tertiary') also needs to be considered. This is where stakeholders beyond the primary victim are affected by crime in some way. For example, the family or friends of a victim of violence or murder suffer also, and can be said to be a victim of sorts. Beyond that, a community as a whole, or even society as a whole, might be said to have been a victim in some sense, hence tertiary victimisation. Also keep in mind, representations of victims and offenders within public discourses, such as those within the news-media and other forms of media, as well as within political circles. Chapter 8 explores some this in relation to media, while Chapter 6 considered the politics of law and order, which help to frame the identity of the victim and offender.

BOX 7.2   CASE STUDY

Sexual violence

The notion of ideal victim appears to be particularly apparent within the context of **sexual violence**, where there appears to be a category of '**real rape**', involving a stranger (male) attacking a young attractive woman who is vulnerable. The reality presented within the data suggests that this form of attack makes up only a small proportion of rapes; most acts are committed by a known party. Yet the 'real rape' conceptualisation is the dominant one within the media, and within the CJS. Research has shown that high levels of acceptance of such 'myths' among police, judges, barristers and jurors, can lead to rape scenarios being dismissed because they do not conform to the 'real rape' stereotype (Ellison and Munro, 2009).

Clearly there are significant justice implications in this, and the low numbers of convictions in relation to rape are hardly surprising. Furthermore, Tempkin et al. (2017) found that rape myths continue to impact on rape trials, used by defence barristers to interrogate the prosecution's case. Furthermore, challenges to such assumptions were reported to be low among the prosecution and judges within the research.

(*Source*: adapted from Bows, 2018: 64–5)

The blurring of the boundary between offender and victim must also be considered. It is natural to see the two categories as distinct from each other, in a similar vein to Nils Chrisite's model of an ideal victim. But in practice, the processes of becoming an offender can be linked to processes of victimisation, and vice versa. The examples of sex work, gangs, and the homeless, are helpful in making this point. We know, for example, that youths are generally more likely to be both victims and offenders than other groups, but this is particularly evident in the instance of gang membership. We also know that those engaged within precarious occupations, especially sex work, are not only engaged in illegal behaviours through their role, but also that those workers are heavily victimised (rape, violence, abuse, robbery) in the course of their job, and also, often victims of social inequalities, and abuse/violence in early life and within relationships (Phoenix, 2018: 27; Rumgay, 2005: 16). Homelessness is a case study within Chapter 10, which considers the interactions between the homeless and the criminal justice system in one way or another.

The experiences of women within offending is explored by Judith Rumgay, who examined a large body of work that points to an entangled relationship between female offenders and their own victimisation (see Rumgay (2005) for a brief summary of a much larger report). The types of victimisation experienced by female offenders included childhood emotional, physical, and sexual abuse, and intimate-partner violence. The CJS is ill-equipped, and ideologically unable to reconcile this relationship between victimisation and offending. For example, Rumgay (2005: 16) notes how:

> the tension inherent in a contradictory dual identity as both victim and offender has presented a considerable obstacle to the development of coherent policy and practice, particularly in the fields of sentencing and rehabilitation. The criminal justice system relies heavily on a clear distinction between the totally innocent victim and the totally guilty offender ... When this distinction blurs, so that a victim appears less than fully innocent and/or and an offender less than fully blameworthy, difficulties arise concentring the attribution of culpability and the distribution of punishment.

Feminist writers have raised questions concerning the status, experiences and treatment of women within crime and justice processes. Feminist positions challenge the male-centred nature of the criminal justice system, and highlight the unique offending and victimisation experiences of women, and the iniquitous workings of criminal justice processes. They often also point to the patriarchal nature of society, which serves to victimise women in specific ways (see MacKinnon, 1987). Rumgay's paper reflects that point. Feminist authors have sought to account for the specific offending and victimisation experiences of women as witnessed in the statistics. Women suffer most from domestic violence and abuse, and sexual violence, while they are more likely to engage in low-level, often property-related offences. Steffensmeier and Allan (1996) seek to explain such gender differences in offending within their work, while Maher (1997) considers more expansively the ways in which structures of gender shape men's and women's lives, and the crime implications of such.

Gender-based theories can also focus explicitly on male offending and victimisation patterns; these are theories of masculinity. Such approaches offer a way of understanding both violent offending, and victimisation of males. Hegemonic masculinity in particular, describes the nature of being male, and the dominant characteristics of 'maleness' within society. As Messerschmidt (1993; 2000) notes, this is related to being tough, being dominant, even being violent. Men seeking to live up to ideals of being male can become involved in violence, both as offenders and victims. As shown within the ONS data earlier in the chapter, men, young men especially, are the group most likely to be both offenders and victims of violent crime.

7.4 UNCONVENTIONAL OFFENDERS AND VICTIMS

BOX 7.3   ADDITIONAL INFORMATION

Corporate crime

Defined as: *Illegal acts or omissions, punishable by the State ... which are deliberate decision-making or culpable negligence within a legitimate formal organization ... in accordance with the normative goals, standard operating procedures and/or cultural norms of the organization; and are intended to benefit the corporation itself.*

Can include: *financial crimes, crimes committed directly against consumers, crimes arising directly out of employment relationships, and crimes against the environment.*

Implications: *a focus upon corporate crime entails continual scrutiny of the coverage and omissions of legal categories.*

(Adapted from Tombs and Whyte, 2013: 81–3)

Considering the nature of victimisation and offending, and therefore victims and offenders, it is important to think expansively and beyond the confines of formal conceptualisations of crime. Thus, the value of the concept of harm is helpful in identifying offending and victimisation: the HSE data presented in Chapter 5 (Figure 5.1) is useful to revisit here, because as authors such as Tombs and Whyte (2013) note, incidents

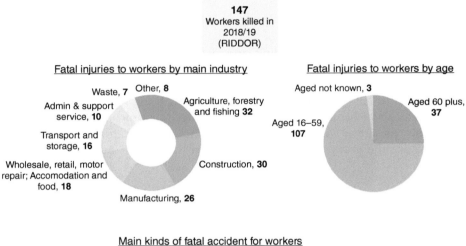

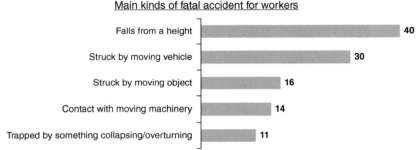

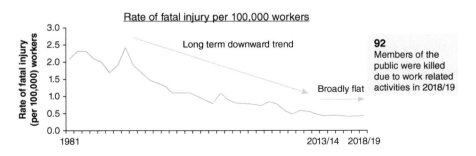

Figure 7.3   Deaths at work

(*Source:* adapted from HSE, 2019)

such as deaths at work can often be a result of negligence and practices imposed by employers, and a lack of proper health and safety consideration. Hence data such as that in Figures 5.1 and 7.3 also reflect processes of victimisation, perpetrated by corporations. It is just that such data does not feature within formal crime statistics.

The example of the demise of the construction giant Carillion reflects the power of big firms, and the harms they can cause. Carillion took government money for public projects and services, and ultimately, mishandled them, and they falsely declared profit levels. The outcome of this has been the loss of jobs, and contractors and taxpayers being left out of pocket. The firm went into insolvency in early 2018, after it ran out of money and could not afford to run its contracts, nor deal with its spiralling debts. This was a consequence of the firm winning contracts at prices that were artificially low to undercut competitors and offered unrealistic chances of project completion and profit-making. The firm misled investors and the government regarding its financial health. The demise of Carillion is significant: it held 450 private–public partnership contracts, and had 43,000 employees and 30,000 sub-contractors. The scandal put the jobs and pensions of thousands at risk, both Carillion core staff and sub-contracted employees (e.g. see Brummer, 2018).

Figure 7.4   Protesting for justice for Grenfell

(*Source:* Worthington, 2018)

Another high-profile case that might also be considered here is that of the fire at Grenfell Tower, in London in 2017. Ultimately, negligence through unsafe practices by contractors, such as the use of flammable cladding, led to the deaths of many residents. The local authority and State more generally also appear to have some culpability through contracting-out improvement works, but not ensuring that the work was completed to a safe standard. They also failed to ensure that safety features such as sprinklers were installed. In addition, there were previous warnings regarding the dangers of possible fire at Grenfell which were ignored.

The scenario of the State as offender is also important to consider, and this can have international dimensions. State crimes are 'forms of criminality that are committed by states and governments in order to further a variety of domestic and foreign policies' (McLaughlin, 2013: 445). This is dealt with more expansively in Chapter 11, but it is worth signalling here that there are a range of crimes committed/facilitated by the State in some way, which criminologists have increasingly given attention to. The most serious of which can be collectively referred to as peace crimes:

- genocide – an attempt to eradicate a population based on ethnicity, nationality, etc.;
- crimes against humanity – systematic and widespread attacks on civilians using extreme violence, such as murder, rape, torture, enslavement, etc.;
- war crimes – crimes committed in the course of war (violations of the laws of warfare), and;
- the crime of aggression – unlawful invasion, or military occupation. (Short, 2017: 287)

It might also be argued that society as a whole, or at least groups within it, can be collectively responsible for the harms experienced by specific groups or communities, i.e. the processes of social injustice some face. The examples of climate change and elements of consumerism are relevant here. In relation to climate change, the habits and practices of the many (heavy energy use, car ownership, being wasteful) has resulted in environmental damage that impacts on everyone, but disproportionately the poor. Consumerism drives global market forces that create global inequalities. Western consumerists enjoy benefits of labour exploitation and harmful working conditions in the Third World, where goods are produced cheaply. In both instances, the global poor are subjected to harms (hence victimised) created by the behaviours of the many. Those creating such harms thus might be understood as offenders in some sense.

7.5 CONCEPTUALISING THE *VULNERABILITY* TO VICTIMISATION AND OFFENDING

A number of themes emerge from considering the discussions above, including from domestic statistics on offenders and victims. The same themes are also apparent within more expansive forms of victimisations, such as those described in the context of corporate and State crime. Indeed, the themes also emerge in relation to both domestic and international forms of victimisation and offending. Those themes are class, inequality, power, and community. Such ideas are useful in allowing us to make sense of events, and crucially, consider *why those victims*, and *why those offenders*:

- Class: in a broad sense, this relates to the ways in which people are socially and economically divided, and usually placed into associated identity groups. This can be in terms of wealth/income, but also in relation to culture, ethnicity, ability/ disability, and so on. It is possible to recognise how those who are victimised in relation to both domestic and international processes of victimisation tend to be marginalised economically, or in terms of status. While offenders who feature within formal criminal statistics tend to be from the same groups, those who feature within other measures such as those related to corporate crimes, are from elite social groups. This is developed further in Chapter 11, particularly in conjunction with the concept of social justice.
- Inequality: describes the unequal distribution of resources, opportunities, recognition, respect and other outcomes between people and groups within societies. Usually, there is a fairness aspect to this, i.e. unequal outcomes are unfair outcomes. This is closely related to class, in the sense that identification with a specific class group can shape a range of outcomes. There appears to be significant differences in likelihood of victimisation based upon an individual's social group or class, whereby traditional offending, and corporate, State and other harms disproportionately impact on the poorest and marginal. Furthermore, there appears to be an inequality of protection and justice for the poorest. Offending similarly appears to be linked to economic and social inequalities, and theories such as strain theories can offer some insight into this. In addition, studies by Houchin (2005) and the Irish Penal Reform Trust (IPRT, 2012) demonstrate how criminal justices processes draw in the poor. Houchan demonstrates how prisons in Scotland are disproportionately housing those from the most deprived wards, while the IPRT demonstrate how the very laws in Ireland have specifically penalised the poor, e.g. through criminalising debt defaulting and vagrancy/begging.
- Power: relates to the ability that people have to influence their own lives and the lives of others. This is related to the notion of agency, which is a term used by social scientists to describe the ability that people have to make choices and shape their own lives. Another related concept is that of structure, which relates to social processes and relationships that influence, shape, or constrain people's lives. When considering processes of victimisation, it is often the least powerful in society who become victimised, those with least agency, and those most constrained by structure. This is the case in relation to mundane crimes, but also processes such as people-trafficking (Chapter 11) and corporate harms: those who are least able to mitigate such victimisation and least likely to have a voice in terms of justice processes.

- Community: relates to a specific geographic place or, more helpfully perhaps, a cultural or social group of some form, with a specific identity. This can relate to specific cultures, ethnicity, country of origin, religion, occupational status, type of residence or area, and so on. Some communities are viewed as 'risky' or 'problem populations' by society and within law enforcement processes. They are thus drawn into the criminal justice system. Some communities are more likely to suffer victimisation of crime or harms than others, because of who they are/the community to which they belong.

Community

The notion of community requires further examination here. The other concepts above are explored in detail within Chapter 11. The concept of community is a fairly complex one, given the multiple ways in which this can be defined and understood. For instance, in relation to geography, shared culture, in relation to citizenship, or even as being related to processes of inclusion and exclusion (see Mooney and Neal, 2008: 25). However, taking a common-sense view on this, community is related to specific geographic and cultural groups, and it is both a site of victimisation and a source of offending, as well as a possible mitigating factor against offending and victimisation. What does this mean?

Starting with the victimisation aspect of 'community', some forms of victimisation are specific to or more likely within some communities. For example, the impacts of social harms, such as global environmental damage, or corporate negligence, can disproportionately affect some communities; it is the poorest, most marginalised communities who often bear the brunt of such processes. It is also possible to think about victimisation in relation to social justice; one strand of social justice is that people have the right to be protected from harms by the State and other actors (Open University, 2008). Yet, there are systematic failures; some groups or communities are not protected. The State, whether national governments, or international bodies of governance, are thus negligent through not safeguarding specific communities. They are then also, in effect, themselves victimising such communities in a sense.

Indigenous populations within former colonial states, such as Australia, the USA and Canada are a strong example of how victimisation is linked to specific communities. Taking the situation in Australia, one researcher, Harry Blagg, has demonstrated how Aboriginal women were 45 times more likely to be victims of violence than non-Aboriginal women, much of which is linked to alcohol misuse by perpetrators (Blagg, 2008, within Hughes, 2008: 125). This example also shows how the link between community and offending is a powerful one. A range of evidence from government and independent sources shows how Aboriginal peoples are much more *vulnerable* than Australians in general to some forms of offending, and engagement with the criminal justice system. For instance, data from the first few years of the twenty-first century demonstrates that about 2 per cent of the population were classified as being Aboriginal, but such groups constituted about 20 per cent of the prison population (Hughes, 2008: 125).

Similarly, in Western Australia specifically, 4 per cent of the youth population were classified as Aboriginal, but they made up 80 per cent of all youths in custody (Hughes, 2008: 125). This is seemingly part of a bigger process, globally. As Hughes has argued, official statistical data from all over the world points to the over-representation of indigenous groups within criminal justice systems. This links to processes such as social and economic disadvantage, family violence, abuse, unemployment, poor educational outcomes, and so on (Hughes, 2008).

Coming back to the statistics outlined earlier within the chapter, some communities appear to be more crime-strewn than others, and offending of different sorts seems to be linked to certain groups within society. A crude link might be the one often made between inner-city and poorest communities and high levels of crime, thus *demonstrating* the criminogenic nature of such places, and some people within those places. The statistics appear to support this in some way. Yet, it is important to be mindful of the flaws within statistics, and processes of criminalisation. The work of the Chicago School (Chapter 3) offers a contribution to such patterns of offending. Linking crime to environments and social conditions is a crucial aspect of arguments within the Chicago School analysis. The so-called zonal hypothesis model helps to explain heightened levels of crime in the poorest areas of cities, because of processes such as social disorganisation within those places. And indeed, the transmission of negative or antisocial attitudes within some communities must be kept in mind.

It is also possible to recognise the ways in which policy-makers have sought to focus on 'community' within policy-making around law and order. The notion of community cohesion, fostering strong and active communities, and so on, have been part of government agendas in recent times, from Tony Blair and the New Labour government's focus on communitarianism, to David Cameron and the Coalition government's notion of the big society. In effect, this is concerned with recognising the need to build strong communities in order to prevent issues such as crime; whereby strong communities foster civic responsibility and order, and weak communities foster disorder and antisocial processes.

The example of terror is also relevant here. The UK government's approach to dealing with terrorism is embodied with the CONTEST strategy (Gov.uk, 2018). This is an overarching framework for how terrorism and extremism are to be dealt with on a number of different levels, from preventing people from becoming radicalised in the first place, through to responding to terror events and dealing with the aftermath. The element of this that deals with prevention is labelled 'Prevent', and this has proved to be controversial because it places emphasis on the monitoring of and the reporting of specific communities.

7.6 SUMMARY AND IMPLICATIONS

This chapter has explored what is meant by the labels victim and offender. There are common-sense understandings of them, but the process of defining a victim or offender is a complicated one, related to personal characteristics and group identity. Different forms of statistics on crime and victimisation help to paint a picture of the typical victim and offender, but these are broad simplifications, and subject to the perils of collecting data on crime and victimisation. Nonetheless, some patterns do emerge, which disproportionately link certain types of offending and victimisation to specifics groups. It is also important to think about harms within any such analysis, as well as legally defined categories of crime. Processes of victimisation and offending on a global level must also be considered. Some important themes emerge from thinking about processes of victimisation and offending, both locally and globally: class, inequality, power and community. And they are all related to the notion of vulnerabilities in one way or another. Such ideas can contribute to our understanding of *why that offender, why that victim*? Within all this, there appears to be a noticeable link between economic and social marginality, for both offending and victimisation. There is, then, a link back to the critical approaches block of ideas covered in Chapter 3. Most of all, it is vital to think about offending and victimisation in an expansive manner.

RECOMMENDED READING AND FOLLOW-UP MATERIAL

Read

- Davies, P., Francis, P. and Greer, C. (2007) *Victims, Crime and Society*. London: SAGE.

  (Read Chapter 1,' Victims, crime and society', and Chapter 3, 'Social class, social exclusion, victims and crime'.)

- Hughes, G. (2008) 'Community safety and the governance of "problem populations"', in Mooney, G. and Neil, S. (eds), *Community: Welfare, Crime and Society*. Maidenhead: Open University Press.

  (This gives a strong overview of the relevance of 'community' in the context of offending and victimisation.)

Listen

- Danny Dorling, 'Peak Inequality' podcast, available at: www.lse.ac.uk/website-archive/newsAndMedia/videoAndAudio/channels/publicLecturesAndEvents/player.aspx?id=4430

CHAPTER REVIEW QUESTIONS

1. How might the notions of 'victim' and 'offender' be defined?
2. Who, typically, are victims, and offenders?
3. What patterns of offending and victimisation can be noted, in relation to specific groups?

REVIEW ACTIVITIES

1. Visit the list of video sources that explore the Bhopal disaster, its aftermath, and the culpabilities of various stakeholders, available at: www.bhopal.net/resources/films/

   This builds on what the chapter has covered in relation to thinking about victimisation and offending in a broader manner, and it will set up the discussions presented within Chapter 11. Watch some of the documentaries listed; there is a link to watch the documentaries for free. Do also, if you are able, watch the feature film listed, *Bhopal: A Prayer for Rain* (2014) starring Martin Sheen (review available at: www.imdb.com/title/tt0839742/)

   When watching the material, keep in mind the links to:

   The social harm perspective;

   The concept of corporate crimes;

   The ways in which such events seem to link to class, power, inequality and community;

   The ways in which international processes of law and order are problematic in terms of dealing with such actions.

2. Write a list of the ways in which the processes of victimisation and offending can become entangled, including those examples raised in the chapter, and think about how is it possible for a person to occupy both the victim- and offender-label categories.

CHAPTER CONTENTS

8 MEDIA AND CRIME

Image 8.1

(*Source:* Levy, 2011)

offenders and victims. Another might be who is influenced by representations of crime, and how. Another might lead to discussions of ideas from previous chapters in this book that are somehow relevant to this topic. Add as much as you can think of. You will be able to come back to this at the end of the chapter.

8.1 INTRODUCING THE MEDIA AND CRIME LINK

If nothing else, take from this chapter the following points: first, when considering 'media' in relation to crime, this inevitably means thinking about the news-media, but news-media is only one part of the story. Many other forms of media represent crime or law and order issues in some way, with notable outcomes. Social media particularly is of increasing importance. Second, it is possible to recognise how the ways in which crime is selected and presented within various media formats can influence the public, policy-makers and criminal justice agencies and, the actual nature of offending itself. In relation to the general public, this influence is evident within how the public understand crime, including who a victim or an offender might be, the prevalence of crime and the typical effects of it, and attitudes regarding what ought to be done about law and order issues. For policy-makers, politicians and criminal justice agencies it is possible to recognise demands on them to respond to public (and media) anxieties about crime.

This plays out often, through tough talk and tough (or 'punitive') responses in relation to law and order issues, and often in relation to specific groups who are deemed to be problematic. Thus, how victims and offenders are dealt with, and what is done about law and order issues, are outcomes of this. Chapter 6 explored this at some length, and used the concept of penal populism. Third, it is possible to see impacts of media representations as somehow influencing crime itself. This might be in relation to fuelling levels of offending, or shaping offending behaviours in some sense. Deviancy amplification and moral panic processes can be considered here, so too can processes such as copycat offending, and desensitisation to violent offending behaviours. Also important within this are theories such as cultural criminology (explored in Chapter 3), because within the theory images and representations of crime are at the heart of understanding crime and responses to it; offending, and the responses to it, is connected to the cultural landscape whereby crime media is a prominent influence (see Ferrell et al., 2015).

The broad picture

There are a series of links to earlier chapters that should be kept in mind when reading this chapter, particularly: theories of crime (Chapter 3); counting crime (Chapter 5);

and the politics of law and order (Chapter 6). The news-media is important in terms of framing and informing what we know about crime. Most of us draw our knowledge of crime from the media, and particularly news-media. The news-media is important in helping the public to define the events and activities deemed to be problematic, that is, what the prevailing threats are; the issues worthy of having a light shone on them. The news-media also plays a role in shaping understandings of who is problematic – individuals, or groups in society who pose a risk. Furthermore, news-media can also directly fuel or amplify crime issues by causing individual and social reactions to what is reported and how. This could be copycat-style acts, where individuals mimic events reported on in the media (or encountered through other media formats, such as gaming). Or, this could be resultant from other social or psychology processes; a consequence of reporting might be the flaming of tensions and fuelling of passions where injustices seem to be apparent, while desensitisation to violence and learnt behaviours through media exposure can also be considered.

News-media is also pivotal in shaping *what ought to be done* about all of this, that is, the policy responses (see Chapter 6). Stuart Hall and colleagues' work demonstrates how criminal justice policies and practices were shaped by media reporting, public concerns and a political reaction to such (Hall et al., 1978/2013). Anxieties regarding the threat of mugging, which had been whipped-up by the media, had some form of influence on the nature of the policies employed by the State in responding to the threat. Within that example, ethnicity played an important role in terms of who was defined to be a threat to society. Ethnicity was crucial, with the media identification of the 'black mugger'. In a sense, those three elements of society (media, public and government) are locked in a cycle of mutual influence, whereby they each feed into one another.

It is useful to think about news-media in the sense of:

- its influence on our thinking about crime;
- its influence on what or who is deemed to be problematic;
- defining what ought to be done about it; and
- something which has the capacity to create reactions – whether this is about influencing policies on law and order matters, or influencing actual offending behaviours.

Case studies related to issues such as welfare-benefits claimants and gaming, which are considered later in the chapter, are useful in demonstrating the above, but equally there are many others which do the same: terrorism; aspects of youth cultures; sexual predators; immigration, and so on. Some of these are touched on in the chapter, and elsewhere in the text.

However, the news-media is only one part of a much larger story. The term 'media' refers to a diverse set of institutions, processes and mediums. It is true that the literature, including other textbooks in criminology and sociology, often use the term 'media' loosely, but mostly they focus discussions (narrowly, and perhaps unhelpfully) around research and theory on news-media only. It is not only the news-media that has the capacity to influence thinking on crime, and to influence reactions to it. It is important to keep in mind film, music, television, gaming and, increasingly, social media. These mediums are noteworthy sites of investigation for criminologists, as set out in section 8.3.

The very decision to make and air specific television programmes, and the stories they portray, has the potential to influence thinking on law and order issues. The level of violence within television, film and computer games has been argued to desensitise people to violence, and the consequences of violence, impacting on offending in some way (Krahé et al., 2011). The glamorisation of violence and crime within music, film, television and gaming is also of interest, and links back to cultural criminology.

8.2 CRIME WITHIN DIFFERENT MEDIA FORMS

Crime features prominently in most forms of media. It is possible to find heavy representation across the following forms of media:

News-media: printed press; television news; online news sites; and radio bulletins. Some elements of the media are ideologically aligned to the *right* and this political bias often means that they discuss law and order issues in a tough and moralistic manner. Robert Reiner (2002: 402) has argued that most newspapers have *more or less overtly C/conservative political ideology*, where tough law and order practices help to preserve a *British way of life*. There are distinctions in terms of content, style and social attitude between news publications that are *left*- or *right*-leaning in ideology (the *Telegraph* vs. the *Guardian* for instance), but also between the 'red-tops' or 'tabloids' (e.g. *The Sun* and *Mirror*) and the broadsheets (e.g. the *Telegraph* and *Guardian*).

Although printed press is eventually declining and newspaper content is shifting online – plus, newspapers are increasingly being accessed through social media, blogs and phone apps – printed newspapers are still common, and many titles are given away free to commuters.

Television and radio productions: dramas; soaps; documentaries; public information platforms (such as *Crimewatch* and *Rogue Traders*) must be considered here. The decision to cover certain topics and stories, to offer specific angles or frame certain victims and offenders, has the potential to influence what the public understand of those issues. Reality-based shows, whether it is those seeking the support of the public to catch offenders, or those exploring the methods and the minds of serial killers, such as those fronted by criminologist David Wilson, including *Killer Psychopaths*, can capture the public's imagination in relation to

Image 8.2

crime. This also relates to the notion of public criminology, which is concerned with making criminology engage with the public as opposed to it being something that is only aimed at academia.

BOX 8.2   ACTIVITY

Access the following, as examples of recent televised crime content:

- The *Serial* podcasts available online at https://serialpodcast.org/
- The *Making a Murderer* programme (if you have access to Netflix).

Consider how exactly consuming such content might influence thinking on crime and justice in some way.

Film: a significant proportion of top-grossing films are dominated by themes of crime and violence. The ways in which characters are framed, their stories, their role, and so on, must be considered. Jackson Katz (2016) for example, has described the lack of positive depictions of black males within film and other media formats, and the links to masculinities theory (plus, also labelling theory), as explored within Chapter 3, whereby dominant models of what being 'manly' looks like can influence behaviours.

Gaming: popular video games are often extremely violent and the protagonists within them engage in crime; this includes Manhunt, Grand Theft Auto, and Postal. The extent to which engaging with such media platforms might influence behaviours is debated, but theories related to copycat offending, desensitisation to violence, and cultural criminology can all be considered here.

BOX 8.3   ACTIVITY

Go online and research *Manhunt, Grand Theft Auto,* and *Postal*. Have a look at the still images, and the description of the nature of what happens in the games via the available **YouTube** clips of game-play.

Social media: social media can be used for raising awareness concerning crime threats, or appeals in seeking to catch perpetrators. However, considering the 2011 English riots, the use of social media was notable in mobilising people in acts of wanton criminality, according to one perspective, or in political protest against the State and processes of inequality according to another view (see Andrews, 2014). Similarly in the so-called Arab Spring, political protest against authoritarian (and criminal) actions of the State was mobilised via social media, and the events were shared with the world. To explore the wider origins of the Arab Spring, see Joffe (2011). Further, social media can offer a platform for offending through the sales of stolen or illicit goods, while the proliferation of hate speech through social media apps is also noteworthy. So too is its role within gang criminality – see the discussion of social media later in this chapter.

Internet sites: although all of the other formats can exist on the Internet in some form, other elements of Internet content can also be significant in terms of crime content. For example, sites dedicated to illegal pornography. The so-called dark web for example, is content on the World Wide Web that exists on 'dark nets' networks and other hidden parts of the web, which require specialised software to access. A study by Owenson and Savage (2015) demonstrated that a significant amount of access to *Tor*, one of the main dark net networks, was related to child pornography. Plus, here it is also possible to consider mainstream sites such as YouTube, which may host violent video content.

Music: violence, crime and status derived from such, are often depicted in some genres of music, notably rap music, e.g. artists such as Tupac Shakur, 50 Cent and Jay Z often have messages of crime, violence and gang membership within their lyrics. Such artists are often viewed as coming from deviant or criminal backgrounds, and those lifestyles are glorified. A reoccurring question here has been the extent to which such representations influence lifestyle choices, aspirations and offending behaviours of those who consume this music. Grime music and RnB are also good examples.

Other media formats can also be considered here, including literature, where depictions of crime can be notable.

8.3 CRIME CONTENT WITHIN THE MEDIA

In summarising the content within media coverage of crime, it is possible to identify the following key themes:

1. Stories about crime are prominent in most forms of media; the news-media is one obvious example, but as demonstrated in the previous section, this also includes television dramas, documentaries, soaps, film and video games.
2. News stories concentrate overwhelmingly on serious crimes, and particularly violent crimes against the person, such as murder and gun and knife attacks. This gives a warped sense of how common such crimes are – certainly if we compare this with official recorded data on crime, or crime survey data (see Chapter 5).

3. The demographics of offenders and victims within media tend to be atypical of what the crime statistics (see Chapter 5) tell us regarding who typical offenders and victims are in relation to certain offences. For example, linking drugs and gang offences to the issue of ethnicity.

4. The risk of victimisation is exaggerated in comparison to what official statistics and survey statistics tell us. Most people are unlikely to ever become a victim of a serious crime, and the data on this tells us that certain groups (usually those who are the most disadvantaged or marginal within society) have heightened risks of victimisation. It is easy to forget this in the context of news reporting on crime, or indeed representations of crime in popular television programmes or film.

5. The media (particularly the news-media) historically tended to present a positive image of the success and integrity of the police and criminal justice system. And this is still the case in some respects – particularly when reporting on crisis or threats to social order; in the aftermath of the 2017 terror attacks in Manchester and London for instance. Yet also, recently, negative representations of the police and justice system are offered, in relation to corruption, lack of integrity, and miscarriages of justice. Coverage of the famous child sexual-exploitation scandals in Rochdale and Rotherham of the past 20 years or so for example, reflect this. The police were seen to have been reluctant to investigate and protect victims (see Tufail, 2015 for a good overview of these events). Thus, there is a contradictory process at work here.

6. A focus on individual victims and their suffering increasingly provides the motive force for crime stories. A range of accounts, often covering the victimisation of children, including those of James Bulger, Holly Wells and Jessica Chapman, and Rhys Jones, have been particularly prominent. This reflects Nils Christie's discussion of an 'ideal victim' (1986) presented in Chapter 7.

7. Particular issues or concerns are reoccurring focal points for media coverage of crime; terrorism; organised crime; child harm and abuse; and benefits crimes, which feature heavily within news-media. Terrorism and organised crime feature heavily in film, and murder features heavily in soap operas, reflecting the public interest in such issues, and their saleability.

BOX 8.4   ADDITIONAL INFORMATION

The **James Bulger** murder in 1993 shocked the country because of the torture and murder of a child by two other children. The national press covered the story at length, including the use of now-iconic images of James and his killers. This case was also among events that had an influence on policy changes in the period.

The case links to points 6 and 7 in this list, given the important role of children within the story, as victim and offenders, and the heavy focus on the suffering of James. Points 2 and 3 are also important.

8. Much of the above can be understood in light of the news-media having an over-riding imperative to sell newspapers, or to attract visitors online. This means that stories must entice and interest audiences. The public have a fascination with crime – which in part is fuelled by media coverage of it, as well as prevailing anxieties brought about by neo-liberalism – and so the coverage of crime stories is a tried and tested way of drawing in audiences. There are also imperatives that form the type of crime story to be included, and how this should be presented in terms of language, style, imagery, and so on, in addition to the wider themes noted above.

9. The concept of newsworthiness is a crucial idea; this is 'A term that encapsulates the perceived "public appeal" or "public interest" of any potential news story' (Jewkes, 2011: 285). As an over-arching concept, this captures much of what the other points above tell us.

BOX 8.5 ADDITIONAL INFORMATION

Steve Chibnall (1977) for example, presents **8 imperatives (or driving forces) of news-media reporting on crime**: *immediacy; dramatisation; personalisation; simplification; titillation; conventionalism; structured access; and novelty*. The more of those criteria that a story reflects the more attractive it is to report on.

Yvonne Jewkes has revised this, bringing it up-to-date (Jewkes, 2015). Within her account, she uses 12 'news values': *threshold; predictability; simplification; individualism; risk; sex; celebrity or high-status persons; proximity; violence or conflict; visual spectacle and graphic imagery; children; conservative ideology and political divergence*.

Activity: Using the list of sources at the end of this chapter, find Chibnall's text and Jewkes' text and explore those various imperatives/criteria of newsworthiness.

Impact on public perceptions

The public's understanding of the level of threat posed by crime can be distorted in terms of the prevalence of serious crimes. Generally, the public believe that there are more serious offences than the various crime statistics suggest (Chapter 5). In a related way, the public's understanding of who is likely to be an offender can be distorted, particularly when specific crimes are heavily associated with certain groups within the media. Thus, there are misunderstandings regarding offending behaviours in relation to class, ethnicity and other background characteristics (e.g. Hall et al., 1978/2013). In a similar way, the public's understanding of who is likely to be victimised, and how, can also become distorted as the media offer a disproportionate focus on some types of victims, e.g. the ideal victim (Christie, 1986).

BOX 8.6   ADDITIONAL INFORMATION

Yvonne Jewkes (2015) uses the analogy of a **prism** to show how crime stories become distorted in some way through media handling and reporting of them; the details enter the prism, and come out the other side having been refracted or edited in a manner fitting to the agenda and stance of the newspaper.

Media as criminogenic

The issue of media being criminogenic, that is, it can create crime, is a much-debated area. On one level, there may be a relationship between crime and media whereby some people are influenced to commit crime in relation to copycat-style offending, as a consequence of media portrayals of crime. Ray Surette (2014) and Chadee et al. (2017) explore this in some detail, picking up on the various ways in which this might happen. Yet, the simplest way of understanding this is when people copy specific actions they see within the media; this could be unusual crime acts, specific modus operandi, or crimes against specific targets or groups. Here news-media is important, but so too is film, gaming, television and other strands of media.

The example of Georgia Williams, a college student in Telford who was murdered by a friend in 2013 in his home, is a useful example to consider. The perpetrator, Jamie Reynolds, was seemingly influenced by content he viewed online. Reynolds was addicted to 'snuff' movies online, which depicted women being tortured, killed and sexually violated. After hanging Georgia, Reynolds was believed to have had sexual intercourse with her body in various rooms of his home. Clearly, the Internet was not the only ingredient within Reynolds' offending, some underlying psychological issue was at play, but the Internet helped to fuel his offending.

BOX 8.7   ACTIVITY

Follow up on the Georgia Williams murder by watching the Channel 5 documentary *Killed on Camera*, which aired in July 2018. You can watch it online through the 'My5' app: www.channel5.com/episode/killed-on-camera/

A further way in which consumption of media might influence offending behaviours is through processes of desensitisation (see Krahe et al., 2011) because of heavy exposure to images of crime and violence. Thus, exposure to such images, particularly over a period of time, might take away the initial shock factor, and in fact, begin to create a sense that such behaviours are acceptable. In the case of the James Bulger murder, there have been claims around this, and the extent to which the offenders had watched violent media before torturing and killing James – the film *Child's Play* is often cited. Although, the evidence in that case is questionable. Video games such as Grand Theft Auto (GTA), which is one of the most successful video-games franchises ever, have attracted sustained criticism. GTA is argued to glorify violence and crime, is thought by some to be linked to crimes, including murders. As such, lawsuits have been filed against the makers of GTA.

Another way in which media might directly influence offending behaviours comes through consideration of the power of media to create perceptions of injustice; where people feel as though they, or specific groups, are unfairly treated by society, or the authorities. For example, a key follow-up study to the 2011 English riots conducted by Tim Newburn and others (e.g. see Lewis et al., 2011), pointed to the feelings of injustice, inequality and resentment towards the State on the part of some of the rioters. The early media coverage of events fed into this, with a rapid expansion of rioting over a period of a few days.

Finally, taking the example of social media specifically, a clear and accessible platform is offered for the facilitation of crime. The illicit drugs trade is a firm example of where social media formats, such as Instagram, Snapchat and Yellow have been used by dealers to promote their products and organise deals. An investigative journalism piece for BBC3 in 2017 presented by Stacey Dooley, uncovered the use of such apps for drug dealing, and the relative ease with which dealers could operate. The term digital dealers is used within the documentary to describe this new form of dealing, and seemingly with good justification (BBC, 2017). Social media also offers a route to offending through hate speech/statements, harassment and other forms of interpersonal victimisation. Also gang activities can be aided through social media – explored later in the chapter.

8.4 MORAL PANICS AND DEVIANCY AMPLIFICATION

Key within the literature on media and crime are discussions of moral panics and deviancy amplification. The two are closely related, with a process of 'deviancy amplification', or a 'deviancy amplification spiral' connected to a 'moral panic' process. As can be seen, moral panic is somehow an outcome of interactions between the public (including their anxieties and concerns), the media (and their imperative to sell stories, and the importance of newsworthiness) and the political dimension of law and order issues (Chapter 6). The outcome of this is a disproportionate reaction to a perceived or actual threat posed by a group or a phenomenon within society. The important aspect within this is how there is some form of moral outrage caused, so the phenomenon or groups under examination must somehow, seemingly, pose a threat to prevailing moral and decent values of society. Also, there must be a reaction of some kind – further public anxieties, further media reporting, political rhetoric, and policy responses.

BOX 8.8   ADDITIONAL INFORMATION

Stan Cohen (1972) famously examined the notion of moral panic, which came about through interactions between media reporting, and public and political reactions. Cohen used the label **folk devils** to describe the groups deemed to be troublesome. He focused on episodes of disorder among the **Mods** and **Rockers**. His work has become a classic in criminology, and is often drawn on by academics and students when discussing **moral panic.**
    Stan Cohen more generally was one of the true giants of British criminology.

Moral panics are said to arise suddenly and they can almost as easily subside. They can, however, often be revived, as new events or new examples of the phenomena come to light. Consider the example of youth culture; a series of authors, including Stan Cohen, have written about this in relation to moral panic. Geoffrey Pearson's text (Pearson, 1983) for instance, shows how concerns for the behaviours of young people have historical roots – in effect, such concerns are not new because examples of media reactions can be found over many generations. In recent times, these have been linked to drug use; antisocial behaviour; and gang violence.

In the second decade of the twenty-first century, moral panic processes can be identified in relation to immigration from places such as Syria, Iraq and North Africa, and the range of issues associated with such migration. Notably, the issue of terrorism, with movements of people across Europe has been a prominent concern. Another example is that of Operation Yewtree, which is related to the explosion in numbers of historic child abuse cases linked to media figures, including Jimmy Savile. This captured the public imagination and unearthed a legacy of historic sex abuse perpetrated by previously well-respected and high-profile celebrities. And to a lesser extent, it raised questions about the law-enforcement bodies tasked with protecting the public who were found, in some cases, to have ignored or even covered up complaints.

Moral panic: welfare benefits

A prominent example has been that of welfare benefit claimants. An entire genre of media has now emerged, concerned with those on welfare benefits, often painting them in a negative light in terms of being profligate, too lazy to work, and morally bankrupt. Tracey Jensen and colleagues have used the term poverty porn to label this genre (for example, Jensen, 2014). Productions such as *We Pay your Benefits; Benefits Street; On Benefits and Proud*; and *Britain on the Fiddle* are typical of the genre, and they reflect the public fascination with welfare benefits, particularly from a position of moral judgement.

Tabloid media also does a good job of framing welfare claimants in a specific light; according to Jensen's analysis, creating and perpetuating 'common sense' narratives of welfare benefits and fecklessness. Any quick Internet search or Nexis database search will reveal many thousands of newspaper front pages or large stories dedicated to the threat and the problems caused by those in receipt of welfare benefits. Here are a few examples of front-page headlines:

75% of incapacity claimants <u>are</u> fit for work
(*Daily Mail*, 27 October 2010)

Vile product of welfare UK
(*Daily Mail*, 3 April 2013)

Benefits cheat couple claimed £47k and spent it on holidays
(*Express* online, 14 August 2017)

£72,000 'benefit cheat' is caught out winning a gold medal at karate
(*Express* online, 24 October 2017)

Brit who bagged £150K benefits escapes jail – thanks to her 12 KIDS
(*Daily Star*, 8 July 2016)

Typical among the depictions of welfare-benefit recipients is a sense of them playing the system, claiming unnecessarily, and the capacity the system has for creating or allowing such things to happen. As well as fostering antisocial attitudes and behaviours. The first headline is a *Daily Mail* front-page story which claims that the vast majority of those claiming disability benefits are doing so unnecessarily. The second headline comes from another *Daily Mail* front page, related to notorious Mick Philpott, who torched his own home, and in doing so killed six of his own children. The story reports on how the welfare benefits system allows/creates such despicable characters through welfare dependency and allowing people to get away with being antisocial, lazy, and 'vile'.

Such reporting, though sensational and capable of whipping-up a frenzy among segments of the population, harks back to earlier commentary on the underclass, where authors such as Charles Murray (1989) have made links between the problem behaviours of elements of the poor and the perverse nature of the welfare system in contributing to it (see Prideaux, 2010). MacNicol (1987) and Murphy (2015) offer a useful overview of how the poor, historically, have been framed in a negative light, in-keeping with Murray's underclass narrative. The next two headline examples report on a similar theme to the first, claiming that people are cheating the system. The third example relates to a couple who claimed benefits but who were caught taking a series of luxury holidays together. They had also reported to officials they were separated, which enhanced their entitlements.

The fourth example is of a common type within this genre, reporting on incapacity claimants who are in fact at the same time engaging in physically demanding activities – thus, showing that their claim to benefits is fraudulent. Within this story, the claimant is described as winning a tournament, despite stating that she was too ill to go out on her own. Investigators were said to have seen her smoking, and walking without difficulty to her karate sessions, three or four times per week, though she claimed to be stricken with severe asthma, high blood pressure and diabetes. Her statement to the Department for Work and Pensions is provided: *It's always lurking, waiting to strike when it wants, taking the air that I breathe.*

The final headline reports on not only how benefits cheats are seemingly *getting away with it*, which is a common theme in news reporting, but that the system is encouraging irresponsibility and fecklessness – having 12 children who the State has to pay for. The mother was said to have received *'breathtaking' amounts of handouts she wasn't entitled to by pretending to be a single mother.*

BOX 8.10   ADDITIONAL INFORMATION

Those elements of the news-media that are ideologically aligned to the **right**, often paint a picture of offenders as morally and culturally different to the rest of society, and this accounts for their offending behaviours. The **individual pathologies** and the **social pathologies** theories could both be considered here; people being shaped by their wider innate characteristics and their negative environments, as covered in **Chapter 3**.

Strands of the **social pathologies** block can allow us to recognise links between offending and social conditions, and there is a flavour of this in relation to some news-media coverage, particularly those which are aligned ideologically to the *left*, which might be more sympathetic in tone.

Choice and decision-making models are also a useful lens here. This is reflected within some accounts, particularly news-media which is ideologically aligned to the *right* – benefits claimants choosing to cheat the system because they can. Media campaigns calling for tougher sentences to deter criminals, and the need to tighten-up the benefits system are evident.

In considering the example of welfare benefits, and the moral panic they represent, or indeed any other example in relation to moral panic theory, the below diagram (Figure 8.1) is useful. This brings together much of the thinking on the matter, and sets outs what might be viewed as a cyclical process.

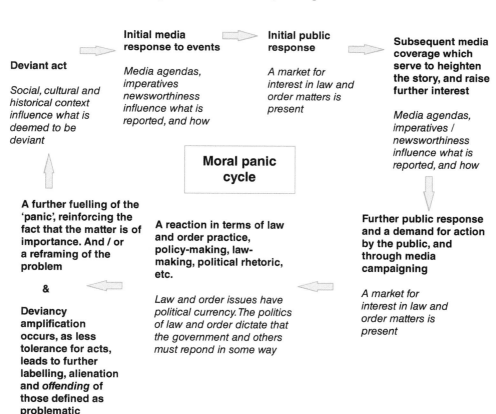

Figure 8.1   Moral panic process

The 'deviant act', considering Jensen's argument, is simply the state of being on benefits, and the problematic status this creates. The sense of 'crime', actual or perceived, relates to fraudulent or unnecessary reliance on welfare benefits, or antisocial behaviours perpetrated while on benefits. The media interest in events is fuelled by their imperatives to publish, and linked to the idea of newsworthiness. This fuels public interest in events, which then fuels further media coverage, and subsequent public outcry, usually accompanied by media campaigning. The public interest in the issue of welfare benefits – particularly where the system is being cheated – coupled with the broader newsworthiness of headlines such as those given above, create a market for reporting on the topic. The deviancy amplification comes through targeted television shows and reporting on *problem* families and estates, where the media go after such novel stories. And exceptional case studies, such as that of Mick Philpott, and the wider public perceptions that this creates, add to it.

The political nature of law and order, then, necessitates a political response in the form of tough talking around the matter of welfare benefits, and new policies must follow; in this case, justification for stringent welfare benefit policies; as witnessed through the 2010 Coalition government, and 2015 Conservative government welfare-reforms. Stringent 'back to work' tests and the famed 'bedroom tax' are examples, and tougher punishments for welfare benefit cheats. Then the re-framing of the issue or the embedding of its status follows. As Jensen (2014) has described, this then contributes to 'common-sense' understandings of the issue – common sense linking between claiming welfare benefits and being feckless or antisocial, when, in fact, this is an ideological creation, and not the reality of the situation for the great majority of those in receipt of welfare benefits.

Moral panic: gaming

As indicated earlier, video-gaming has attracted some interest, and captured the public imagination owing to concerns regarding possible adverse effects on people from playing such games. The possibility that playing violent and crime-focused games might desensitise gamers is one issue. Another, and in some ways related, is that gamers might try to replicate some of the things they see and engage with through the game. The research evidence concerning these processes is not clear-cut.

BOX 8.11   ADDITIONAL INFORMATION

Strands of **positivism**, those related to psychology, can allow us to make links between offending and psychological processes, such as in relation to copycat

offending, desensitisation to violence, social learning theory and differential association, in terms of the transmission of offending behaviours.

The ideas within the **social pathologies** (sociological positivism) block of theory
can also help us to make sense of some of this, because at its core is the notion that
actors are somehow shaped by the environment (social, cultural, consumerist or
otherwise) around them.

There is also a clear link from here to earlier discussions of cultural criminology:
understanding offending, and also the responses to it, in view of the cultural landscape whereby crime media is a prominent influence. Furthermore, the 'thrill' or
excitement of the act of offending or 'transgressing' is also described. Engagement
with violent and crime-laden video-gaming, and possibly playing these out in real
life, might offer that thrill and provide some meaning for those involved. Jewkes
remarks, through this lens: *crimes become a participatory performance, 'a carnival',
and the streets become theatre* (Jewkes, 2010: 35). Film, music and television feature
heavily within this discussion, but gaming represents a useful case study in itself. The
actions, style, thrill and excitement experienced through violent and transgressive
gaming formats (the virtual world) might then somehow translate or be lived-out in
real life.

The Grand Theft Auto series is among the most controversial. Commercially, this
has been extremely successful, but a number of lawsuits have been filed against the
makers, 'Rockstar', because the game series has been linked to a number of crimes,
predominently, murders. Media and political pressure have been placed on the makers of such games. Just one example is that of Fox News reporting in 2005 on a story
about a teenager who had shot to death two police officers and a dispatcher, appar-
ently influenced by/replicating what he had experienced within the game format. The
offender, Devin Thompson, was quoted as saying, on being apprehended: *Life is a
video-game. You've got to die sometime* (Fox News, 2005). This type of gaming continues to prompt debate regarding the need to better regulate violent and
crime-focused gaming.

Academics such as Stephen Kline have written extensively about the issue of moral
panics in relation to computer gaming. But recently, Patrick Markey and Christopher
Ferguson in their book *Mortal Combat: Why the War on Violent Video Games is
Wrong* (Markey and Ferguson, 2017) wrote on the need for caution here. They note
how the panic related to school shootings and other episodes of violence claimed to
be emergent from video-game playing must be tempered with the research evidence,
which does not present such a clear link. The authors for example describe the
'Grand Theft fallacy'.

8.5 SOCIAL MEDIA AND CRIME

Social media, though a relatively newly emergent focal point for investigation, clearly has implications for the ways in which law and order issues are viewed and understood. This chapter has already touched on it in a number of places, but it is worthwhile developing this further here. It is one of the most dynamic areas of focus within the wider area of media and crime. An obvious example of why social media is so important is the example of the Arab Spring (2011) within which a series of dictators in Middle-Eastern/ North African countries were overthrown by popular uprising, and others were subjected to severe pressure (see Joffe, 2011). Global attention (and reaction) was created by social media coverage of events on the ground. Worldwide exposure was given to events, and the use of social media contributed to neighbouring and international responses to those events. Social media was also used to mobilise protest.

Also notable is how social media can be a vehicle for offending, or organising offending behaviours. The Stacey Dooley example considered earlier relates to this, linking the selling of stolen or illicit goods to social media use. But also, its use for grooming minors, hate crimes, or even also the supposedly mass mobilisation of rioters during the 2011 riots across England; see the discussion of the 'Blackberry riots' in Andrews (2014). The term Blackberry riots emerged from those 2011 riots because Blackberry Messenger was said to have been used to spread news and information, and mobilise rioters. The authorities struggled to intercept such messages.

Some authors have explored the relationship between social media and hate crimes. Muller and Schwarz's paper (2018) explored the role of Facebook within hate crimes. Focusing on Germany, where the far-right movement has recently adopted a significant social media presence, the authors note a link between Facebook use and hate crimes: 'right-wing anti-refugee sentiment on Facebook predicts violent crimes against refugees in otherwise similar municipalities with higher social media usage' (2018: 1). Social media is said to differ from traditional media because it allows for:

> user exchange [and] self-select into preferred topics and viewpoints ... Our findings provide evidence for real-life negative effects of social media filter bubbles ... we find that the deliberation of extreme viewpoints on social media increases polarization. We show that hateful sentiments are not only propagated through these networks, but also associated with more hate crimes. (2018: 5–6)

Other authors such as Jonathan Intravia (2018: 158) have explored the link to fear of crime. Within his study, he used data collected from a multi-site sample of mostly young adults, and found that overall there was a significant link between social media consumption and fear of crime.

Authors such as Desmond Patton and colleagues have considered the relationship between social media and gangs. In one 2016 paper, for example, Patton et al. (2016: 591) note how youths are using sites such as Facebook, Twitter and Instagram 'to brag about violence, make threats, recruit gang members and to plan criminal activity known as Internet banging'. The authors interviewed outreach workers in Chicago, who described behaviours such as: 'taunting rival gangs, posturing and boasting about violent crimes'. It was also shown how social media could be of value when used in crisis-interventions work in violent communities, if there were trusting relationships developed between the workers and youths (Patton et al., 2016). A later paper also argued that Internet banging had resulted in: 'serious injury and homicide' and that 'violence may be disseminated in Chicago through social media platforms like Twitter' (Patton et al., 2017: 1000).

8.6 POLICING AND THE MEDIA

The relationship between the media and the police

Historically, policing has been very much about responding and investigative work in relation to events such as property crimes, and crimes against the person. Thus, the increasing complexity of media, and the threats presented by this, has created a range of problems for law and order agencies. Traditionally, the police and the media have enjoyed a positive relationship (primarily here in terms of news-media, film and television). This played-out in positive depictions of the police and policing processes, with a focus on their pro-social function, a commitment to safeguarding the public, and a simplistic representation of them as being on the side of 'good'.

From the second half of the twentieth century, representations of the police became more pluralistic. Jewkes (2015) presents a good overview of this changing depiction of law and order agents and processes. Stories of corruption, and failure, became more prevalent in the press and within television and film. For example, criticism of the police for their involvement in political disputes, such as in the miners' strikes in the late 1970s and early 1980s damaged their reputation. We can add to this their role within the Hillsborough disaster, and subsequent cover-up (see Scraton, 2013). In the miners' strikes the police were viewed by many as agents of the State, enforcing their political will, as opposed to them being a force for the people, made up by the people. Similarly, scandals related to discriminatory practice and attitudes have also done some damage. Examples include, stop and search practices which disproportionately impact on BAME groups, and the handling of the Stephen Lawrence murder in 1993, leading to the labelling of the Metropolitan Police as institutionally racist by the MacPherson Report. Plus, investigative journalism such as that of the BBC's 2003 Panorama episode, *the Secret Policeman*, exposed an ugly side of policing, and the media was quick to pick up on this.

BOX 8.14   ADDITIONAL INFORMATION

In *the Secret Policeman*, Mark Daly (a journalist) went undercover and trained for seven months as a police officer, and filmed racist behaviour among officers in Manchester. This was commissioned by the BBC in the aftermath of the 1999 MacPherson Report, which was scathing of the Metropolitan Police.

'Policing' the media

Given that media plays an important role in terms of informing the public on law and order issues, shaping perceptions on a range of issues related to this (and indeed many other social issues), the extent to which media should have a free hand to do as they please has been much debated. Indeed, the extent to which elements of the media should be regulated or controlled in some way is now a well-rehearsed discussion. On the one hand, freedom of the press, and freedom of expression and choice would dictate that news-media and entertainment-media alike should be free to write and produce media output as they see fit. On the other hand, common-sense checks and balances should be in place to ensure that what is reported is accurate and fair, and to ensure that entertainment-media outputs are appropriately placed, and not unnecessarily harmful to those who consume them (and wider society).

Often, this discussion is centred on news-media. For example, there has been scandal relating to the media giant News International, and their part in the phone-hacking of celebrities and crime victims; child murder victim Milly Dowler's voicemail was hacked, and so too was Sarah Payne's mother's voicemail. Prime Minister David Cameron launched the Leveson Inquiry in 2011 to investigate historic phone-hacking incidents, and police bribery that took part in relation to this, associated with the *News of the World*, one of News International's titles. The *News of the World* was closed down because of the revelations that emerged.

The current ownership models and political affiliations of news titles might be said to create a situation whereby the interests of defined groups become embodied within news reporting. Yet, one safeguard are bodies such as the Independent Press Standards Organisation in the UK, who are in place to regulate news-media content in some way.

The Internet is a more complex system to regulate. The size and structure if it; its international and entangled nature; and the technological complexity of it, makes it difficult to police in any real way, excluding State-led black-outs as seen in countries such as China. *Whose responsibility is it to monitor and police an international, interconnected system with perpetrators impacting on people in different countries? Furthermore, with different legal systems and ethical and moral standards, and who will pay for this?* Units such as the National Cyber Crime Unit are responsible for policing aspects of the Internet nationally within the UK, dealing with specific threats. International/intra-national bodies, however, are also in place, though limited in their role and impact.

Social media, similarly, is a complex arena to police. Facebook, WhatsApp, Twitter, Instagram and other social media platforms have expectations placed on them regarding safeguarding and responding to criminal behaviours, but the extent to which these platforms can and should be governed is still very much a fluid debate.

Policy-making and legislation is slowly compelling further responsibility on the part of both owners and users of social media platforms to monitor and police their own sites. The Criminal Justice and Courts Act (2015), for example, deals with the issue of revenge porn, and responsibilises those who would share without consent explicit images of a third party. Interestingly, law enforcement bodies are themselves increasingly using social media platforms as investigative platforms, where users leave digital footprints, or information that can support investigation and prosecution. The aftermath of the 2011 riots is a good example of this, where social media platforms were used to identify and round-up rioters afterwards.

Policing, media and 'surveillance'

Jewkes (2015), and others, have discussed the surveillance function afforded by media. That is, the possibilities that media formats allow for law enforcement bodies to monitor citizens and gather information on them. The Edward Snowden case is a useful example here. Snowden was arrested and prosecuted for illegally downloading files from the US government. These showed the extensive nature to which the USA and UK were unlawfully collecting data (through hacking and intercepting information) about citizens from Facebook, Google searches, from phones, and so on. This information was passed on to journalists for them to report on. Cyber-surveillance more widely, as conducted by agencies such as SOCA, MI5, MI6, GCHQ, and elements of the armed forces in the UK, and by the NSA, FBI, CIA and others in the USA, is generally accepted as a necessary process to prevent terrorism, organised crime and illegal/offensive content. Yet, human rights and civil liberties campaigners are quick to raise caution about where this takes us (see Jewkes, 2015, Chapter 8, for a detailed overview of this).

8.7 SUMMARY AND IMPLICATIONS

Although the topic of 'media' and crime is a very large one within the field of criminology, this chapter presents some of the most important ideas within the topic. The following points have been covered in some way:

- There are different forms of 'media' that depict crime and justice in some way.
- Video games, music, social media and television and film are increasingly important to consider, and not just 'news-media', although 'news-media' is still very important.
- There are over-riding imperatives that influence news-media reporting on crime.
- 'Newsworthiness' is important in shaping what features within news-media.
- Media can be argued to be 'criminogenic' in several ways.
- 'Deviancy amplification' helps us to understand how media can fuel crime.
- 'Moral panic' processes can occur through media coverage of crime.
- Copycat offending may occur as people see crime representations within media.
- Desensitisation towards violence is thought to be linked to media depictions of crime.
- Cultural criminology considers the relationships between media and crime.
- Media, politics and law and order policies are related to one another.

RECOMMENDED READING AND FOLLOW-UP MATERIAL

Read

- Jewkes, Y. (2015) *Media and Crime* (3rd edn). London: SAGE.

  (For a good overall coverage of media and crime, and the various sub-topics within this, Jewkes's text is a good place to start your reading.)

- Hall, S., Critcher, C., Jefferson, T., Clarke, J. and Roberts, B. (eds) (1978/2013) *Policing the Crisis: Mugging, the State and Law and Order*. London: Macmillan.

  (This is a classic reading which deals with the notion of moral panic, and explores the issues of ethnicity and politics.)

- Chibnall, S. (1977) *Law and Order News: Crime Reporting in the British Press*. Tavistock: London.

  (This offers a useful discussion of what ends up in the news-media and why.)

Watch

- Elizabeth Yardley's SAGE Knowledge video on 'Media and Crime', available at: http://sk.sagepub.com/video/media-and-crime

CHAPTER REVIEW QUESTIONS

1. How do the news-media present issues of law and order, and why?
2. What are the consequences of the ways in which law and order issues are presented within the media?
3. Name three relevant authors from the chapter, and describe their input on this topic.

REVIEW ACTIVITIES

1. Revisit the map you created at the beginning of this chapter. Now will create a more comprehensive summary map of this chapter, covering key discussion points, themes, concepts and theories, and links to authors and case studies. Include some arrows to demonstrate the links between the various discussions where relevant.
2. Using the Internet, follow-up on the examples of the 'Arab Spring' and the English riots of 2011, and make notes on the role of social media in terms of both fuelling behaviours, and recording and presenting events.

PART 3

DEALING WITH CRIME AND JUSTICE

CHAPTER CONTENTS

9 PUNISHMENT

Image 9.1

(*Source:* Reprieve, 2018)

9.1 POWER, AUTHORITY AND LEGITIMACY TO PUNISH

The matter of responding to crime appears, on the face of it, a simple issue: a person or group commits a crime or crimes, and the logical response to this is that the State, or some other body, seeks to punish that person or persons through a sanctioned penalty, such as imprisonment. However, the matter of punishment is much more complicated than that. *Why we punish, and what punishment should look like, as well as who should be doing the punishing*, are all important issues to grapple with. So too must we consider how punishment relates to the nature of societies themselves, and indeed, broader international trends. As well as that, it is important to keep in mind the influences of the politics of law and order (Chapter 6), historical legacies, and so on. Criminologists use the term penology to describe this complex study of punishment, and it operates as a sub-discipline within criminology.

The first issue to consider, *who should punish*, is related to who has the power and authority to deliver punishment, and where legitimacy for doing so comes from. This can be explored by asking the following questions:

- Who has the power/authority to punish?
- Where does that power/authority come from?
- In what ways is this legitimate, and where does such legitimacy to punish come from?
- Who should have the power/authority to punish?
- What happens when the legitimacy to punish is contested?

It is generally accepted (but not universally – consider anarchist movements for example) that States have such power, authority and legitimacy, stemming from their role as governors of a nation, and their duties in protecting its citizens. Famously, Thomas Hobbes within his Leviathan thesis (Hobbes, 1985 [1651]) described how, left to their own devices, people are essentially antisocial and a 'war or all against all' ensues if people are not kept in check. The State therefore has a role in controlling populations. Legitimacy is gained through citizens consenting (albeit tacitly) to the governance processes of the State. The analogy of the social contract is used to demonstrate this compliance; individuals submit to the State and adhere to rules in return for receiving protection from the State.

A common way that States, and agencies representing the State such as the police, courts, prisons, and so on, receive public backing is through elections, where mandates for policy decisions are created. That is only so within democratic countries. In other countries, North Korea being a good example, such power, authority and legitimacy derives from strong autocratic leadership, whereby a ruler has supreme power and decision-making authority. Similarly, in nations such as Saudi Arabia, theocratic leadership is evident, whereby there is a strong influence of religion – countries can have both autocratic and theocratic governance at the same time.

The matter is complicated further when considering the issue of privatisation. This is where corporations have a role within the management and running of criminal justice processes, which raises questions regarding legitimacy of punishment. Notably, the UK witnessed privatisation of aspects of probation from 2014, which followed earlier processes of privatisation within the prison system and police work. The UK is not alone in this respect: in the USA for example, there is a much more embedded culture of privatisation of criminal justice processes. Private companies receive the power and authority to deliver processes of punishment from their contract issued by the State, but does this mean that they have legitimacy according to the people to *deliver justice*? The answer ultimately depends upon one's ideological position.

A linked influence is that of managerialism: a phenomenon which has permeated all areas of public and social policy over the past few decades in the UK and elsewhere.

In short, this relates to an agenda concerned with efficiency, improvement and value-for-money, and usually entails the imposition of targets, auditing processes and ranking measures, and a focus on 'risk' as a means of informing the management and practice of services. McLaughlin et al. (2001) offer a good discussion of this in the context of criminal justice. A reoccurring issue within such an agenda has been the impact on the mission and empowerment of CJS practitioners in performing their roles. Both privatisation and managerialism are, in effect, related to seeking to use the resources, expertise and tools of the private sector to get better or more cost-effective outcomes from the justice system. Yet, the issue of private firms being involved in justice processes, with a profit motive, is controversial.

9.2 PUNISHMENT AT AN INTERNATIONAL LEVEL

The power, authority and legitimacy to punish can of course operate within an international context. States might pursue perpetrators across the world for their crimes, sometimes with legal authority to do so and other times without. This might include conventional law-enforcement activities, but it might also include measures such as war fighting and targeted assassinations (see 'Additional information' box below), which we should think about as criminal justice processes, albeit within a more expansive notion of criminal justice given the role of such activities as a mechanism for bringing perpetrators to justice in some way. The 2001 invasion of Afghanistan, for example, might be viewed in that context, with both the Prime Minister of the UK, Tony Blair, and President of the USA, George Bush, framing conflict in relation to bringing those responsible for the terrorist attacks on 9/11 to justice, and also, the global war against drugs given Afghanistan's role in flooding Western markets with opium (e.g. see Glenny, 2006).

In addition to individual states, the United Nations and other organisations have (according to most states anyway) an accepted role in policing a range of criminal and harmful behaviours. They receive their power, authority and legitimacy for such, for instance in the case of the UN, through nation states signing up to international agreements concerning conduct, and their continued procedural participation within the UN. Often, the UN itself, or individual states within it, receive authorisation to police or pursue in relation to specific issues or perpetrators. The UN's role within the various Yugoslavian conflicts in the 1990s is a good example of this and so too has been its continual presence in Cyprus, policing the border between the Greek and Turkish territories.

Yet there are examples where State actors have failed to receive such authority through failing to receive the backing of individual member states. Thus, their eventual actions are deemed to have been illegal according to international law. The most famous example of this is the 2003 invasion of Iraq, by a coalition led by the USA.

The UN failed to reach an agreement to provide a mandate for the military actions that followed. The military action was eventually declared 'illegal' by the United Nations Secretary General, Kofi Annan. Domestically also, the actions were deemed to be illegitimate, following the revelation that the evidence presented to the UK parliament to grant backing for the war, concerning the capacity of the Iraqi state to deploy weapons of mass destruction, had been modified to play-up the threat (see MacAskell, 2016; MacAskell and Borger, 2016).

BOX 9.1   CASE STUDY

Targeted assassinations: the death of reyaad khan

Taken from the Joint Committee on Human Rights report on *The Government's Policy on the Use of Drones for Targeted Killing* (Second Report of Session 2015–16) (UK Parliament, 2016: 5):

'On 21 August 2015 Reyaad Khan, a 21-year-old British citizen from Cardiff, was killed by an RAF drone strike in Raqqa, Syria. He had appeared in a recruitment video for ISIL/Da'esh and was suspected of being involved in plotting and directing terrorist attacks in the UK and elsewhere.

Deploying the UK's Armed Forces is a prerogative executive power, but the Government has chosen to observe a recently established constitutional convention that, before troops are committed abroad, the House of Commons should have an opportunity to debate the matter, except when there is an emergency and such a debate would not be appropriate. Pursuant to this convention, the House of Commons in August 2013 debated the possibility of airstrikes against President Assad's forces in Syria after their use of chemical weapons but both the Government's motion and the Opposition's amendment (which did not rule out airstrikes) were defeated. When voting in favour of military action against ISIL/Da'esh in Iraq in September 2014, the House expressly did not endorse UK airstrikes in Syria and resolved that any proposal to do so would be subject to a separate vote in Parliament. At the time of the drone strike that killed Reyaad Khan, the Government therefore had the express authorisation of the House of Commons to use military force against ISIL/Da'esh in Iraq, but airstrikes in Syria were expressly not endorsed without a separate Commons vote.'

An enduring legacy of the war on terror, which the above example reflects, has been the use of a highly controversial system of arrest, detention and interrogation of terror suspects. The use of rendition of suspects (in effect, illegal abduction) and torture to extract information are both legally problematic, but seemingly have been used often by USA and some intelligence agencies. However, it is the operation of Guantanamo Bay, which is perhaps the most controversial. Guantanamo Bay in Cuba has been used by the USA to detain terror suspects, but without formal justice processes being initiated. Inmates have spent many years in detention, in brutal conditions, without formal charge or prosecution:

> Since 2002, 779, including at least 15 children, have been imprisoned at Guantánamo. The vast majority of them were sold to the US for large bounties – typically, around $5,000 for each man. So far just 4 detainees have been convicted of a crime – fewer than the number who have died in detention. No one has ever been held accountable for the illegal detention and abuse at the prison camp and it remains open to this day. (Reprieve, 2018)

Such actions can be recognised as criminal justice processes, albeit highly controversial in nature, and international in dimension given how suspects 'rendered' or otherwise brought into Guantanamo are multinational, and have been taken from different countries to that facility.

Image 9.2   Protesting for the closure of Guantanamo Bay, outside the White House

(*Source:* Worthington, 2018)

9.3 WHY PUNISH?

The specific reasons for seeking to punish can be multiple. Added to that, the outcomes of punishment can be equally as varied. On the most basic level, punishment can be either something concerned with the here and now moral reckoning that an offender receives – getting what they deserve in a sense; or, something related to the future, in terms of preventing crime in the future. This can be described as a dichotomy between retribution (revenge) and reductionism (reducing crime). This is a very simple way to think about punishment and, in reality, the nature of punishment in modern criminal justice systems reflects aspects of both. In examining this further, there are a range of rationales for punishment that link to that retribution *versus* reductionism dichotomy. The following are possible aims:

- Retribution: in essence, this relates to how there is moral justification for inflicting punishment upon a wrongdoer, and it is linked to an 'eye for an eye' mentality, without necessarily looking to future consequences. Within the writing of the early Classicists, such as Beccaria writing in the eighteenth-century (Beccaria, 1995[1767]), there was a reaction to the overly retributivist nature of criminal justice in that period, which was brutal and ineffective at dealing with the crime problem.
- Deterrence: at both the level of an individual who has committed a crime, and also society more widely. The principle here is that individuals are dissuaded from committing crime through the nature of the punishment that follows. This is an important feature of Classicist thinking, where imprisonment is advocated as a method of deterrence.
- Rehabilitation: this is concerned with dealing with the factors that are thought to have had an influence on the offender. This could be about changing attitudes and outlook on life, as well as specific issues such as mental illness, and drug and alcohol abuse. This is more in line with positivist positions on crime, as explored within the individual pathologies block of theory in Chapter 3.
- Incapacitation: both temporary and permanent: this is linked to preventing an offender from reoffending by removing them from society. Imprisonment is an example of this, both short and long sentences, as well as more permanent measures, such as life in prison and the death penalty. This can be linked to both Classicist and positivist approaches: Classicism in relation to the extent to that the incapacitation aspect of imprisonment also acts as deterrence and is not a brutal form of punishment, and positivism where influences on offending behaviour cannot be treated and so the offender cannot be rehabilitated. Or perhaps where imprisonment is needed in order to facilitate rehabilitation.
- Restoration/reparation: the intention is to move things back, as far as possible, to where they were before a crime occurred; repairing the damage caused to communities, victims and other stakeholders. The notion of restorative justice is

important here, and itself is seen as a specific penal approach, involving removing the monopoly of criminal justice from the State through involving communities. This is in line with accounts within the critical approaches block of theory, in terms of taking power away from the State.

There are arguably other aims of punishment which sit outside that retribution *versus* reductionism dichotomy, and these are *mostly* more in line with arguments presented within the critical approaches block of theory examined in Chapter 3. These are:

- Social control and warehousing the poor: in line with a range of perspectives within the critical approaches block. Processes of punishment can be viewed as mechanisms for exercising control over populations, primarily the poor and marginal, who might pose a threat to social hierarchy. Loic Wacquant's thesis (2005) presents such an argument within which the policing of urban, poor black populations, and their imprisonment, represents them being warehoused in the context of being viewed as dangerous.
- Disciplining populations to the demands of the economy: punishment for some critical authors is closely linked to creating populations subservient to demands of the economy (capitalism). This is said to be related to disciplining people to adhere to the rules and etiquette of the workplace. Linebaugh (2003) examined this in relation to eighteenth-century English society, while Lea (2015) brought this up-to-date, and linked it to welfare benefits policies also.
- Affirming moral standards and societal boundaries: rather than fitting with a critical theoretical position, punishment in this vein is linked to functionalist accounts of crime and punishment, such as that of Emile Durkheim (see Garland, 1991). Crime and processes of responding to crime are said to aid the functioning and advancement of healthy societies.

In practice, the aims of punishment are multiple, whether this is an individual punishment mechanism, or a nation's penal approach more broadly; they involve a mixture of those various rationales. For example, the following justifications for punishment within the UK are set out within the Criminal Justice Act 2003 (s.142):

Punishment (*retribution*) Reduction of crime (*deterrence*)

Reformation (*rehabilitation*) Protection (*incapacitation*) Reparation

9.4 TYPES OF PUNISHMENT

How individuals are brought into the criminal justice system (CJS), how they are processed, and the steps leading up to an individual receiving a sentence of punishment, and the management of that sentence, is a fairly complex process. In short, taking the UK as an example, this involves processes of law-making, enforcement of laws through agencies such as the police, and then the processing, defence and sentencing of suspects via a system involving the crown prosecution service and the court system, and the instruments for delivering punishment, such as prisons and probation. And then also, there are various agencies whose role it is to manage or inspect those processes, such as the multiple HM Inspectorates, e.g. HM Inspectorate of Constabulary and Fire and Rescue Services, who inspect the police and the fire and rescue services. Further exploration of the UK model is beyond the scope of the chapter. For a more expansive coverage see Chapter 20 of Case et al. (2017); and the entirety of Hudson (2013).

BOX 9.2   ADDITIONAL INFORMATION: POLICING

The nature of policing is not expressly explored within this text, although it is a vital element within the CJS. Within criminology, it has been an increasingly important area of study and research.

Criminologists who research policing, such as **Janet Chan, Tim Newburn** and **Robert Reiner,** have tended to focus on aspects such as the organisation of the police, police powers, different models of policing and themes such as police effectiveness, and police cultures, corruption and privatisation. Tim Newburn, pictured, who, in addition to generally being one of the leading British criminologists, is an expert on policing (and other areas also, including **youth justice**).

Image 9.3   Tim Newburn

One of the best sources of further information on policing is Newburn's *Handbook of Policing* (Newburn, 2008).

It goes without saying that there are a broad range of mechanisms or responses which that may be used in responding to crime and they vary greatly according to their level of severity, the types of crimes they tend to be used in relation to, their specific aims (as considered in section 9.3) and their outcomes and consequences. Figure 9.1 presents some of these different punishment forms.

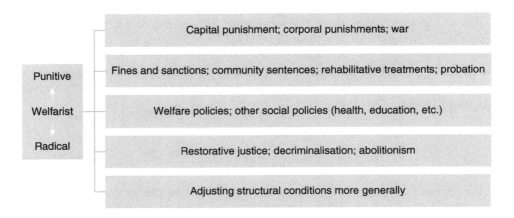

Capital punishment	involves the death penalty of one form or another.
Corporal punishment	involves non-lethal physical punishment including beatings and brandings.
War & international sanctions	relates to the attempt to prosecute States and other offenders across international boundaries through military action, e.g. 2001 invasion of Afghanistan, and economic and other sanctions.
Imprisonment	involves holding offenders in dedicated residential units (prisons) either in the short-term or for extended periods.
Fines and sanctions	monetary or regulatory conditions imposed on individuals or organisations.
Community sentences	linked to the above, involves an offender serving a sentence based within the community, such as project work, having behavioural conditions imposed on them, or improving the local community.
Rehabilitative treatment	involves processes designed to reform an offender and deal with the influences upon their behaviour, such as changing attitudes, or drug and alcohol recovery. This could be done in isolation, or in conjunction with imprisonment.
Probation	involves the supervision of an offender within the community, either as an alternative to prison, or on release from prison, and is connected to the notion of rehabilitation.
Welfare system policies	involves using the welfare system to punish harmful behaviours (withholding benefits), or to incentivise positive behaviours. (*This is explored within the next chapter.*)
Other social policy interventions	involves using interventions in fields such as education or health to tackle offending; e.g. health interventions to tackle offending linking to drug abuse, and parenting support programmes (within Sure Start settings) to deal with both parental abuse of children and future offending of children. (*This is explored within the next chapter.*)

Restorative justice	involves restoring things back, or as close as possible, to how they were before a crime occurred. This entails a range of stakeholders who are related to the crime event in some way, coming together to express their feelings, and to seek closure. This can be used in isolation, or in conjunction with imprisonment.
Decriminalisation	involves changing the law so that certain activities are no longer deemed to be illegal. Drug use is a good example of this, whereby a range of countries, such as Chile and Canada, have decriminalised the medicinal and recreational use of cannabis. (See **Chapter 6** where the issue of decriminalising drugs is used in relation to the **politics of law and order**.)
Abolitionism	involves getting rid of the CJS in its entirety, or, more commonly, the use of capital and corporal punishment. It can also relate to removal of other specific aspects of punishment, such as imprisonment for non-violent offenders.
Adjusting structural conditions within society more generally	involves changing the nature of the economy, and overarching processes within society, such as job markets, the education system, and so on, in order to tackle root causes of offending (linked to acute social inequalities).

Figure 9.1   Mechanisms for responding to crime

Some of the responses to crime are punitive, that is they are tough on offenders, while others are more welfarist, that is, they are concerned with the wellbeing of offenders and communities more generally. Others are radical in terms of changing the current state of affairs or social arrangements. In reality, criminal justice systems use a mixture of responses that are punitive, welfarist and radical in nature, although the balance between these different types of response varies between different criminal justice systems, and over time.

9.5 OUTCOMES AND CONSEQUENCES OF HOW WE RESPOND TO CRIME

Given what was covered in section 9.3, a key outcome of punishment can be viewed in relation to impact on crime in some way. For those various rationales linked to a reductionist approach, reducing crime numbers through stopping offenders from reoffending and preventing others from offending in the first place is the anticipated outcome. Yet, there are other outcomes from punishment. For example, those punishment strategies linked to rehabilitation and restoration are also concerned with the wider welfare of offenders and communities, beyond the specific measure of crime numbers. In addition, other strategies, such as decriminalisation and abolitionism, are more concerned with changing the status quo around punishment, which are presented as being unfair.

In the main, we tend to assess the outcome of punishment in relation to:

1. overall crime numbers, for a specific crime category, or crime as a whole;
2. reoffending levels of those who complete a sentence of punishment, known as recidivism.

These tend to be the *common-sense* measures of punishment effectiveness and in practice, political, policy and public discussions around crime and punishment tend to be linked to these. How such measures are arrived at links back to Chapter 5, where the focus was on measuring crime. Both police recorded data on crime in a given time period, as well as victimisation survey data, can inform us about crime numbers, even though in practice, linking the effect of individual punishment strategies to crime numbers is fraught with difficulty. For example, how exactly do you make a direct causal link and control for a whole range of other possible influences on crime numbers, such as the state of the economy and social change? Focusing on reoffending rates is perhaps less problematic in that sense, but there are a range of factors beyond simply the punishment type an offender receives that can have an impact on their eventual outcome, as well as gaps in the data where reoffending is not recorded. Nevertheless, determining whether an individual has been charged or convicted of a crime in a standard time period following completion of a sentence (usually within 12 months) has value.

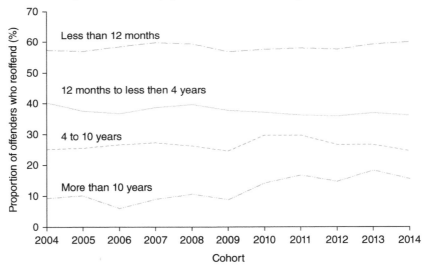

Proportion of adult offenders released from custody who commit a proven reoffence, by custodial sentence length, 2004 to 2014

Figure 9.2   Reoffending and sentence length

(*Source:* MoJ, 2017b)

Exploring the measure of reoffending, it is possible to see significant differences in recidivism levels across different punishment types and in relation to different types of offender; across age for example. Data for England and Wales for 2014 showed that from 488,000 people who completed a sentence of one form or another, 125,000 had been *proven* to have reoffended within a year, at a rate of 3.2 offences per offender (MoJ, 2016). There was significant variation based on age, with younger offenders generally more likely to reoffend. There was also variation in relation to whether an offender had been in custody, or served a community-based sentence; community-based sentences resulting in less reoffending. The variations in outcomes according to prison sentence type are also revealing, as Figure 9.2 shows.

Shorter-term sentences appear to be the most problematic in terms of reoffending levels. Why might this be the case? Such a sentence is likely to be received for lower-level offending, often habitual offending, where unless the wider causes of offending are addressed, an individual is likely to come out of prison after a short period of incapacitation, and enter back into old ways. Plus, there is the question of how well rehabilitative processes can be delivered within short sentences. Plus, there are endemic issues of overcrowding in prisons, under-resourcing, and under-staffing, which also detract from any rehabilitative process that might otherwise occur. At the other end of the spectrum, individuals who go to prison for a long sentence tend to have committed less common and more serious offences, and it is unlikely that they will repeat it, e.g. murder.

Work by Jonson (2012) supports this. That study, which involved bringing together the large body of research conducted on the effects of imprisonment, demonstrated the following:

- imprisonment does not reduce reoffending and, in fact, can be seen as criminogenic – especially in the instance of low-risk offenders;
- most systematic reviews have found that imprisonment has a 'null to slight criminogenic' effect on subsequent reoffending;
- custodial sentences 'generally result in more post-release offending behaviour than non-custodial sanctions';
- Harsher prison conditions result in greater recidivism.

BOX 9.3   ADDITIONAL INFORMATION: YOUTH JUSTICE

The use of punishment in relation to children is one controversial issue. *'At its simplest "juvenile justice" is the subdivision of criminal justice that focuses specifically on law, policy and practice in respect of child offenders'* (Goldson, 2013: 242)

(Continued)

(Continued)

In England and Wales, the age of criminal responsibility is 10, meaning that no child under that age can be deemed to be guilty of a crime. Then, between ages 10 to 18 offenders are processed through a separate court system to that of adults; in effect, a separate justice system. This system involves the use of Youth Offending Teams, community-based sentences, restorative justice practices, as well as custody. A key aim is that of adopting a welfarist-based approach, and diverting young offenders away from formal criminal processes as far as possible. Although, high levels of youth detention (although, it has to be noted that this has reduced significantly in recent years) and reoffending levels, and concerns for conditions (including lack of adequate mental health support) are worrying issues.

For further information, see Goldson and Muncie's (2015) text *Youth, Crime and Justice*.

Beyond counting crime

Aside from the impact on crime numbers, other outcomes of punishment might also be considered. The role of the various Inspectorates, for instance, also relates to the extent to which the police, prison service, probation system, and so on, adhere to best practice, foster fairness and equality within their practice, spend public money efficiently, and so on (see Criminal Justice Inspectorates, 2018). It is possible also to consider outcomes such as public confidence, albeit, such outcomes are less obvious and seemingly less concrete than crime numbers, but crucial given what Chapter 6 demonstrated on the politics of law and order, linked to penal populism.

Social outcomes/costs of punishment, as Garland (1991) notes, must also be taken in to account. This relates to a range of consequences, intended or unintended, which go beyond the issue of crime numbers and the plight of an individual offender. For example, taking Garland's point and building on it, the following outcomes could be included:

- Civil liberties and human rights implications where punishments impact basic rights and freedoms.
- Social inequalities in terms of punishment disproportionately affecting some groups, e.g. disparities in terms of ethnicity and socio-economic status within prison populations.
- The labelling of some groups as 'risky' or dangerous as a result of their disproportionate involvement with CJS processes, e.g. prison populations again, where disparities across ethnicity can be witnessed.

- Damage to families or communities as a result of a punishment, e.g. families being broken up, or communities divided.

Thus, it becomes apparent that any assessment of punishment becomes more complicated than simply thinking about crime numbers, or even recidivism. The use of prison sentences is among the most commonly researched and written about form of punishment, and thus it is worthwhile exploring further. Famously, Gresham Sykes (1958) wrote the *Society of Captives*, and within this, explored 5 Pains of Imprisonment: *the deprivation of liberty; the deprivation of goods and services; the deprivation of heterosexual relations; the deprivation of autonomy;* and *the deprivation of security*. From this, it becomes apparent how imprisonment is about much more than a simple loss of liberty. Instead, it is linked to a range of deprivations and loss of rights, and also, a process that can all too often create or exacerbate social problems and individual vulnerabilities.

A paper by Ramaswamy and Freudenberg (2012), which focuses on the US context, reports on how imprisonment is a social response to dealing with a range of social problems – drug use; crime; violence; and mental illness – whereby the poor, particularly the black population, are dealt with through imprisonment. Such an argument reflects that of Wacquant's (2005) *punishing the poor* narrative, explored in Chapter 6. Furthermore, imprisonment and the failure to ensure appropriate resettlement plans serve to further exclude vulnerable groups from society. A paper by Lee et al., (2016) also projects the exclusionary outcomes evident from imprisonment. The authors link imprisonment of a parent to multiple forms of deprivation for children and, ultimately, social exclusion (this is explored in the next chapter). This is even more acute where a mother is sent to prison.

The problems with imprisonment

Looking at the trend in UK prison numbers since 1990, a clear picture emerges: one of continued rise in the prison population, alongside a persistent overcrowding, as depicted within Figure 9.3.

The bottom line denotes the level of accommodation available to house prisoners, constituting 'uncrowded capacity', while the top line depicts the actual prison population, and thus points to overcrowding throughout most of the period in question. Undoubtedly, this raises questions regarding prison conditions and the capacity for fostering rehabilitative processes. That context is even more worrying given what the Prison Reform Trust (2017) has demonstrated regarding the *state* of our prisons; that is, the various problems faced within the modern prison system in England and Wales, but in Scotland and Northern Ireland also. They report on a number of critical issues, which are mapped out in Figure 9.4.

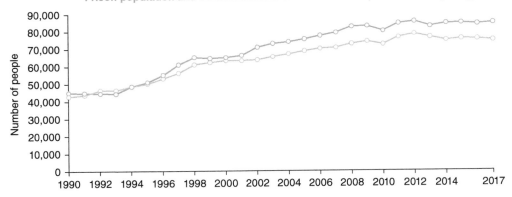

Figure 9.3   Prison numbers and overcrowding

(*Source*: Prison Reform Trust, 2017)

Children in prisons (pp.37–39) At the end of 2017, there were 880 children in custody (although a large drop within the past decade); such children are disproportionately BAME (45%); children in care were five times more likely to be sanctioned for an offence than those within the general population; rates of self-harm and assault amongst children prisoners are on the rise; restraint of children in custody remain high – an average of 380 per month; 90% within young offenders institutes reported having been excluded from school.	**Rehabilitation and resettlement issues** (pp.48–55) For 2014–15, only 16% of people released from prison went into education and training; only 51% of prisons received a positive rating from Inspectors of purposeful activity work (2016–17); time out of cell is limited in local prisons and young adult prisons; In 14 out of 35 adult prisons inspected, there were not enough places for all prisoners to take part in education or vocational training throughout the week; in recent years there had been a 42% fall in prisoners studying Open University degrees (since the change in the funding regime).
Safety (pp.14–15) 300 people died in prison between September 2016 and September 2017; Rates of self-harm are at the highest ever levels – over 41,000 incidents in 2017; serious assaults are at the highest recorded levels at above 40 per 1,000 prison in 2017.	
BAME people in prison (pp.24–25) 26% of the prison population are BAME; the Lammy Review found a clear direct association between being BAME and the odds of receiving a custodial sentence; Black men are 26% more likely than white men to be remanded in custody; a disproportionate number of black people in prison are held in segregation, and held there for long periods.	**Mental health in prisons** (p.44) Self-inflicted deaths in custody are 8.6 times higher than within the general population. 70% of these people had already been identified as having mental health needs; 25% of women and 15% of men in prison reported symptoms indicative of psychosis, versus 4% for the general population; 40% of prisons had inadequate or no training for prison officers to know when to refer a person for mental health support.

Figure 9.4   The state of prisons

(*Source:* adapted from Prison Reform Trust, 2017)

A comparison conducted by the Institute for Criminal Policy Research (ICPR, 2018) using the most recent data (which also includes pre-trial detainees/remand prisoners) showed that England and Wales was placed 20th in the world in terms of total prison population, at 83,014. Its neighbour France had 70,710, and ranked at 26th. The Netherlands by comparison, came in at 93rd, with 10,464. At the other end of the scale, China came in with 1,649,804. However, when considering the imprisonment rate per size of population (using the measure of per 100,000 people), England and Wales was joint 112th in the world, with 140 prisoners per 100,000 people. Seemingly then, the situation, in terms of numbers at least, is not as dramatic as Figure 9.4 might suggest. Similarly, France and the Netherlands also did better on this measure, at 146th and 188th respectively, with rates of 104 and 61. China also dropped down the list when considering total population, at 134th place – but the data is likely to represent an underestimate.

The situation in the USA is also problematic, and the scale of imprisonment there is on another level to that of countries such as the UK. For example, Figure 9.6 depicts the vast increases within the prison population over the course of the twentieth century, and how this continued through into the twenty-first century. The data from the ICPR (2018) – again, this also includes pre-trial detainees/remand prisoners – put the total USA figure even higher than that in Figure 9.5, at 2,121,600, and at a rate of 655 per 100,000 of populations. The USA tops the list for both measures.

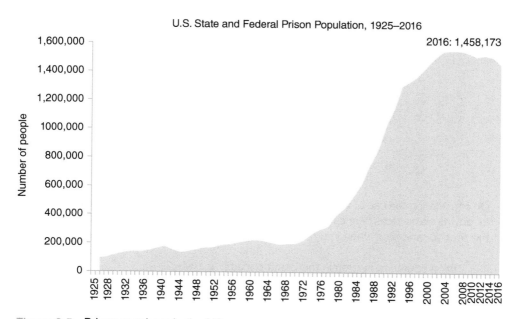

Figure 9.5   Prison numbers in the US

(*Source:* adapted from The Sentencing Project, 2018: 1)

The issue of ethnicity is also significant in the USA, as Figure 9.6 reflects and, indeed, the paper by Ramaswamy and Freudenberg (2012). That paper noted how in New York City young men of colour make up 95 per cent of all inmates. Clearly, there appears to be some form of bias in relation to how ethnicity correlates with likely imprisonment. This is very apparent when factoring in the actual size of groups within the wider populations. For example, the likelihood for all men as a whole, born within the USA in 2001, of being imprisoned at some point is 1/9. For white men specifically, it is 1/17. However, for black men specifically, this become 1/3, and 1/6 for Latino men. Similarly for women, the picture is also very problematic: for all women the odds are 1/56 and 1/111 for white women specifically. Yet for black women it is 1/18, and for Latino women 1/45.

People in state and federal prisons, by race and ethnicity, 2016

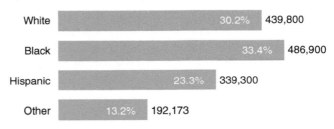

White	30.2%	439,800
Black	33.4%	486,900
Hispanic	23.3%	339,300
Other	13.2%	192,173

Figure 9.6   US imprisonment and race

(*Source:* adapted from The Sentencing Project, 2018: 5)

9.6 THE DEATH PENALTY

BOX 9.4   ACTIVITY

On considering the use of capital punishment, think about the following questions and jot downs some ideas. You can then come back to this once you have finished reading the section, and also when you have done some wider reading around the subject:

- Which countries still retain the death penalty, and why?
- What are the rationales for the death penalty?
- How is it carried out? How are people put to death?
- Does it have a place in the modern world?
- What are the wider implications of it?

The use of death as a means of punishment, or capital punishment as it is known, continues in many countries. Perhaps surprising, is that according to the charity Reprieve, by the end of 2016, 57 countries were still actively administering the death penalty, and another 30 retained its use in principle. And in that year, at least 1,032 people had been put to death (Reprieve, 2018). That figure is likely to be a large underestimate given the lack of transparency in some countries regarding justice processes. The list of countries that retain its use include the USA, and also Japan; some of the most economically advanced nations on Earth.

BOX 9.5   ADDITIONAL INFORMATION

Notice the link back to **Chapter 5**, on counting crime. The role of NGOs, such as Amnesty and Reprieve, in collecting and disseminating information on crime and punishment matters is important, where otherwise such data would not be available to us.

In terms of numbers put to death, according to Reprieve (2018) (using data from Amnesty, and Death Penalty Worldwide), China is thought to top the list, with an estimated 1,000+ deaths per year, although the true figure is unknown. Iran follows at an estimated 567+, and Saudi Arabia is in third place with at least 154 deaths in the same period. To put this into context, the USA is thought to have put 20 people to death in the same period, albeit with a great variation between states, with many having abolished capital punishment, while others retain it but do not use it, and some retain it and actively use it.

All of this might be surprising to us within the twenty-first century, given processes of globalisation (see Chapter 11), sharing of cultures, and the role of mass media and social media bringing the word together. Indeed, those Classicist authors, such as Beccaria (Chapter 3), wrote about the problems of overly punitive responses to crime, and they were particularly critical of putting people to death. In Britain for instance, capital punishment was effectively ended in 1969.

For Beccaria, writing in the eighteenth century, the use of such responses took legitimacy away from the criminal justice system. And yet, fast-forward to the twenty-first century, and such responses to crime are still prevalent globally. Organisations such as Reprieve strive towards total abolition of capital punishment, but there is some way to go for this to become reality. In instances where abolition has occurred, such as within Britain, this has been a consequence of changing social, cultural and political dynamics, as well as notable miscarriages of justice which served to discredit capital punishment as a credible form of punishment. The cases of Timothy Evans and Derek Bentley were two such high-profile cases, where defendants were hanged in error. Evans was wrongly convicted of the murder of his wife and daughter, who were in fact murdered by the landlord; while Bentley was convicted for the murder of a policeman that occurred during an attempted robbery, but it was thought that Bentley neither fired the shot, nor was of sound mind.

Linking capital punishment to rationales and theories

The use of capital punishment is more complicated than we might imagine. For example, it is not possible to point to any one single rationale for its use, but rather, a series of rationales can be identified, and these can vary between different countries. The following are possible rationales, and these are also linked back to discussions of criminological theories in Chapter 3:

- Deterrence: to set a strong example to others in order to dissuade offending.
- Incapacitation: capital punishment is the ultimate form of incapacitation; putting people to death permanently removes their ability to commit crime.
- Retribution: capital punishment is an extreme form of retribution; the ultimate means of making offenders pay for their crimes against society or the State.
- Enforcing morality or religious ideology/exercising the symbolic power of the State/suppressing populations: such rationales, which are linked, are concerned with preserving the current state of affairs within a country, and preventing social/political change.

Generally, Classicists, critical authors, and most Positivists alike would view capital punishment as problematic. Classicist models hold deterrence and incapacitation to be important, but most Classicist writers would view the use of death as a step too far and consider it to be brutal, and detracting from a legitimate process of justice. For positivists, treatment and rehabilitation of offenders, or reforms in society are advocated as responses to crime. Yet the death penalty might have relevance for some when dealing with dangerous offenders, where treating them is not possible. Critical authors generally view such a punishment as repressive, and an extreme example of the control of the State, to the detriment of its people.

Application of capital punishment

In addition to there being different rationales for the use of capital punishment, there are also different ways of carrying it out, and each can tell us something about the nature of those societies. The methods can include: judicial hanging; electric chair; lethal injection; stoning to death; beheading; or use of firing squads. Some appear to be more barbaric and drawn out in nature than others, which might tell us that not only is the sentence of death important in itself, but also, that it is important for individuals who receive it to suffer before they die. *Stoning* is a good example of this, whereby the offender is likely to suffer physically before eventual death. So too might we consider some forms of hanging here: judicial hanging can involve a sufficient drop in order to break an offender's neck and kill them quickly, but it can also entail a slow dangle from a low height, which then entails an offender suffering for some time before they eventually succumb.

What is also telling is how capital punishment can be used for policing behaviours that have a moral or religious element to them, which then makes them an offence within specific countries, but not all countries. Linking to discussions in Chapter 1 on the social construction of crime, this most extreme of punishment types is used routinely in some countries in responding to behaviours not criminalised in other countries. For example, Reprieve (2018) list such behaviours:

- adultery and premarital sex;
- apostasy (abandoning your faith);
- protest; blasphemy; and
- 'homosexual acts'.

Saudi Arabia, Iran, Nigeria, Yemen and Afghanistan are cited as examples in relation to most of those behaviours. Furthermore, the application of capital punishment for children raises further issues. For example, between 2013 and 2018, Egyptian courts have recommended initial death sentences for at least 10 children (Reprieve, 2018).

BOX 9.6   CASE STUDY

Saudi Arabia

- In 2016, at least 154 people were put to death.
- The methods used include **beheading, stoning**, and **'crucifixion'** (beheading followed by public viewing).
- The death penalty can be imposed for 'protest-related offences', including attendance at political protests, and acts such as adultery, blasphemy and sorcery.
- In January 2016, 47 people were executed in one day, including juveniles. At least one – **Ali al Ribh** – was convicted on charges relating to protests; The Saudi authorities did not inform his family of the execution and are keeping the location of his burial secret.

(Continued)

(Continued)

- In April 2019 Saudi Arabia was reported to have executed 37 people in one day, which is thought to have included children and the disabled. Those executed were accused of being involved in terrorism, despite international commentators claiming that confessions were extracted under duress/torture (e.g. see Al Jazeera, 2019; Smith, 2019).

(Source: adapted from Reprieve, 2018)

9.7 CRITICAL ISSUES OF PUNISHMENT

When thinking about punishment, whether this is in relation to imprisonment, capital punishment or any other process, such as community-based punishments, a number of critical issues must be considered. Such issues raise questions concerning the workings of punishment, influences on punishments, and the consequences of how we punish.

The punishment of children and women is an acute problem, particularly given that there tends to be a heightened vulnerability of women and children within the CJS, and particularly prisons in terms of harm and impact on families;

The privatisation of aspects of criminal justice in many countries, and the linked issue of managerialism; both of which are essentially about using a private sector ethos and model to drive standards and efficiencies within criminal justice. This raises questions regarding legitimacy, and the relevance of using a profit motive in relation to justice issues;

The politics of law and order seemingly have some influence on the nature of punishments used (Chapter 6);

Effectively dealing with mental health issues which are linked to offending, or are a consequence of the nature of punishment, such as imprisonment;

Resource and staff shortages in areas such as the prison system, probation and offender support services, impact on the likelihood of rehabilitative pathways developing for offenders;

Processes of penal reform, decriminalisation, and abolitionism;

Wider patterns, over time and internationally, of punishment (think here about Garland's *Culture of Control* thesis (2001) for instance).

Beyond the criminal justice system

There is a wider issue here, and one that becomes obvious should we consider the arguments within the social pathologies block of theory in Chapter 3; that of viewing crime as something linked to social conditions and economic processes. If we view crime in that way, then thinking about punishment as a mechanism for addressing crime only gets us so far. This is because punishment, in the main, is focused on dealing with the outcomes, rather than causes of crime. Certainly, rehabilitative pathways might be fostered alongside imprisonment or community-based punishments, but nevertheless this is a reactive process, rather than a pro-active one.

If we view crime as in some way being a product of social processes such as inequality, failing job markets, failing educational systems, and so on, then it stands to reason that those processes should be addressed to impact on crime. Those sorts of policies and interventions thus sit outside of the CJS. The CJS undoubtedly has a role to play, but so too do other policy areas. That sense of needing to go beyond the criminal justice system is the main theme in the next chapter, which considers welfare benefits, health, education and other policy areas in relation to dealing with, and preventing crime.

9.8 SUMMARY AND IMPLICATIONS

The study of punishment, or penology as it is known, is a core part of criminological enquiry, and draws together thinking on the aims and rationales of punishment, different strategies for punishing, criminological theories on offending, and considerations for the outcomes and consequences of punishments. Punishment in a modern sense should be concerned with positive social outcomes, although this is not always the case. The ways in which societies seek to punish can tell us much about the social, cultural and political dynamics within those societies, as well as broader shifts in attitude and policy-making. The use of imprisonment proves to be particularly controversial given what we know about the historically high numbers we see in the USA, UK and elsewhere, and the concerns regarding prison conditions, reoffending and the social outcomes from mass imprisonment. The death penalty is also an interesting case study, considering its continued use in many countries, and the moral and ethical questions it raises. The idea that 'punishment' can only get us so far in dealing with the crime problem is an important one, particularly when we view crime as being linked to wider social conditions and processes.

RECOMMENDED READING AND FOLLOW-UP MATERIAL

Read

- Hudson, B. (2003) *Understanding Justice: An Introduction to Ideas, Perspectives and Controversies in Modern Penal Theory*. Buckingham: Open University Press.

  (This covers theory, rationales and examples of punishment, and will develop many of the ideas from the chapter in more detail. Read the introduction and then choose some additional chapters at your leisure.)

- Prison Reform Trust (2017) 'Bromley *Briefings Prison Factfile Autumn* 2017'. Prison Reform Trust [online], available at: http://www.prisonreformtrust.org.uk/Publications/Factfile

  (This provides a good overview of the contemporary landscape of prisons in England and Wales, and covers some of the critical issues and concerns.)

Watch

- Clive Stafford Smith's TED talk: 'My Father, Mental Illness and the Death Penalty', available at: https://www.youtube.com/watch?v=gMNIRovT5x4

CHAPTER REVIEW QUESTIONS

1. What are the various rationales for punishment?
2. How might we think about the outcomes of punishment – are there different ways of thinking about the consequences of punishment?
3. What are the pros and cons of imprisonment as a way of responding to crime?
4. Is there a place for the death penalty in the modern world? Why do some people seek to abolish it?

1. Go online and have a look at the abolitionist charity 'Reprieve' via their website https://reprieve.org.uk/

2. Do some research on what the charity does, and what it aims to achieve. Do also look at any news bulletins and short video stories presented on the homepage.

3. In order to consolidate your learning of the topic, produce a poster that maps out the various types of punishment we see globally, and how they link to punishment rationales. Use the chapter and your wider research to add statistics to this, regarding the prevalence of the punishments, and also add information regarding punishment outcomes and consequences. The following box is a useful template to follow.

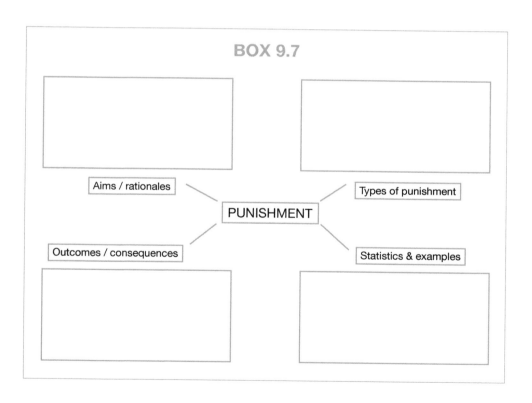

BOX 9.7

Aims / rationales

Types of punishment

PUNISHMENT

Outcomes / consequences

Statistics & examples

CHAPTER CONTENTS

10 SOCIAL POLICY AND CRIME

Image 10.1

(*Source:* Ksicinski, 2017)

LEARNING OUTCOMES

By the end of this chapter, you will be able to:

1. understand how a range of poor social outcomes, including crime, are seemingly linked;
2. recognise where criminal justice policies have relevance for broader social policy areas, such as education and health;
3. recognise where policies located within broader social policy areas, such as education and health, have relevance for law and order issues.

10.1 UNDERSTANDING THE CONNECTION BETWEEN SOCIAL POLICY AND CRIMINOLOGY

Chapter 1 demonstrated how criminology is an interdisciplinary endeavour; one which draws from a range of disciplines in order to explore, explain and respond to law and order issues. It is also possible to describe criminology as a sub-area within social policy, as some do, which is concerned with law and order aspects of society, and policy-making around that. For example, see Baldock et al. (2011), whose best-selling textbook on social policy has a chapter on *crime, justice and punishment*, among others on *housing and housing policy, social care, health and health policy*, and so on.

The policy aspects of criminology, historically, have been viewed, at least in part, as being concerned with crime control agendas, i.e. being focused on preventing crime. Conversely, social policy as a broader field is concerned with social welfare agendas and policies, i.e. focused on peoples' welfare in a broad sense. Yet the nature of modern-day criminology means that it now also includes a focus on wider issues of welfare through its interest in inequalities, social justice and, crucially, harm (see Chapters 7 and 11), which connect criminology to aspects of social policy. Plus, as the previous chapter on punishment noted, understanding both the causes of crime, and how to tackle crime, ultimately leads us to think beyond the confines of the CJS, into the realms of social policy areas, and thus beyond traditional understandings of what criminology should be. Crime might also be viewed as just one of many, connected, social issues.

One obvious area of relevance for thinking about the connection between criminology and social policy is the use of criminological expertise and policies to deal with social problems that sit within other policy domains, such as those in education, health or welfare benefits. Also, it is possible to recognise the opposite scenario, whereby expertise and policies within other domains are used to deal with law and order issues. For example, scenarios could include sanctioning parents for failing to ensure their children participate in schooling, and using health and wellbeing interventions (e.g. drug and alcohol recovery programmes) to deal with offending. Furthermore, it is important to consider the effects of specific policies, where outcomes can cross over into different domains. For example:

> Social welfare policies presented as meeting social needs can be experienced by users and claimants as punitive, and they can have criminalising effects. Similarly, crime control policies presented as deterring people from crime and maintaining law and order may also have distinctive 'welfarist' or rehabilitative dimensions. (Open University, 2008)

Hartley Dean's overview

Some specific examples of policies are explored later within the chapter, but the broader point concerning the relationship between the two disciplines is developed further by Hartley Dean. Dean (2012: 106–8) for example, presents three clear areas where criminology and social policy overlap. These are:

First, there is the issue of community safety and the importance to human wellbeing of physical security. The criminal justice system plays an important role in providing a safe and congenial local environment in which to live. The concept of 'community safety', initially framed in the Morgan Report ... captures the sense in which the criminal justice system may be thought of as an element within a holistic approach to social justice. Specifically, the Morgan Report suggested that crime prevention and reduction strategies should be situated within a broad social policy framework and based on local multi-agency collaboration between human service industries. Elements of this approach were implemented in the UK from 1998 onwards, when local authorities and community-based agencies were given a role in partnership with the police in developing crime reduction and prevention strategies ... It is an approach that links crime reduction and prevention to housing, public health, community education and social service issues.

Dean demonstrates a link back to Chapter 7, which covered the relationship between the notion of community and offending/victimisation. In addition, Dean is also leading the discussion back to the logic within a social pathologies understanding of crime, and thus, what ought to be done about crime; locating the development and continuation of crime as being something connected to aspects of communities and a range of social issues:

the development of common theoretical understandings about the disciplinary effects of administrative processes and of prevailing shifts in policy. Post-structuralist analyses ... have contended that criminal justice systems and welfare systems were equally implicated in the development of the disciplinary techniques by which modern societies were governed. Penal and welfare institutions had certain things in common, not least the significance they attach to the surveillance of the individual human subject, and the way they succeed in stigmatizing certain social groups ... The essentially populist policy response has constituted what David Garland (2001) characterizes as a 'culture of control'. The new approach is characterized, on the one hand, by 'tougher' and more tightly regulated sentencing of offenders, but also by new methods in policing, based on 'zero-tolerance' of even minor offences, such as begging and antisocial behaviour (see Squires, 2006). This new authoritarianism has its counterpart in certain elements of the social policy developments ... in the shift towards 'workfare' ... in aspects of the treatment accorded to lone parents ... but also in what Peter Dwyer (2004) has called the 'creeping conditionality' of social policy, a process that might yet extend, it has been suggested, to include the withdrawal of welfare benefits as a sanction for antisocial behaviour.

Here Dean is referring to how criminal justice polices, in the same way as other policies, such as welfare benefits policies, have seemingly become increasingly punitive in how they function, and as a consequence, the outcomes for those who they affect. This is particularly in relation to shaping behaviours. All of this is described as being part of a broader shift in society, away from welfarist approaches of dealing with social issues, and towards a more punitive, crime control/behavioral control model. Garland's (2001) work has been considered in a number of chapters within this text, e.g. in the context of punishment, and the politics of law and order.

> The third reason that Social Policy and Criminology need to be studied together relates to the way that both criminal justice policy and crime itself tend to bear in often disproportionate ways upon the poorest and most vulnerable in society (Grover, 2008). The relationship between poverty and crime is contested and complex. Following the riots that occurred in several English cities in the summer of 2011, the British Prime Minister David Cameron insisted that the riots 'were not about poverty'. And yet an analysis of court cases involving those accused of violence against the police and looting revealed that the majority of suspects apprehended and charged with offences came from deprived areas (Taylor et al., 2011). Data from the UK demonstrate that the country's growing prison population is characterized by alarming levels of past disadvantage, illiteracy and mental health problems ... (cited by Prison Reform Trust, 2010: 20). Policing and the criminal justice system, it may be argued, are directly implicated in a process of 'punitive segregation' (Young, 1999) by which significant numbers of the most vulnerable or deprived people are physically excluded from society through periods of imprisonment. At the same time it is the residents of the poorest neighbourhoods that suffer most from crime (Pantazis, 2000), and high levels of crime and antisocial behaviour within a neighbourhood may, in turn, exacerbate the process of neighbourhood exclusion (Lupton and Power, 2002).

Finally, Dean reflects arguments covered in Chapters 3 and 7 related to not only how we can view offending and victimisation processes through the lens of social pathologies, but also, how the negative consequences of policies, whether within the criminal justice system or other social policy domains, tend to disproportionately affect the most marginal in society. The value of the concepts of inequality and social justice are therefore apparent.

10.2 POLICY OVERLAPS

In light of the discussions above, it then becomes apparent that there is a need to think expansively about the nature of policies. Specifically:

- What are policy aims or goals?
- What are the policy mechanisms and institutions, i.e. how they are implemented or put into practice, and by whom?
- What are the policy outcomes: both within the specific policy domain where the policy has been created or targeted, and also within other policy domains?

Although Table 10.1 is by no means exhaustive, it covers a number of recent policies that cross over into different policy domains, and it is likely that many of them will be familiar to you. You can also add to this list as you read around the subject, and as you see examples of new policies in the news

Social policies with law and order implications	Criminal justice policies with social welfare implications
Sure Start and other early interventions: designed to deal with **child abuse and neglect** (by parents/carers), as well as **preventing offending in the future** (by children). The Sure Start programme began in the UK in 1998, and was inspired by a US scheme 'Head Start'. It involves a range of child and parent interventions, to develop parenting practices, child–parent relationships, and positive outcomes for both, as well as communities more widely (e.g. see Smith, 2018). This is closely linked to government agendas around child and parent outcomes framed within the documents **Every Child Matters HM** (HM Treasure, 2003), and **Every Parent Matters** (DfES, 2007). In relation to child outcomes, this links to the aspects of both the **individual pathologies** and **social pathologies** analyses of crime. That is, on the one hand, there are psychological factors associated with attachment and learning theories (individual pathologies), and on the other hand, there are broader cultural and community aspects (social pathologies).	**Enforcing school attendance**: For example, the Education Act 1996 notes: *If a child of compulsory school age who is a registered pupil at a school fails to attend regularly at the school, his parent is guilty of an offence. If ... the parent knows that his child is failing to attend regularly at the school and fails ... to cause him to do so, he is guilty of an offence ... A person guilty ... is liable ... to a fine ... or imprisonment for a term not exceeding three months, or both.* This is linked to children's right to education, and their development.
Troubled Families' programme: a programme of targeted intervention for families with multiple problems, including crime, antisocial behaviour, truancy, unemployment, mental health problems and domestic abuse (UK Parliament, 2018a). This demonstrates the relationship between crime and other social issues.	**Ban on smoking in cars with minors** (age below 18 years) from 2015 onwards in the UK. This is a child-health issue being enforced through criminal justice sanctions. This example, and the one above, can be described as part of a process of **juridification**, i.e. **net-widening** of the law to bring more behaviours into the gaze of the law. Some of this process can be viewed as positive in terms of protecting citizens from **harm**, as the examples here might represent (and also a focus on **hate crime**). While other aspects might be viewed in the sense of a more controlling and punitive State, e.g. regulating behaviours that are not harmful.
Drug and alcohol treatments: used to help to rehabilitate offenders, for which the evidence on their effectiveness seems to be compelling – for example, see O'Connor (2017). This links to the **individual pathologies** analysis of offending, i.e. offenders are influenced by biological or psychological factors of some form.	**Ban on smoking in public places in England**: from 2007, following the Health Act 2006, and earlier bans in other countries, e.g. Ireland in 2004. This is a public health issue being enforced through criminal justice sanctions.

Social policies with law and order implications	Criminal justice policies with social welfare implications
Education as a route away from antisocial behaviour/offending: for example study programmes within prisons – such as Open University degrees. Another example is that of the **NEETs** agenda: concern for young people who are not in education, employment or training (see Mirza-Davies and Brown, 2016). This is linked to viewing the development of offending, but also desistance from it, within broader policy areas, e.g. education and work.	A range of **environmental protection laws**: linked to public health and safety, and economic prosperity. This is an example of where **social harm** has been embedded within formal law-making. The sub-discipline of **green criminology** focuses on environmental damage and protection, and associated processes of offending and victimisation.
Welfare benefits system: e.g. aspects of **welfare conditionality** (see www.welfareconditionality.ac.uk/) where sanctions can be applied to welfare recipients. And, sanctioning of antisocial behaviours through the withholding of benefits. And conversely, policies of wealth redistribution to tackle poverty, which can be seen as driving social issues (such as crime), linked to a **social pathologies** approach. There is also a **Classicist** logic to some of this, in seeking to shape behaviours through incentivisation and deterrence. ***Universal Credit.**	A range of **employment** and **health and safety laws**: linked to worker safety, wellbeing, and rights, enforceable through criminal justice sanctions. This links to the **harms** approach, as considered throughout this text. Also, consider the HSE data example within the early part of **Chapter 5**.
Local multi-agency collaborations on crime: partnerships involving different agencies who collectively seek to address offending, and related issues. One example is that of **Crime and Disorder Reduction Partnerships** (CDRPs), set up by the Crime and Disorder Act 1998. This demonstrates the influence on crime of wider social issues.	Tackling **benefits fraud**: linked to the appropriate use of public monies, and ensuring resources reach those who need it – ensuring that social welfare is best served at an aggregate level.

Table 10.1   Examples of policy overlap within the UK

*As this text is going to press, an unfolding issue is that of the shift towards Universal Credit, which is an attempt by the Conservative government to replace a raft of individual welfare benefit payments with one single payment. For example, see Millar and Bennett (2017). This is under trial at present, but has already proved to be controversial because of fears that it can push claimants into financial difficulties. The wider consequences of Universal Credit are still being considered. Any future edition of this text will be able to report on this in greater detail, but it is worth flagging-up now because this is one of the most significant welfare reforms in recent times.

The types of examples within Table 10.1 have increasingly entered the criminological fray. The value of thinking about harm comes through here, but also an application of the logic of criminological theories on offending and desistance within social policies. Reflecting this increased interest within criminology, a number of key texts have sought to explore the overlaps between criminology and social policy. Chris Grover's text *Crime and Inequality* (Grover, 2008) offers a strong coverage of the relationship between inequality and crime, exploring the relationship in terms of parenting, education and youth policies, welfare benefits policies, homelessness, and so on. Paul Knepper's 2007 text *Criminology and Social Policy* focuses on a range of social policy areas to explore the connection, such as health, housing and youth policies. Emma Wincup's text *Understanding Crime and Social Policy* (Wincup, 2013) is a more recent effort, and offers an excellent coverage of the topic, considering among other things, the Troubled Families agenda, the resettlement of prisoners, and various examples of the regulation of behaviours through criminal justice policies.

Social exclusion as a key concept

Common within analyses of the crime that consider the connections to social policy, is the concept of social exclusion. Ruth Levitas (2005) explores the concept in some detail, and considers the different ways in which the concept is understood. In essence, this is a label used to describe disadvantage faced by individuals and communities which is multi-faceted in nature; i.e. disadvantage in relation to a range of different social outcomes and processes, e.g. health, education, crime and victimisation, political engagement, and so on, all at the same time. This is a useful concept, although not uncontested, in demonstrating the relationship between various poor social outcomes, and thus, how crime and victimisation are just one of several consequences of poverty and inequality.

Accounts of social exclusion vary in terms of how they present the causes of exclusion, and thus, the *causes* of crime, and the solutions. Levitas summarises these different accounts as RED, MUD, and SID. RED relates to the redistributive discourse, that is, arguments about social exclusion being related to the distribution of wealth, and so to tackle social exclusion a better distribution of wealth is required through welfare policies. MUD relates to arguments of a moral underclass discourse, that is, social exclusion is about individuals/groups who are antisocial and culturally different. The blame for this lies at the feet of those excluded, as well as failings of the welfare system in creating dependency. Therefore, such individuals and groups need to be dealt with punitively, and the State should reform the welfare benefit system to make it tougher. Finally, SID is the social integrationist discourse, that is, social exclusion is linked to a lack of inclusion through absence of employment. Therefore, the solution to a range of social problems all at once is getting people into productive work (Levitas, 2005).

10.3 INEQUALITY MATTERS

As has been suggested throughout the chapter so far, social inequalities matter in terms of shaping outcomes for individuals and society more widely. The concept of social exclusion is essentially about processes of inequalities creating adverse outcomes for marginalised groups. Many of the policies and agendas explored in Table 10.1 disproportionately affect those who fare worse from social inequalities, especially economic inequalities. This is supported within a body of research. For example, Philip Alston (2015) reporting for The UN's Human Rights Council, notes the compelling link between income disparities and reduced skills development, opportunities for education, and indeed social mobility (para. 30). Alston also reports on the link between inequality and crime, where Alston cites the work of Elhar and Aitken (2011); Melamed and Samman (2013), and earlier UN research, within which a consistent relationship between inequality and homicides and robberies is claimed (paras 27, 28).

The UN's Committee on Economic, Social, and Cultural Rights (2018), in their assessment of the situation within the UK in 2016, noted particular concern regarding austerity measures witnessed in the UK, following their implementation in 2010 onwards by the Coalition government. In their view, such measures seriously, and disproportionately, impacted on disadvantaged and marginalised groups. Some studies have shown the importance of thinking about inequalities not only in relation to adverse outcomes for marginalised groups, but for societies as a whole. Wilkinson and Pickett's text *The Spirit Level: Why Equality is Better for Everyone* (2010) reports on negative social outcomes across a range of areas, including health, well-being, education, and law and order, all of which is said to be linked to economic inequalities.

Their work, which draws on data for countries across the world, demonstrates that societies with high levels of economic inequality suffer from higher levels of negative social outcomes – not just the poorest people within those societies. In the context of law and order for instance, countries with high levels of inequality have higher 'homicide' rates, and higher rates of imprisonment. This also tells us something about the nature of punishment and its link to different types of societies (Wilkinson and Pickett, 2010). The USA, Portugal and UK are among the most unequal societies according to the authors' measurement of inequality, and they also score the worst on the aggregate social problems score.

Classic studies within criminology have reported on the relevance of inequality and/or poverty specifically in relation to crime. For example, Box (1987) states that income inequality is strongly related to criminal activity; Hansen and Machin (2002) found a statistically significant link between changes in crime and the extent of low pay; Grogger (1998) reported on falling wages in real terms as a determinant of rising youth crime during the 1970s and 1980s; Carmichael and Ward (2000) suggest a systematic positive relationship between burglary rates and male unemployment; whilst Farrington and colleagues (e.g. Farrington, 2005) within their work for the Cambridge Study in Delinquent Development (as covered in Chapter 3 and elsewhere) found higher crime levels for periods of unemployment versus periods of employment at an individual level – particularly in relation to crimes involving material gain.

Figure 10.1   **Rough sleeping**

(*Source:* Homeless Link, 2018)

One issue that exemplifies the overlap between criminology and wider social policy is that of homelessness. This issue not only demonstrates how a range of social issues appear to be connected together, but also how processes of offending and victimisation are heightened in relation to one of the most vulnerable (and marginalised) groups within society. There is a tendency to think about homelessness in purely a domestic context; this is an issue that has local dimensions within virtually every country throughout the world, but also, there are often international dimensions to it. There are also international drivers of homelessness within countries. Bulman (2018) offers insight into this problem, and in particular, how punitive UK government policy has been exacerbating the situation. Data cited within work shows that a quarter of those using night shelters are refugees.

The UN Special Rapporteur on the right to adequate housing (Farha, 2015: 1) describes homelessness as:

> an egregious violation of human rights occurring in all countries, threatening the health and life of the most marginalized. Homelessness is the unacceptable result of States failing to implement the right to adequate housing. It requires urgent and immediate human rights responses by the international community and by all States.

A three-dimensional definition of homelessness is presented by the Special Rapporteur (Farha, 2015: 1):

1. The first dimension addresses the absence of home in terms of both its physical structure and its social aspects.
2. The second dimension considers homelessness as a form of systemic discrimination and social exclusion, whereby 'the homeless' become a social group subject to stigmatization; link to social injustices.
3. The third dimension recognizes homeless people as resilient in the struggle for survival and dignity and potential agents of change as rights holders.

The first dimension reflects how being homeless is not simply about a lack of a physical resource, but that there are a range of social processes linked to having a fixed address. Apparent within the second dimension is a more explicit link back to the concept of social exclusion in relation to how homelessness can result in many forms of disadvantage, and limit the life experience of those who are homeless. Indeed, Lynch (2005: 116) has noted how 'there are clear causal and consequential links between homelessness and social exclusion. Social exclusion can cause, contribute to, exacerbate and maintain homelessness'. Lynch examines the ways in which the state of being homelessness is at odds with the meeting of individuals' human rights. One of the areas where this is apparent is in relation to the right to equality and non-discrimination; where individuals face exclusion from a range of services as a result of not having a fixed address, as well as being treated less favourably within processes of law. The third dimension suggests that those who are homeless can still be agents of their own change, rather than simply viewing these groups as having things done to them; they have some capacity to help themselves.

The trends in homelessness are themselves a concern. Taking England as an example, Figure 10.2 demonstrates estimated rises in the number of those homeless across almost all regions of England between 2010 and 2017, and the numbers cited are likely to be underestimates.

St Mungo's report on homelessness (2016: 10–11) points to a number of factors driving increases in homelessness. Important factors include 'welfare reforms; the cost of housing; a shortage of supported housing; the splitting-up of homeless services; more foreign nationals ending-up on the streets', and so on. 'The breakdown of relationships and release from temporary accommodation and prison' are also very significant (p.15). Central within all this, is also the issue of mental health.

The link to the criminal justice system among the homeless is significant. In the UK for example, the use of criminal law and civil measures to tackle antisocial behaviour, effectively banning activities linked to being homeless, such as begging, has served to criminalise the homeless according to a UK parliament briefing paper (UK Parliament, 2018b). The Vagrancy Act 1824, and the Anti-Social Behaviour, Crime and Policing Act 2014 have been important within this. It has been noted for example, that the number of prosecutions under Section 3 of the Vagrancy Act 1824 increased substantially between 2006–7 and 2015–16: from 1,510 to 2,365 (UK Parliament, 2018b). Also:

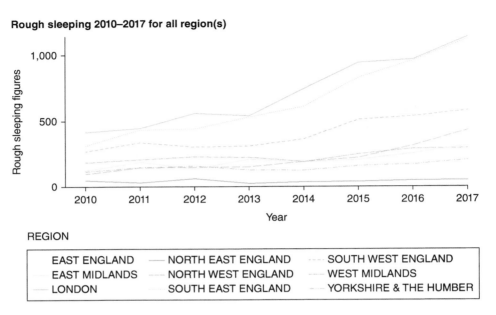

Rough sleeping 2010–2017 for all region(s)

REGION

EAST ENGLAND	—— NORTH EAST ENGLAND	··· SOUTH WEST ENGLAND
EAST MIDLANDS	---- NORTH WEST ENGLAND	-- WEST MIDLANDS
—— LONDON	SOUTH EAST ENGLAND	·· YORKSHIRE & THE HUMBER

Figure 10.2   Regional trends (England) in homelessness

(*Source:* Homeless Link, 2018)

a survey of local authorities in England and Wales by the national homelessness charity Crisis in 2016 found that 36% (29 out of 81) of respondents had specifically targeted rough sleeping with enforcement measures. This was reported to be a response to increasing levels of rough sleeping alongside reported rises in anti-social behaviour such as begging and street drinking.

Thus in many cases, the homeless are actively targeted, or put in other words, actively victimised. The briefing paper also points to a range of other punitive measures designed to target the homeless. They include:

- Physical deterrents (sometimes referred to as 'defensive architecture'): street furniture and the urban environment may include features such as spikes, curved or segregated benches, and gated doorways, to deter rough sleeping.
- 'Wetting down': spraying and hosing down doorways/alleyways with water or cleaning products to stop rough sleepers using the space.
- Noise pollution: sounds, such as loud music, are projected through speakers to deter rough sleepers.
- Moving-on: security guards/enforcement agencies tell rough sleepers to move out of an area.

- Diverted giving schemes: local authority-sanctioned schemes that promote and advertise in begging hotspots asking members of the public to reconsider giving money to beggars and give to local charities instead.

As the briefing paper notes, such measures are not related to legal sanctions, but they are highly controversial in nature, and effectively victimise the homeless. A report by Irish Penal Reform Trust (2012) has similarly showed how behavioural sanctions and formal law-making can seemingly target the most marginal within society. The report sub-title *Ireland's Disproportionate Punishment of the Poor* is in itself telling. The report points to examples such as: 'imprisonment for non-payment of fines and non-payment of debts; vagrancy laws/begging laws; and uneven application of the law' against those from poorer socio-economic backgrounds. Also within the report is a close examination of the links between homelessness and crime (p.19):

- For some individuals being homeless leads to crime which in turn leads to imprisonment, whereas for others, being released from prison leads directly to homelessness.
- Many of those imprisoned after a period of homelessness are imprisoned for crimes associated with their poverty and lack of stable accommodation such as vagrancy, theft and drug offences.
- 39% of participants in a Focus Ireland study identified homelessness as a direct factor that led them to re-offending.
- Lack of housing results in a lack of stability and this makes it extremely difficult to engage in education, work or training, or to re-integrate into society in any meaningful sense.
- Many programmes for former prisoners require secure accommodation because it is viewed as necessary for being able to engage with services.
- Others may face homelessness after release from prison as they may have lost local authority housing or had family or other relationships break down while they were incarcerated.

Apparent within the above discussions is the idea that homelessness is strongly connected to both offending and criminalisation, and all of this sits within a wider milieu, or matrix, of social circumstances/disadvantage. This, in turn, demonstrates the deep connection between criminology and social policy. The solutions to acute social issues such as homelessness, offending, and a range of other poor social outcomes, lie within a number of different policy domains all at once. The criminal justice system and the tools at its disposal are just one of many strands required to tackle such issues; therefore, there is a need to think about responding to crime beyond the criminal justice system; a traditional notion of punishment (Chapter 9) can only get us so far.

10.5 SUMMARY AND IMPLICATIONS

The relationship between criminology and social policy is evident within a range of different processes examined throughout the chapter. Policies have the potential to cross over into different domains in terms of their aims and outcomes, but there exists an acute issue of both criminal justice and social policies disproportionately affecting the poorest; whether this is by design or through unintended consequences. Criminal justice policies can have social welfare outcomes, just as social policies can have punitive or criminalising effects. The example of homelessness is useful in terms of showing much of this crossover, but other examples also, such as welfare benefits, and youth policies. The concepts of inequality and social exclusion are particularly significant within all this.

RECOMMENDED READING AND FOLLOW-UP MATERIAL

Read

- O'Connor, R. (2017) 'How alcohol and drug treatment helps to reduce crime'. Gov.uk [online], available at: https://publichealthmatters.blog.gov.uk/2017/11/02/how-alcohol-and-drug-treatment-helps-to-reduce-crime/

  (This offers an interesting and recent discussion of evidence regarding how drug and alcohol interventions – health and wellbeing policies – can have a strong reduction impact on offending.)

- Wincup, E. (2013) *Understanding Crime and Social Policy*. Bristol: Policy Press.

  (Particularly Chapter 7, which explores the 'Troubled families' agenda, and Chapter 8, which explores the regulation of a range of behaviours.)

Watch

- Adam Foss's TED talk, 'A Prosecutor's View for a Better Justice System', available at: www.ted.com/talks/adam_foss_a_prosecutor_s_vision_for_a_better_justice_system?referrer=playlist-truths_about_the_us_prison_system

- Alice Goffman's TED talk, 'How We're Priming Some Kids for College – and Others for Prison', available at: www.ted.com/talks/alice_goffman_college_or_prison_two_destinies_one_blatant_injustice?referrer=playlist-truths_about_the_us_prison_system

  (both videos demonstrate the wider link between crime, justice and other policy areas.)

CHAPTER REVIEW QUESTIONS

1. In what ways might it be argued that criminology and social policy are connected?
2. What is meant by the idea that criminal justice policies can have welfarist aims and outcomes?
3. In what ways can both criminal justice policies, and wider social policies disproportionately affect the most vulnerable or marginal groups in society?
4. Why is the example of homelessness a useful one for considering the connections between criminology and social policy?

REVIEW ACTIVITIES

1. Visit St Mungo's website, specifically the section on 'publications and research': www.mungos.org/homelessness/publications-and-research/
2. Read some of the reports you find there, and consider how they help to show the connection between homelessness, crime, victimisation and a range of other social issues.
3. Make a list of all the policies you have read about in this chapter, or within your wider reading, which in some way demonstrate connections between social policy criminology. To help with this, you might want to think about policy aims; policy mechanisms; and policy outcomes.
4. In order to help consolidate your learning on this topic, prepare a short series of PowerPoint pages covering the key ideas and examples presented within the chapter. You might like to imagine that you will be using these to deliver a short presentation to peers, and envisage how you would cover the material and present it succinctly, and with clarity.

CHAPTER CONTENTS

11 GLOBAL JUSTICE

Image 11.1

(*Source:* International Campaign for Bhopal, 2014)

LEARNING OUTCOMES

By the end of this chapter, you will be able to:

1. understand the ways in which law and order issues can operate internationally;
2. recognise the need for analysing and responding to some law and order issues in an international way;
3. understand the importance of thinking about human rights and social justice in relation to law and order issues, and the concept of harm;
4. recognise processes of offending and victimisation perpetrated by powerful actors, such as States and corporations.

11.1 THE NEED TO THINK 'GLOBAL'

This chapter develops some of the ideas raised in previous chapters, taking up discussions of human rights and social justice in more detail, and considers the international or global nature of crime and justice processes. Social justice is an important idea related to ensuring fairness and protection for all, regardless of who they are. Similarly, the notion of human rights has become a vital aspect of how we understand what basic rights and dignity should be afforded to all. It is possible to argue that human rights are an aspect of social justice, i.e. *a socially just situation is one where human rights are upheld.* In one sense, human rights, and indeed social justice, represent an international standard against which nation states and other actors can/should be held to account. The United Nations have been vital in driving a human rights agenda, from within the aftermath of the Second World War. This has entailed the creation of a rights framework, monitoring processes to determine whether or not actors adhere to the rights frameworks and, mechanisms for policing/responding where rights are violated.

On a domestic level, it is possible to consider how law and order policies and practices might respect or disregard such standards, such as the extent to which an over-crowded and under-resourced prison system can afford those basic rights and dignity; or, how welfare benefits policies are impacting peoples' lives. But also, international events and processes of victimisation and harm must be considered here. These include: the trafficking of people, and cybercrimes committed by organised crime groups; war crimes such as torture and genocide by State actors; terrorism; corporate crimes and harms, environmental damage which impacts on people, and so on. They can all have international dimensions to them, and they all have both human rights and social justice aspects to them.

BOX 11.1 ADDITIONAL INFORMATION

Terrorism is undoubtedly a vital part of any discussion on global aspects of law and order. However, other examples are instead developed within the chapter. Terrorism is considered in **Chapter 7**, and mentioned briefly at points in this chapter. For more coverage of it do read David Whittaker's *The Terrorism Reader* (2012), and read the UK's CONTEST strategy (as discussed in **Chapter 7**).

Central also within this, is the concept of globalisation. In short, it:

describes processes of the world becoming ever-more connected and inter-dependent, and this can be seen in relation to the sharing of cultures and ideas, linked financial, political and education systems, and so on, and the rapid development of technology and information systems which have aided much of this.

For criminologists this is important because it has implications for the ways in which offending can occur; trafficking and cybercrimes are good examples of this. It also has implications for responding to crime; crime processes cross borders and so too must policing and justice processes, such as laws and policing collaborations. More fundamental than that, globalisation can be argued to have changed the very ways in which we live, and lots of implications stem from this. The workings of law and order processes are just one area of this.

Although the actual meaning, and the noted processes and consequences of globalisation can be debated (there are different theoretical approaches to understanding it; see Potter, 2017), the following offer a useful way of framing globalisation:

- Giddens (1990: 64): the intensification of worldwide social relations which link distant localities in such a way that local happenings are shaped by events occurring miles away and vice versa;
- Newburn (2007: 868): set of changes that give the feeling of a shrinking world;
- Potter (2017: 289): the increasing interdependency and interconnectedness of individuals, social groups, states and economies across the world ... the single most compelling force behind globalization is the movement of capital and credit resulting from investment, and resource and profit extraction by multinational corporations in global markets.

It is now vital to think globally about law and order issues, as criminologists increasingly have done. Brisman et al. (2017: 228–9) note how long-standing areas of focus within criminology, such as exploring effects of inequality and culture on offending, especially in the light of consumerism and commodification (see Chapter 3), must be understood in the context of globalisation. Globalisation is now central within many issues and topics within criminology. Globalisation seemingly has the impact of eroding aspects of human rights, impacting on natural environments and working conditions, and so on. But also, globalisation can help to create and proliferate international standards.

Crucial within this, many economies across the world have become dominated by the central narrative of neo-liberalism (free markets economics), which has served to give corporate actors more power. It has also helped to entangle governments and corporations in the development of economic *progress*, and indeed, the provision of services (see discussion of privatisation in Chapters 6 and 9). As a consequence, new harms and processes of injustice can emerge. Meanwhile, there have been new threats emerging, or at least increasing, linked to a globalising world, such as forms of organised crime and terrorism. Katja Aas (2013) offers an excellent source on further discussion of the criminology–globalisation interface. Figure 11.1 offers a simplified overview of some of the relevancies of globalisation for law and order matters. Within the points below there are clearly both positive outcomes and opportunities, but at the same time, new dangers and threats.

Offending (across borders or in several countries at once)	Victimisation (across borders or in several countries at once)	Law-making (international laws)
Policing and investigation (collaboration between countries)	International standards (human rights; social justice)	Punishment (international courts, sanctions, conflict)
Increasing focus on, 'risk', security, and exclusion (as dominant ways of thinking about law and order)	Global international penal trends (policy-sharing; common policy directions e.g. see Garland, 2001)	

Figure 11.1   Global dimensions of law and order

BOX 11.2   ACTIVITY

Thinking about those various points in Figure 11.1, consider the possible implications of them:

- How might 'positive outcomes and opportunities', and 'new dangers and threats' be created?
- Is it possible that inequalities might be created in some form?

Global inequalities

One key concern of a globalised/globalising world is the extent to which it fosters negative outcomes and inequalities. A connected world improves life for citizens and states alike, but it also creates new dangers. More connectedness and interdependence creates new opportunities, but also new vulnerabilities. Global inequalities can be understood much in the same way as the earlier discussions of inequality in Chapter 10. The distribution of resources and opportunities, and the ways in which people and groups are treated are significant in an international sense, just as they are domestically. This links to the subsequent discussion in this chapter on social justice. Some of the ways in which global inequalities can be seen within law and order processes include:

- New opportunities and means by which criminal activities can be conducted and new forms of associated victimisation, particularly for the most vulnerable groups, who have least power; the later section in this chapter on people trafficking typifies this. Cybercrime is also a good case study here.
- Globalisation affects the workings and nature of the nation state, which can mean that they lose some power and control, which has consequences for policing and

justice processes, and the abilities of the State to protect all. For example, increasing corporate power raises the possibility of increased corporate harms, usually against the poorest/least powerful.

- Globalisation gives rise to new insecurities and a focus on 'risk' (Beck, 1992), and this impacts on some communities more than others in terms of how law-enforcement practices operate. Some communities are viewed as risky populations, or dangerous, and so criminal justice policies and other policies, e.g. immigration policies, target them. Plus, long-standing and new processes of negative identities (which are imposed on groups) and prejudices for specific groups can be exacerbated by globalisation. For example, in relation to ethnicity and immigration, and in a related way, terrorism.

- Inequalities in wealth, development and power have emerged, and these are linked to global markets and trading, and political processes. Thus, just as criminologists consider the links between inequality and crime, and victimisation, through models such as strain theory, such ideas can also be used on an international level. Thus, international processes of offending and victimisation can be related to differentials in power, and status (i.e. class): e.g. victims of people trafficking.

BOX 11.3   CASE STUDY

Cybercrime

[also see discussions of the Internet and crime in Chapter 8]

- A type, or series of types of crime which have been created or facilitated by emergent technologies, and is closely linked to globalisation. Yvonne Jewkes (2013: 112) defines this as 'illegal acts committed with the assistance of, or by means of computers, computer networks, the internet, and web-based information and communication technologies'.
- There are two types: 1) where a computer is the target, e.g., a virus, malware, hacking to retrieve information, etc.; 2) where people are the targets and the technology is used as a vehicle to access them, e.g. fraud, hate crime, abuse, attacking critical infrastructures that may then cause harm, terror propaganda and recruitment, etc.
- The advantages of using such technologies are the stealth of use and anonymity; access to many users quickly, and with low risk; the lack of regulation of cyberspace; the ability to offend across borders, which raises problems in terms of different law enforcement jurisdictions, and cooperation.

- Responding to cybercrimes is made difficult by the lack of resources invested in this by governments; the sheer volume of web traffic; the ability for offenders to use encryption and act anonymously; the problems of crossing jurisdiction; the politics and practicalities of cooperating with other nations; and the technology gap between the criminals who are innovating, and law enforcement who are generally trying to play catch-up.

11.2 INTERNATIONAL STANDARDS: *SOCIAL JUSTICE*

Social justice

One positive of globalisation has been the development and proliferation of global standards. Arguably, a heightened focus on social justice has emerged within academic, policy and public domains (e.g. on social media). When thinking about inequalities, as outlined in Section 11.1, the concept of social justice is useful. Although this can be quite a complicated concept, Peter Taylor-Gooby (2012: 29) helpfully describes this as related to 'who ought to get what' within society. That is, a socially just situation is one where people receive fair outcomes in relation to economic distributions, but also in other aspects of life. To aid understanding of this, think back to Chapter 7 which focused on victims. It was shown how a number of themes emerge from considering the statistics on offenders and victims. For example, it is possible to recognise how those who are victimised in relation to both domestic and international processes of victimisation tend to be marginalised economically, or in terms of status, or both. It thus seems that the poorest often receive less (i) protection from states and its institutions, as the first two bullet points in the previous section indicate.

This is particularly apparent given the role of corporations who are sometimes able to exploit lower regulatory, safety and pay standards in poorer countries, but also, where corruption and poor governance structures operate at a State level. The working of competitive global markets has implications for the (ii) distribution of wealth (bullet point 4), and associated resources, with less economically advanced countries, and especially the marginal populations within those countries losing out. Furthermore, linked to that, the ways in which society or institutions value communities differently (think about discrimination and labelling), means that there are inequalities in terms of peoples' abilities to (iii) exercise capabilities, i.e. being able to play a full role in society (bullet point 3), and how people are treated and represented within discourses of media, politics and policy-making: their level of (iv) recognition (bullet point 3).

Those four points all in some way connect to the notion of social justice. A socially just situation is one where all people and groups are able to be supported in respect of those four areas. Figure 11.2 is a useful way of putting all this together, describing what social justice looks like in relation to each of those areas, and conversely, what issues of injustice looks like.

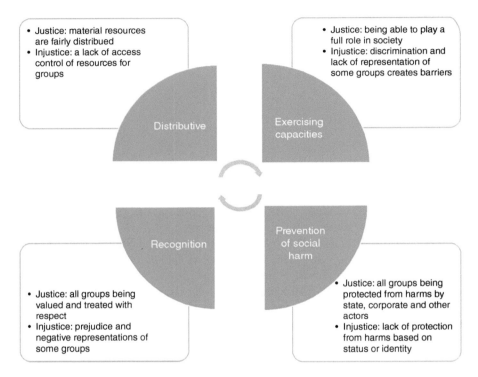

Figure 11.2   Domains of social justice

(*Source:* adapted from Open University, 2008)

Within Figure 11.2 it is apparent that the notion of social justice can relate to a range of different aspects of life. The simplest way of thinking about it relates to economic distribution. Clearly then, economic inequalities exist between individuals and groups within a country, but also, between individuals and groups across countries. But such inequalities also exist in relation to peoples' abilities to exercise their capabilities, or put differently, their ability to fully participate in society based on their identities (linked to class, ethnicity, culture, and so on). Third, the extent to which individuals and groups are treated with respect and receive appropriate recognition in society can also vary in relation to their social and cultural identity. Finally, the extent to which individuals and groups are protected from crimes and harms can also vary according to social and cultural identity.

The last point is typified on a domestic level within the data for deaths on probation (Gelsthorpe et al., 2012; Philips et al., 2017); it is possible to argue vulnerable groups not only fail to be protected by the State, but they are also actively victimised by CJS processes. The data on ethnicity and imprisonment (Chapter 9) also clearly reflects this. On an international level, examples such as people trafficking, genocide and corporate crimes/harms also clearly reflect that sense of marginalised groups receiving fewer protections, and in some cases, are actively victimised because of who they are. That broad conceptualisation of social justice goes some way towards explaining the victimisation patterns evident both on a domestic and an international level; those who fair worse in relation to economic distributions, and who are least protected, and least valued, are likely to be those we see within official data on victimisation and offending. And indeed, they are most likely to be victimised according to other measures, such as other CJS data, work and industrial-related injuries/deaths, corporate failures, outcomes of environmental damage, and so on.

A recent high-profile example of where there are clear social justice implications is that of the flooding of Kerala, a region of India, in August 2018. Although this happened within the notorious monsoon season, which ordinarily brings high levels of rainfall, the levels of rain in 2018 were unprecedented (42 per cent more rain than usual) coupled with soil erosion. This caused hundreds of deaths, over a million evacuees, and billions of dollars' worth of damage (Parsons and Skinner, 2018). This was immediately claimed to be a consequence of climate change by scientists and governmental actors alike, including the UN Secretary General (UN, 2018). The social justice implications relate to how it is regions such as Kerala, and other less economically developed regions of the world, that disproportionately face the consequences of environmental damage, harms from industry and government policies alike. For example, flooding in Bangladesh from rising sea levels consequent from global warming (melting ice caps), and the climate change-induced desertification of areas such as the Sahel in Africa. Within such cases, and others, it is the poorest who often reside in the places most vulnerable to consequences of climate change, and also, the poorest that are least able to respond.

The following boxed case study of the Bhopal tragedy in India, which began in 1984 but still persists to this day in terms of its consequences and legacy, is another powerful example of how the poor and voiceless are often those who suffer from avoidable harms. This was resultant from corporate negligence. What makes the episode all the more telling is how over 30 years of campaigning for justice has ensued because of the power and status of those responsible for the events, which has allowed them to evade justice. The concepts of power, class, inequality, and community are useful in making sense of how such events can unfold, who the offenders and victims are, and why justice is often so hard to enact.

BOX 11.4   CASE STUDY

Corporate crime – Bhopal

On December 3rd, 1984, in the middle of the night, thousands of people were gassed to death **because of a catastrophic chemical leak at the Union Carbide pesticide plant in Bhopal, India.**

More than 150,000 people were left severely disabled, and 22,000 people have since died of their injuries. For these reasons the Bhopal gas disaster is widely acknowledged as the **world's worst-ever industrial disaster.**

What Leaked and Why?

More than 27 tons of methyl isocyanate and other deadly gases turned Bhopal into a gas chamber. None of the six safety systems at the plant were functional, and Union Carbide's own documents prove the company designed the plant with 'unproven' and 'untested' technology, and cut corners on safety and maintenance in order to save money.

Inadequate Compensation

In 1989 a settlement was reached between Union Carbide and the Government of India, awarding each survivor only $500 for life-long debilitating injuries.

This means survivors have been given less than 5 cents per day – the cost of a cup of tea – to pay for decades of medical bills. Many have lost the ability to work because of their health problems and live in dire poverty. On top of this, a study in the *Journal of the American Medical Association* confirmed that the next generation – children of gas-affected parents – are themselves afflicted by Union Carbide's poison. Yet these children have received no help from Union Carbide or the Government of India.

Water Contamination

Union Carbide abandoned Bhopal and did not clean up its factory site. For years it had been dumping chemicals and wastes around the factory grounds, and these have leaked into the soil and contaminated the drinking water of 30,000+ people. Tens of thousands of people drank the water for years, and Union Carbide told no one of the risks. Testing published in a 2002 report revealed poisons such as 1,3,5 trichlorobenzene, dichloromethane, chloroform, lead and mercury in the breast milk of nursing women living near the factory. Many of the people who drank the water have become too sick to work, but they have received no help. Meanwhile, the contaminated land has never been cleaned up, and families too poor to move live on top of the contaminated soil.

Cancers and Birth Defects

Recent reports confirm that the contamination is getting worse. Water from one hand pump in Atal Ayub Nagar, already lethal by 1999, has become seven times more toxic since then. The rate of birth defects in the contaminated areas is ten times higher than in the rest of India. Cancers and other diseases are rife.

Dow Refuses to Pay

In 2001, Dow Chemical purchased 100% of Union Carbide. The survivors, as well as the governments of India and Bhopal's state Madhya Pradesh, told that Dow Chemical acquired Union Carbide's liabilities through the purchase. Indeed, immediately after the acquisition, Dow set aside $2.2 billion to meet Union Carbide asbestos liabilities in the USA. However it bluntly refuses to accept Carbide's liabilities in Bhopal – or even admit that they exist – even though there is still a pending criminal court case against Union Carbide currently in Bhopal. Union Carbide has refused to show up to court, and Dow Chemical is considered to be hiding a fugitive from justice.

To this date, Dow/Union Carbide has refused to: clean up the site, which continues to contaminate those near it, or to provide just compensation for those who have been injured or made ill by this poison; fund medical care, health monitoring and

(Continued)

necessary research studies, or even to provide all the information it has on the leaked gases and their medical consequences; provide alternate livelihood opportunities to victims who cannot pursue their usual trade because of their exposure-induced illnesses; stand trial before the Chief Judicial Magistrate's court in Bhopal, where Union Carbide faces criminal charges of culpable homicide (manslaughter), and has fled these charges for decades.

(*Source*: Reena Shadeen, International Campaign for Bhopal, 2014)

11.3 INTERNATIONAL STANDARDS: *HUMAN RIGHTS*

Although the notion of human rights in some form pre-dates the twentieth century, it is the founding of the United Nations and the drafting of the Universal Declaration of Human Rights (1948), and the later additions of the International Covenant on Civil and Political Rights and the International Covenant on Economic, Social and Cultural Rights, which have been of most significance within the consideration of human rights. Together, they form the International Bill of Human Rights, which sets out a list of human rights. Human rights are *rights*, or *entitlements*, against which governments have obligations to ensure/protect. Such rights are universal, in that they apply to everyone, they are non-negotiable, and they are legally binding. They are related to the protection and dignity of all people, but they also relate to the ensuring of opportunities for people to thrive and to participate in key aspects of society. The International Bill of Human Rights cites:

The right to equality and freedom from discrimination

The right to life, liberty, and personal security

Freedom from torture and degrading treatment

The right to equality before the law

The right to a fair trial

The right to privacy

Freedom of belief and religion

Freedom of opinion

Right of peaceful assembly and association

The right to participate in government

The right to self-determination

The right to social security

The right to work

The right to form trade unions and work under favourable conditions

The right to an adequate standard of living

The right to education

The right to health

The right to food and housing

The right to take part in cultural life

The right to benefit from scientific progress.

(See UN OHCHR, 2018)

BOX 11.5   CASE STUDY: GENOCIDE RWANDA 1994

the world's governments stood by and watched as an estimated 800,000 people in Rwanda were massacred in the space of a hundred days. Aid agencies saw what was happening, but it was in vain that we lobbied to persuade Western governments to fulfil their obligations under the 1948 Genocide Convention and intervene to stop the killing.

The Oxfam campaign poster for the crisis in Rwanda

GENOCIDE IN RWANDA

Oxfam fears that up to half a million people may have been killed or are in grave danger of their lives in Rwanda.

70,000 Tutsi refugees have fled the country. As many as two million are displaced internally. Maurice Herson, an Oxfam Emergency Officer, reports from the border: *"People will be killed or they will starve. They face extermination."* Alfred Sakafu, Oxfam's Country Representative in Tanzania, reported that the river which forms the border with Rwanda *"is full of dead bodies, so we cannot use the water to supply refugees".*

HOW HAS OXFAM RESPONDED?

We are helping Rwandan refugees in Zaire, Burundi, and Tanzania. We have already flown out all the water and sanitation equipment in our emergencies warehouse. Our staff on the borders are ready to go back into Rwanda as soon as it is safe to do so. We are already spending £1.6m and expect to spend more.

HOW HAS THE UNITED NATIONS RESPONDED?

When the violence started, the UN had 2,500 peace-keeping troops in Rwanda. On 21 April the UN decided to **reduce** the number of troops to 270. Some Belgian UN soldiers were so disgusted at the decision to withdraw them that they tore up their UN berets in protest.

WHAT WILL YOU DO? SEE OVER ▶

OXFAM

(Source: Oxfam, 2014)

(Continued)

(Continued)

With the number of deaths rising daily, we pressed for an urgent reinforcement of the tiny and helpless United Nations force ... But the UN Security Council members would not commit their own troops, Nor would they deliver the necessary logistical support.

(*Source*: Oxfam 2014)

CASE STUDY: GENOCIDE – SYRIA

(*Source*: adapted from Stop Genocide Now, 2018)

The Facts

When: 2011 — Present
Location: Middle East
Estimated dead: 200,000+
Displaced persons: 10 million

Current Conflict

- The Syrian government and the Islamic State of Iraq and the Levant have been targeting and killing civilians based on either ethnic background, religious identification, or political designation.
- The Syrian government has imprisoned and killed over 11,000 political opponents and has used barrel bombs and cluster munitions to attack civilians.
- At least 17 confirmed incidents of mass killings have been carried out by government forces.
- In August 2013, government forces fired rockets filled with sarin gas at several suburbs surrounding Damascus, killing between 300 and 1,400 people.
- The Islamic State has targeted ethnic and religious minority groups, in an attempt to eradicate non-Sunni Arabs in Syria. Over 5,000 members of these minority groups have been executed in separate instances since the onset of the civil war.
- Islamic State are using child soldiers as well as employing young women as sex slaves throughout the Islamic State territory.
- The Islamic State has also destroyed multiple historic sites within Syria.

The importance of thinking about human rights within criminology is crucial both at a domestic and international level, and it links to both the idea of social justice, and harm. On a domestic level, areas of interest here include the nature of CJS policies and practices, and the extent to which they respect basic rights, or foster negative outcomes for some groups. Imprisonment in the UK, USA and elsewhere is a good example of how policy and practice might conflict with a human rights agenda, given what Chapter 9 presented on the nature of imprisonment in those countries. Responding to the threat of terrorism is also a strong example; where disregard for the human rights of suspects can be an outcome of punitive monitoring and detention processes. On the flipside of this, creating new protections for groups via defining new offences, such as those of hate crime, which is an example of juridification (net-widening), can actually help to safeguard peoples' rights.

On an international level, activities such as peace crimes, which include genocide – an attempt to eradicate a population based on ethnicity, nationality, etc.; crimes against humanity – systematic and widespread attacks on civilians using extreme violence, such as murder, rape, torture, enslavement, etc.; war crimes – crimes committed in the course of war (violations of the laws of warfare); and the crime of aggression – unlawful invasion, or military occupation (Short, 2017: 287) have clear human rights implications. Clearly, State actors have the capacity to engage in such behaviours, hence the notion of State crime: 'forms of criminality that are committed by states and governments in order to further a variety of domestic and foreign policies' (McLaughlin, 2013: 445). The two boxed examples (above) are drawn from an alarming number of such cases over the course of the twentieth and twenty-first centuries.

The International Criminal Court (ICC) plays a role in responding to such actions, where states are unwilling or unable to do so (Short, 2017). The ICC has almost universal sign-up from countries but, notably, the USA, India and others have not yet become member states. They have not signed up to Rome Statute (UN General Assembly, 1998), which defined the various peace crimes, and eventually established the ICC in 2002. However, the ICC remains an important instrument for prosecuting those who have perpetrated some of the worse crimes possible. A simple examination of the cases dealt with by the Court via the ICC website reflects this: www.icc-cpi.int/. Yet, all too often, responses to tackling such heinous events are slow and reactive in nature, rather than being pro-active and swift.

11.4 PEOPLE TRAFFICKING

Increasingly, organised crime networks are implicated within systematic violations of rights, and indeed, processes of social injustice, through activities such as people trafficking and the sex trade. People trafficking can be defined as a form of 'new slavery in the global economy' (Bales, 1999), and it relates to illegal movements of people across regions or borders through organised crime networks, sometimes with the voluntary participation of those trafficked, but often, without. The purposes for doing so include domestic labour and servitude, forced agricultural labour or other labour, and significantly, the sex trade. Even where voluntary participation of those trafficked is seemingly apparent this is often under false pretences regarding work opportunities. Such examples clearly represent violations of rights of freedom, privacy, and the protection from degrading behaviours, as well a series of other rights as a consequence of having lived outside of mainstream society. That is, access to health, education, democratic participation, and so on, are linked to being a legally recognised resident, and having a relevant abode.

Emergent from much of the discussion around both social justice and human rights, is the notion of vulnerabilities and this becomes very apparent within the people-trafficking example. That concept was important within the focus on victimisation within Chapter 7. Considering processes of injustice or human rights violations, this is often linked to status or class. Those who suffer from corporate exploitation and harms are economically vulnerable, and this can explain their involvement in low-pay and often unsafe work in many instances, which makes them more vulnerable to exploitation and harm. Those who suffer from human rights violations in the course of policing and criminal justice processes (e.g. imprisonment; stop and search) are disproportionately poor and from minority groups. Those who suffer at the hands of unscrupulous states through attempted genocides, torture, systematic abuses, and so on, are usually the marginalised ethnic and religious populations within a country. Whereas those who are trafficked for the sex trade or slavery are disproportionately the poorest sections of the poorest countries, and disproportionately women and children (see UNODC, 2016). Such groups have least power and agency.

Developing the example of people trafficking, it is has been estimated that between 2012 and 2014 alone, about 23,000 victims of trafficking for sexual exploitation were detected and recorded (UNODC, 2016: 31). This is likely to be a vast underestimate; think about the discussions in Chapter 5 on the problems of producing accurate crime figures, especially involving more hidden types of crime. Yet the sex trade is only one driver of trafficking, as reflected in Figure 11.3, which shows the main reasons and recent trends. Clearly, the demands of the sex trade are crucial, but labour is also significant. 'Other forms' of trafficking relate to organ removal, begging, sham marriages, baby selling/illegal adoption, and so on.

The information within Figure 11.4 shows how the flow of people appears to be, in the main, people moving from less economically developed countries to more economically developed countries, signifying how illicit global markets work. The poorer and less protected groups are used to service more affluent consumer markets – sex trade or otherwise. Thus, the notion of vulnerabilities fits here, so too, again, do ideas of power, class, inequality and community; those who sit at the bottom of class hierarchies become victimised:

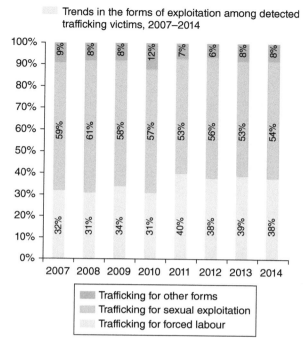

Trends in the forms of exploitation among detected trafficking victims, 2007–2014

Trafficking for other forms: 9% (2007), 8% (2008), 8% (2009), 12% (2010), 7% (2011), 6% (2012), 8% (2013), 8% (2014)

Trafficking for sexual exploitation: 59% (2007), 61% (2008), 58% (2009), 57% (2010), 53% (2011), 56% (2012), 53% (2013), 54% (2014)

Trafficking for forced labour: 32% (2007), 31% (2008), 34% (2009), 31% (2010), 40% (2011), 38% (2012), 39% (2013), 38% (2014)

- Trafficking for other forms
- Trafficking for sexual exploitation
- Trafficking for forced labour

Figure 11.3   Reasons for people trafficking

(*Source:* UNODC, 2016: 10)

in order to recruit those who are to be trafficked there is often a strong motivation to want to go – as a result of their economic situation – and those people are thus vulnerable to being duped by a trafficking gang. Or, the poor law enforcement landscapes enable gangs to snatch people against their will and offer little in terms of investigatory follow-up. Especially in rural areas (Kiley, 2005). This might be a result of acute shortages in resources, or competencies, but also complicity or 'selective law enforcement'. (Murphy, 2019)

Social injustice is experienced because it is the poorest who are systematically victimised and under-protected, and linked to this is their lack of recognition and ability to exercise capabilities because of the way they are identified and treated within societies. For example, Sam Kiley's (2005) documentary for Channel 4 *Land of Missing Children*, is a powerful example of how class/status of poor girls in some regions of India places them at great risk of victimisation through trafficking. The law-enforcement responses witnessed within that example were woefully inadequate, and actually reflect aspects of corruption and complicity among law enforcement bodies.

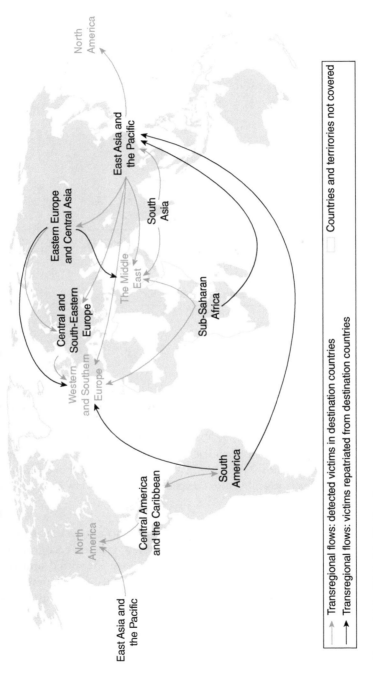

Main destinations of transregional flows and their significant origins, 2012–2014

North America

East Asia and the Pacific

Eastern Europe and Central Asia

South Asia

Central and South-Eastern Europe

The Middle East

Western and Southern Europe

Sub-Saharan Africa

North America

Central America and the Caribbean

South America

East Asia and the Pacific

→ Transregional flows: detected victims in destination countries

→ Transregional flows: victims repatriated from destination countries

☐ Countries and territories not covered

Figure 11.4   Global trafficking flows

(*Source:* UNODC, 2016: 13)

Furthermore, weak states – those where they are unable to maintain conventional processes of governance over their lands – create vulnerabilities to criminal networks (Aas, 2013). Areas of weak governance are attractive grounds of operation for criminals because they are less likely to be stopped, and less likely to be prosecuted within such places. The notion of state–crime nexus is also relevant here, where corruption of government agencies can result in collaboration between them and organised criminals (see Aas, 2013). This can then result in selective law-enforcement (Muller, 2012, within Aas, 2013) and other forms of cooperation.

11.5 APPLICATION OF CRIMINOLOGICAL THEORIES

It is possible to apply a range of criminological theories to an example such as people trafficking, but also other forms of trafficking, terrorism, and other international processes of offending. In understanding the vulnerabilities of victims, but also the motivations for offending, and the difficulties of preventing such activities, it is important to understand the social, cultural, political and economic processes which have created the conditions for offending/victimisation. This is of particular importance whereby the poor, and women and young girls are under-protected in relation to trafficking, and whereby criminal organisations can flourish. Stark inequalities in wealth and power lead to inequalities in protection, and also motivations for offending, which reflects aspects of both strain theory and critical criminological perspectives. However, it is also possible to consider a rational choice-based approach theory in order to develop a fuller understanding of events. Just as Chapter 3 noted the possibility of integrating models of crime together (integrated approaches block), the example of trafficking offers a good focus to show this in practice.

Murphy (2019) does this, using routine activity theory (a rational-choice/decision-making based model) as the starting point, with aspects of the social pathologies and critical approaches blocks drawn in for a fuller analysis. Routine activity theory (RAT) holds that in order for a crime to take place, there needs to be a motivated offender, a suitable target, and the absence of capable guardianship (Cohen and Felson, 1979). This model is ordinarily used to explain mundane and specific acts of offending such as theft, in making sense of the question *why that target, in that place, and at that time*? There is little consideration for how a motivated offender actually comes about, and the broader factors that create the vulnerabilities of a *suitable target*. Within Murphy (2019) the model is used more expansively in order to consider more dynamic types of crime, e.g. trafficking and terrorism, and to account for both the motivation of an offender, and the vulnerabilities of a target (victim). Figure 11.5 consolidates this into the form of a diagram, but this should be read in conjunction with the discussions of victimisation and offending in Chapter 7.

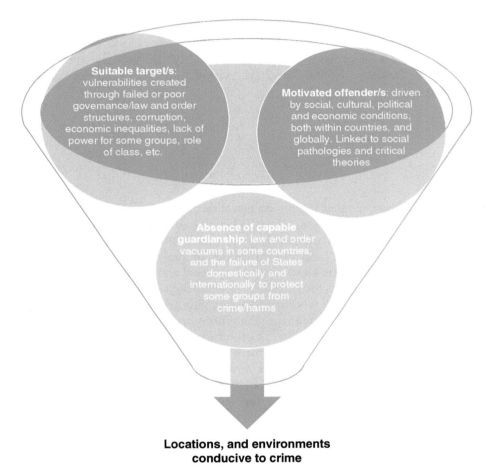

Figure 11.5 A revised routine activity model

(*Source:* adapted from Murphy, 2019)

As Figure 11.5 shows, understanding how such issues of social injustice and human rights emerge requires consideration of a range of factors, both domestic and international in focus. So, too, must responses to such activities be international in nature. The United Nations Office on Drugs and Crime is a good source for both the details of trafficking and terror worldwide, as well as strategies and campaigns to respond on a global level: www.unodc.org/

11.6 SUMMARY AND IMPLICATIONS

Understanding the globalised nature of crime and justice, and international standards, such as social justice and human rights, has become increasingly significant within criminology. It is important to recognise how the processes of offending and victimisation can operate across national borders, and so too, processes of justice must follow in that vein. But also, international standards have been increasingly considered and imposed, and used as a framework for evaluating what States, corporations and private actors do. The United Nations and a wider human rights agenda have been important within this. The chapter has explored the role of corporate and State actors, as well as organised crime groups, within offending and victimisation processes. Crimes types/harms such as cybercrime, genocide, and people trafficking have been considered to show how the criminological focus has widened in recent decades.

RECOMMENDED READING AND FOLLOW-UP MATERIAL

Read

- Aas, K. (2013) *Globalization and Crime* (2nd edn). London: SAGE.

  (This offers a strong coverage of the international dimensions of criminology, and the consequences. Start with the introductory chapter and then have a look at a few others, subject to how much time you have.)

- Craig, R. (2014) 'The global markets in modern day slavery', *Criminal Justice Matters*, 97, available at: www.crimeandjustice.org.uk/sites/crimeandjustice.org.uk/files/09627251.2014.950509.pdf

  (This is a short but effective exploration of some of the chapter themes in the context of 'modern slavery'.)

Watch

- Videos housed within the NGO Human Rights Watch's video repository at www.hrw.org/video-photos

  (These are all very short, so watch as many as possible because they explore the contemporary challenges to human rights in a range of different countries.)

CHAPTER REVIEW QUESTIONS

1. Why is it important to think globally about crime and justice issues?
2. What are some of the global injustices witnessed in recent times?
3. What is the value in thinking about human rights as a guide for recognising and understanding injustices?
4. Why might crimes carried out by States and corporations be described as crimes of the 'powerful', and what are the motivations for such actions?

REVIEW ACTIVITIES

1. Using the Internet, research the International Criminal Court (ICC), and consider its role and activities. Start with the ICC website at www.icc-cpi.int/ and read some of the reports and case studies which are available there.
2. Revisit Chapter 7 (related to 'victims' and 'offenders') and make some notes regarding how the issues explored within that chapter overlap with those within this chapter. In particular, think about how it is important to move beyond common-sense notions regarding who victims and offenders are, and the need to think on a global level about crime and harms.

CHAPTER CONTENTS

12 CONCLUSION

12.1 SUMMARY OF THE TEXT

The intention of this text has been to present a brief introduction to the contemporary nature of criminology. The intention has not been to cover every single area or strand of criminology, nor every issue and topic of relevance to criminologists, nor every single facet of the areas discussed within the book. That level of detail is beyond the scope and aims of the text, and arguably, that represents a different pedagogical philosophy. The role of the text is to provide students with a broad introduction to some important themes and issues within criminology which are of value for the here and now, as well as foster a critical mind-set. Along the way, some key authors, concepts and theories have been explored, and the text has demonstrated the diverse and expanding nature of the criminological gaze. This is linked to a central purpose of preparing students for studying criminology in a broad and a critical way; both in terms of content and analytical thinking.

The reason for approaching the text in such a way is the product of a decade or more teaching undergraduate students on introductory criminology courses across a number of universities. My experience has been that the type of resources commonly used by students (traditional textbooks), with their depth of coverage and language and presentation style, and the ways in which this shaped teaching of criminology, was sometimes a barrier to student enjoyment and understanding of criminology. Of course, those more comprehensive texts do have a very important place, but they need to be used appropriately by students and tutors alike to avoid overwhelming students with information.

This text has sought to introduce some of the most pertinent ideas within the field, without providing excessive depth and expansive detail, which in itself can make the key messages disappear among the noise of the vastness of the material. Instead, the attempt here is to show the types of issues of concern within criminology, the connectedness of areas within criminology, and relevance of all this in today's world. To get the most out of the text, follow-up on the key readings and videos throughout, and the activities, and read more widely around the various chapters using the other references given. Use the index to the text and the reference list at the end to aid you with this. Do use the accompanying website for the book (details of this are on the inside-cover page), which has additional resources. Also, those other, longer introductory criminology textbooks can then be used to build the specific detail, once you can appreciate the most overarching ideas within a given topic.

As has been shown throughout, criminology is a complex field of study, which includes focus on an ever-expanding range of issues, both crime and justice specific, and those beyond which still have some wider relevance to the matters of crime and justice, e.g. human rights, social justice, social policies, the nature of cultures and societies, politics, and so on. Criminology began as a much narrower field of enquiry, initially through the intellectual influences and writings of Classicists from the eighteenth century onwards, and Positivists from the nineteenth century onwards.

The twentieth century witnessed the further development of those schools of thought, as well as the emergence of others, and new concerns beyond why people commit crime, and what should be done about it. Such as considerations of the social, cultural and community influences on offending; the wider processes and influences on law-making; CJS practice; the issue of power within society; a focus on gender, ethnicity or other social groups in relation to the law and order matters; concerns with the workings of politics and media; consideration of the influences of economic paradigms and globalisation; the impact of emerging technologies and social trends; consideration of the voices and expertise of those who have experienced offending, victimisation, or encounters with the processes of criminal justice at first-hand; international crime and justice patterns; considerations of international standards such as human rights and social justice, and so on.

At present, criminology reflects all of that and much more. But at its cornerstone, is still the aim of seeking to offer explanation and solutions to problems somehow connected to matters of law and order, it is just that the boundaries are continually shifting to include ever-more sites of focus, and an increasingly diverse set of enquirers across intellectual background and influence. It is useful to come back to the diagram in Chapter 2, which attempted to show how theory in criminology sat within a complex relationship in something called the criminological web of knowledge. In fact, the diagram does more than that, by showing the complexity of criminology more widely, and the ingredients that make up the field, regardless of the specific topics or issues which may emerge over time, or be rescinded from the criminological landscape at any given point in time.

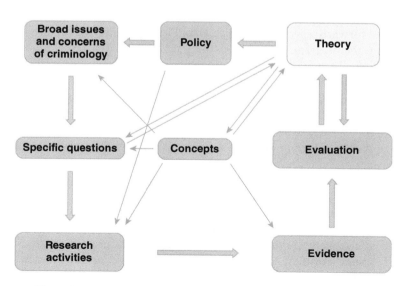

Figure 12.1   The criminological web of knowledge

12.2 PUTTING IT ALL TOGETHER

Having reached the end of the book, your knowledge and understanding of criminology will be stronger, and you should feel more confident as a result of this. However, the next step is to think about how you can *put it all together*, in terms of applying the knowledge and understanding you now have to assessment tasks you will face throughout your studies. There are multiple ways of doing this, and often how you do it depends on the type of assignment being tackled, i.e. an essay *versus* a report, *versus* a poster, *versus* a reflective statement, *versus* a presentation, and so on. However, at the core of all those assessment forms, is researching the topic appropriately, and synthesising ideas with clarity and structure, and often presenting some form of central story, theme or argument.

To that end, a worked example is presented below, which utilises one effective way of doing this; using something that can be referred to as the tree of knowledge. The tree analogy can assist in synthesising lots of material, and keep your work focused on a central story, or theme, or argument. When approaching assignments, the research (reading and familiarisation with the topics) undertaken is crucial in determining the quality of work produced. And so too is the structure adopted. Figure 12.2 essentially states that producing a good essay – let us take the example of an essay given that this is a very common form of assessment – normally involves presenting or exploring a key theme, issue or argument (labelled as the 'trunk' in the diagram). And the way you can demonstrate that is by breaking down the key point being offered through considering a number of smaller issues or themes that in some way build towards the main point, or lead from it; within the diagram these are 'branches'. Finally, in order to effectively demonstrate and support the points put forward, specific examples, detail and evidence are required; these are 'leaves' within the diagram.

Logically then, an overall point is being made or explored in the essay, this is then shown through the discussion of some smaller points, which in turn are developed or corroborated through the examples, detail and evidence presented. This then means that preparation for producing a good essay should entail not only drawing out a main point or argument in relation to a topic, but also, mapping out the steps that must be demonstrated in order to arrive at that point, and explicit detail, examples, and pieces of evidence needed to presented in relation to each of those steps. And this all comes down to engagement with readings, course materials, and developing a comprehensive essay plan.

Let us work through this with an example based on what was covered in Chapter 3. Consider the question *how do critical approaches in criminology explain crime?* The main point or argument could be that critical approaches present crime as a consequence of social conflict, divisions and inequalities, and for many critical criminological positions (but not all) this is influenced by economic forces. So, that is the 'trunk'. Throughout the essay, you would want to try to come back to that

LEAVES: specific examples, detail and evidence in relation to the 'branches', and which will thus help to demonstrate your overall theme or argument presented within the essay.

BRANCHES: secondary themes or issues which build towards or develop the main theme, issue or argument you are putting forward within the essay.

TRUNK: the main theme, argument or point being offered within the essay. It is important to lead off from the trunk, but then come back to it, at the end, and ideally, throughout the essay.

Begin with the 'trunk', which then needs to be built or demonstrated via the introduction of the branches, which in turn, need to be supported through the use of leaves. Although there is a movement out away from the trunk, an effective essay structure means that the essay needs to come back to the trunk throughout in order to stay focused and on track, and to demonstrate the main point you are seeking to make.

The use of 'leaves' help to build and support the discussions of the 'branches', which in turn, helps to present / build the overall theme or argument being offered in the essay. After presenting leaves, an effective essay structure means that you should move back to focusing on the relevant branch, and eventually, the trunk

Figure 12.2   The tree of knowledge

argument in some way, and at the end you will certainly need to revisit that idea within the conclusion. Next, 'branches' are needed. Thus, what might be explored that will help us to build towards that overall argument being presented? There is no exact number required, but the length of an essay will usually dictate how many 'branches' should be used. A 1,000-word essay will require only a few. A 3,000-word essay might require a couple more, or it might require you to spend more time exploring those same few branches, and the associated leaves.

Given the argument regarding critical approaches, one branch could explore the nature of critical approaches broadly, pointing to the range of different perspectives which sit within that block of thinking, related to Marxism, ethnicity, class, and feminism, and so on, and briefly, their overlapping points that link them together. Some leaves would then be presented in order to furnish that, or to put flesh on the bone to so speak. The next branch could be the idea that economic forces shape social relations, creating elite and repressed groups, and offending is a reaction to it, whereby those at the bottom offend to survive. Another branch could be that offending is a political reaction or protest against the social order and unfair nature of society. Another branch could be that economic forces create greed, and those at the top of society commit crime just as readily, if not more so, than those at the bottom, yet it is the poor who are criminalised.

Another branch could consider the very nature of 'crime' itself and show how labelling and criminalising processes against marginalised groups actually creates 'crime'. And so on. It is not necessary to cover everything that has been explored or found out about the topic, but instead, a few well-chosen key points, which are actively led back to the trunk in the course of your discussion. All of the branches mentioned here tell us that 'crime' is, in some way, a result of social conflict, divisions and inequalities; core features of critical approaches. In each case leaves are needed. Taking the branch related to the labelling and criminalisation of the poorest or marginalised groups within society, the essay could cover material that shows disproportionate policing (stop and search suspect statistics for instance); the nature of imprisonment (characteristics of prisoners: the poor, marginal, BAME groups, etc.); and the creation of specific laws that impact on the poorest, and so on.

12.3 CRIMINOLOGICAL FUTURES

Finally, it is important to look to the future, to consider what criminology might look like in the near future. What are the new or recently emergent areas of focus that can be pointed to, which are likely to become important strands within the field? Here are just a few; this is not exhaustive, but instead indicative of the evolving nature of the field, and some of these you will already recognise within discussions throughout the text:

Public criminology: associated with authors such as Michael Burawoy (2005), and Ian Loader and Richard Sparks (2010), this direction of criminology places emphasis on the importance of wider engagement from criminology with public spheres, including social movements linked to social justice, human rights, and so on. But also, this is related to engaging the public with criminological enquiry and knowledge, as opposed to it being a pursuit solely aimed at academia. For instance, David Wilson's media work (Chapter 8) is a good example of this.

Postcolonial criminology: associated with authors such as Biko Agozino (2003), this type of criminology is an attempt to remove the field from its supposed role of serving colonialism, whereby criminology has been argued to have imposed Western ideas and prejudices onto other nations/groups. This approach for example, seeks to shed a light on State crimes and over-representation/criminalisation of marginalised groups.

Queer criminology: associated with authors such as Matthew Ball (2016), this approach posits the value of utilising the knowledge and experiences of the LGBTIQ (lesbian, gay, bisexual, transgender, intersex and queer) communities to understand aspects of victimisation and offending. This is in the context of historical processes of marginalisation and criminalisation of such 'deviancy'. This is linked in a sense to other approaches such as convict criminology, which has focused on the experiences and expertise of offenders in producing criminological knowledge.

Visual criminology: associated with authors such as Eamonn Carrabine (2014), the focus is on the value of visual images, including photography and film within criminology to explore aspects of offending, victimisation and law enforcement. Although the visual tradition is well-established within other fields, criminology is only really now starting to embrace this. Cultural criminology, for example, is an example of the early application of this.

Ultra-realism: associated with authors such as Steve Hall and Simon Winlow (2015), this approach places the issues of intersectionality and harm as central within its analysis, rejecting the extreme left's strong focus on social constructionism of crime, and the right's focus on the legalistic understanding of crime. Instead, a realist approach sits in-between those two positions, but is nevertheless a critical approach. 'Realist' approaches within criminology have been developed previously (e.g. Left Realism – Lea and Young, 1984) but this 'ultra' form is distinguished by the focus on harm (rather than crime), and use of ethnography as the key methodology approach.

FINAL ACTIVITY

Visit the accompanying website for this textbook; details can be found at the start of the book. Work through the 'student' set of materials for each chapter. This will complement the information within the chapters, and also provide you with additional materials, learning and revision activities, and links to contemporary examples of the issues explored within the book.

REFERENCES

Aas, K. (2013) *Globalisation and Crime* (2nd edn). London: SAGE.

ACMD (2018) 'Cannabis-derived medicinal products recommended to be available on prescription', Advisory Council on the Misuse of Drugs, available at: www.gov.uk/government/news/cannabis-derived-medicinal-products-recommended-to-be-available-on-prescription

Agnew, R. (1992) 'Foundation for a general strain theory of crime and delinquency', *Criminology*, 30, 47–87.

Agozino, B. (2003) *Counter-Colonial Criminology: A Critique of Imperialist Reason*. London: Pluto.

Al Jazeera (2019) 'Executed Saudi men confessed under duress: report', *Al Jazeera* [online], 27 April 2019, available at: www.aljazeera.com/news/2019/04/saudi-men-executed-confessed-duress-report-190427072137621.html

Albertson, K., Best, D., Irving, J., Murphy, T., Buckingham, S., Morton, G., Stevenson, J., Crowley, M., Mama-Rudd, A. and Chaggar, A. (2017) 'Right turn veteran-specific recovery service: 5 site evaluation pilot: final report'. Helena Kennedy Centre for International Justice, Sheffield Hallam University.

Alston, P. (2015) 'Report of the Special Rapporteur on Extreme Poverty and Human Rights, United Nations General Assembly: Human Rights Council, twenty-ninth session, agenda item 3', available at: https://www.ohchr.org/EN/HRBodies/HRC/RegularSessions/Session29/Documents/A_HRC_29_31_en.doc

Alston, P. (2017) 'The populist challenge to human rights', *Journal of Human Rights Practice*, 9(1), 1–15.

Amnesty International (2018) 'Sierra Leone: a force for good? Restrictions on peaceful assembly and impunity for excessive use of force by the Sierra Leone police', 3 July 2018, Index number: AFR 51/8590/2018, available at: www.amnesty.org/en/documents/afr51/8590/2018/en/

Andrews, G. (2014) 'Riots and disorder on the street', in Woodward, K. and Clarke, J. (eds), *Understanding Social Lives, Part 2*. Milton Keynes: The Open University.

APCC (2018) *Role of the PCC*, available at: www.apccs.police.uk/role-of-the-pcc/

Baird, V. (2011) 'Riots sentencing: a sinister attempt to upend the judicial process', *Guardian* [online], 18 Aug 2011, available at: www.theguardian.com/commentisfree/2011/aug/18/riots-sentencing-courts

Baldock, J., Mitton, L., Manning, N. and Vickerstaff, S. (2011) *Social Policy*. Oxford: Oxford University Press.

Bales, K. (1999) *Disposable People: New Slavery in the Global Economy*. Berkeley: University of California Press.

Ball, M. (2016) *Criminology and Queer Theory: Dangerous Bedfellows?* London: Penguin.

BBC (2017) 'Stacey Dooley Investigates: Kids Selling Drugs Online'. BBC One [aired 10 August 2017].

Bean, P. (2018) *Probation and Privatisation*. Abingdon: Routledge.

Beatty, C. and Fothergill, S. (2016) 'The uneven impact of welfare reform: the final losses to places and people', Centre for Regional, Economic and Social Research, available at: www4.shu.ac.uk/research/cresr/sites/shu.ac.uk/files/welfare-reform-2016.pdf

Beccaria, C. (1995[1767]) *On Crimes and Punishment and Other Writings*, translated by Richard Bellamy. Cambridge: Cambridge University Press.

Beck, U. (1992) *Risk Society*. London: SAGE.

Becker, H. (1963) *Outsiders: Studies in the Sociology of Deviance*. London: Macmillan.

Bennett, L. (2018) 'The sentence should fit the crime, not the race', The Marcus Harris Foundation [blog] 18 August 2018, available at: https://marcusharrisfoundation.org/blog/f/the-sentence-should-fit-the-crime-not-the-race

Bershidsky, L. (2018) 'Germany must come to terms with refugee crime', Bloomberg [blog], available at: www.bloomberg.com/view/articles/2018-01-03/germany-must-come-to-terms-with-refugee-crime

BJS (2018) 'Data collection: national crime victimization survey (NCVS)', available at: www.bjs.gov/index.cfm?ty=dcdetail&iid=245

Bondy, M., Roth, S. and SAGEr, L. (2018) 'Crime is in the air: the contemporaneous relationship between air pollution and crime', The Centre for Climate Change Economics and Policy, Working Paper no.331 (online), available at: www.lse.ac.uk/GranthamInstitute/wp-content/uploads/2018/04/working-paper-295-Bondy-et-al.pdf

Bowling, B. and Phillips, C. (2000) *Racism, Crime and Justice*. London: Pearson.

Bows, H. (2018) 'Victims and victimisation', in Cooper, V. and Phoenix, J. (eds), *Criminological Theories and Concepts: Book 2*. Milton Keynes: The Open University.

Box, S. (1987) *Recession, Crime and Punishment*. London: Palgrave.

Brisman, A., Carrabine, E. and South, N. (eds) (2017) *Criminological Theory and Concepts*. Abingdon: Routledge.

Brummer, A. (2018) 'Rescuing Carillion would have saved taxpayers hundreds of millions over the long term', *This is Money* [online], available at: www.thisismoney.co.uk/money/comment/article-5326861/ALEX-BRUMMER-real-Carillion-scandal.html

Bulman, M. (2018) 'Home Office policy leaving refugees homeless within days of being granted asylum, report finds', *The Independent* (online), 6 June 2018, available at: www.independent.co.uk/news/uk/home-news/homeless-people-night-shelters-refugees-home-office-policies-sajid-javid-a8368806.html

Burawoy, M. (2005) 'For public sociology', *American Sociological Review*, 70, 4–28.

Carmichael, F. and Ward, R. (2000) 'Youth unemployment and crime in the English regions and Wales', *Applied Economics*, 32, 5, 559–71.

Carrabine, E. (2014) 'Seeing things: violence, voyeurism and the camera', *Theoretical Criminology*, 18, 2, 134–58.

Carroll, L. (2016) 'How the war on drugs affected the incarceration rate', *Politifact*, 10 July 2016 [online], available at: www.politifact.com/truth-o-meter/statements/2016/jul/10/cory-booker/how-war-drugs-affected-incarceration-rates/

Case, S., Johnson, P., Manlow, D., Smith, R. and Williams, K. (2017) *Criminology*. Oxford: Oxford University Press.

Chadee, D., Surette, R., Chadee, M. and Brewster, D. (2017) 'Copycat crime dynamics: the interplay of empathy, narrative persuasion and risk with likelihood to commit future criminality', *Psychology of Popular Media Culture*, 6, 2, 142–58.

Chambliss, W. (1978) *On the Take: From Petty Crooks to Presidents*. Bloomington: Indiana University Press.

Chibnall, S. (1977) *Law and Order News: Crime Reporting in the British Press*. London: Tavistock.

Christie, N. (1986) 'The ideal victim', in Fattah, E.A. (ed.), *From Crime Policy to Victim Policy*. London: Palgrave Macmillan.

Clarke, R.V.G. and Cornish, D. (2001) 'Rational choice', in Paternoster, R. and Bachman, R. (eds), *Explaining Criminals and Crime: Essays in Contemporary Criminological Theory*. Los Angeles: Roxbury.

Clarke, R.V. (2018) 'Regulating crime: the birth of the idea, its nurture, and the implications for contemporary criminology', *The ANNALS of the American Academy of Political and Social Science*, 679, 1, 20–35, available at: https://doi.org/10.1177/0002716218775031

Cochrane, A. and Talbot, D. (eds) (2008) *Security: Welfare, Crime and Society*. Maidenhead: Open University.

Cockburn, J.S. (1994) 'Punishment and brutalization in the English Enlightenment', *Law and History Review*, 12, 1, 155–79.

Cohen, A.K. (1955) *Delinquent Boys: The Culture of the Gang*. New York: Free Press.

Cohen, L. and Felson, M. (1979) 'Social change and crime rate trends: a routine activity approach', *American Sociological Review*, 44, 4, 588–608.

Cohen, S. (1972) *Folk Devils and Moral Panics*. London: MacGibbon and Kee.

Coleman, C. (1996) *Understanding Crime Data: Haunted by the Dark Figure* (Crime and Justice). Buckinghamshire: Open University Press.

Connell, R.W. (1987) *Gender and Power*. Cambridge: Polity Press.

Cornish, D. and Clarke, R.V. (eds) (1986) *The Reasoning Criminal: Rational Choice Perspectives on Offending*. New York: Springer-Verlag.

Criminal Justice Inspectorates (2018) 'Criminal Justice Inspectorates', available at: www.justiceinspectorates.gov.uk/

Daigle, L. (2013) *Victimology: The Essentials*. Thousand Oaks: SAGE.

Davies, P., Francis, P. and Greer, C. (2007) *Victims, Crime and Society*. London: SAGE.

Dean, H. (2012) *Social Policy* (2nd edn). Cambridge: Polity Press.

Dearden, L. (2018) 'Fear of infuriating Trump made UK drop opposition to death penalty for British Isis suspects, court told', *Independent* [online], 8 October 2018, available at: www.independent.co.uk/news/uk/crime/isis-suspect-executioners-beatles-death-penalty-us-uk-drop-opposition-trump-a8574096.html

DfES (2007) *Every Parent Matters*. London: DfES.

DiFilippo, D. (2016) 'Stepping back from vengeance; seeking reformative justice', *WHYY* [online:], available at: https://whyy.org/articles/stepping-back-from-vengeance-seeking-reformative-justice/

Dorling, D., Gordon, D., Hillyard, P., Pantzias, C., Pemberton, S. and Tombs, S. (2008) *Criminal Obsessions: Why Harm Matters More Than Crime* (2nd edn). Centre for Crime and Justice, available at: www.dannydorling.org/wp-content/files/dannydorling_publication_id1047.pdf

Downes, D. (1966) *The Delinquent Solution*. London: Routledge.

Durkheim, E. (1964 [1895]) *The Rules of Sociological Method*. New York: The Free Press.

Durkheim, E. (1984 [1893]) *The Division of Labour in Society*. New York: The Free Press.

Elias, N. (2000) *The Civilizing Process*. Oxford: Wiley.

Emsley, C. (2010) *Crime and Society in England: 1750–1900* (4th edn). London: Routledge.

Farha, L. (2015) 'UN Special Rapporteur on the right to adequate housing: homelessness as a global human rights crisis', available at: www.ohchr.org/Documents/Issues/Housing/HomelessSummary_en.pdf

Farrington, D.P. (2005) 'Childhood origins of anti-social behaviour', *Forensic Psychology*, 12, 3, 177–90.

Faye, G. (2015) 'The migratory invasion, part 3: strong medicine', Counter Currents Publishing [Blog], available at: www.counter-currents.com/2015/09/strong-medicine/

Felson, M. and Eckert, M. (2015) *Crime and Everyday Life*. London: SAGE.

Fergusson, R. and Muncie, J. (2008) 'Criminalising conduct', in Cochrane, A. and Talbot, D. (eds), *Security: Welfare, Crime and Society*. Maidenhead: Open University Press, 93–126.

Ferrell, J., Hayward, K. and Young, J. (2008) *Cultural Criminology: An Invitation*. London: SAGE.

Ferrell, J., Hayward, K. and Young, J. (2015) *Cultural Criminology: An Invitation* (2nd edn). London: SAGE.

Field, A. (2016) *An Adventure in Statistics: The Reality Enigma*. London: SAGE.

Finch, E. and Fafinski, S. (2016) *Criminology Skills* (2nd edn). Oxford: Oxford University Press.

Foucault, M. (1979) *Discipline and Punish: The Birth of the Prison*. New York: Vintage Books.

Fox News (2005) 'Lawsuit: 'Grand Theft Auto' Led Teen to Kill', February 16th 2005, available at https://www.foxnews.com/story/lawsuit-grand-theft-auto-led-teen-to-kill

Francis, P. and Davies, P. (2018) *Doing Criminological Research* (3rd edn). London: SAGE.

Garland, D. (1991) 'Sociological perspectives on punishment', *Crime and Justice*, 14, 115–65.

Garland, D. (2001) *The Culture of Control*. Oxford: Oxford University Press.

Garside, R. (2015) 'Criminal justice since 2010: what has happened and why?' *Criminal Justice Matters*, 100, 1, available at: https://www.crimeandjustice.org.uk/publications/cjm/article/criminal-justice-2010-what-happened-and-why

Gelsthorpe, L., Padfield, N. and Philips, J. (2012) 'Deaths on probation: an analysis of data regarding people dying under probation supervision', Howard League for Penal Reform, available at: https://howardleague.org/wp-content/uploads/2016/05/Deaths-on-probation.pdf

Gerdziunas, B. (2018) 'Three quarters of Brits back dramatic fall in immigration: poll', Politico [online], 22 June 2018, available at: www.politico.eu/article/poll-three-quarters-of-brits-back-dramatic-fall-in-immigration/

Giddens, A. (1990) *The Consequences of Modernity*. Stanford: Stanford University Press.

Gitlin, M. (2017) *The Border Wall With Mexico*. Michigan: Grenhaven.

Glenny, M. (2006) 'Drugs and terror: Britain's role: Tony Blair's ambition to eradicate opium production in Afghanistan has failed miserably. More poppie', *New Statesman* (Politics) [online], 9 October 2006, available at: www.newstatesman.com/node/195620

Goldson, B. (2013) 'Juvenile justice', in McLaughlin, E. and Muncie, J. (eds), *The SAGE Dictionary of Criminology* (3rd edn). London: SAGE.

Goldson, B. and Munice, J. (2015) *Youth, Crime and Justice*. London: SAGE.

Goodey, J. (2005) *Victims and Victimology: Research, Policy and Practice*. Harlow: Pearson Education.

Gov.uk (2018) *Counter-terrorism Strategy* (CONTEST), Home Office, available at: www.gov.uk/government/publications/counter-terrorism-strategy-contest-2018

Grabosky, P. (2001) 'Virtual criminology: old wine in new bottles?' *Social & Legal Studies*, 1, 2, 243–9.

Grogger, J. (1998) 'Market wages and youth crime', *Journal of Labor Economics*, 16, 4, 756–91.

Grover, C. (2008) *Crime and Inequality*. Cullumpton: Willan.

Hall, S., Critcher, C., Jefferson, T., Clarke, J. and Roberts, B. (eds) (1978/2013) *Policing the Crisis: Mugging, the State and Law and Order*. London: Macmillan.

Hall, S. and Winlow, S. (2015) *Revitalizing Criminological Theory: Towards a New Ultra-Realism*. London: Routledge.

Hansen, K. and Machin, S. (2002) 'Spatial crime patterns and the introduction of the UK minimum wage', *Oxford Bulletin of Economics and Statistics*, 64 (Supplement), 677–97.

Henry, S. and Milovanovic, D. (2013) 'Constitutive criminology', in McLaughlin, E. and Muncie, J. (eds), *The SAGE Dictionary of Criminology* (3rd edn). London: SAGE.

HM Prison Service (2018) *Contracted-out Prisons*, Department of Justice, available at: www.justice.gov.uk/about/hmps/contracted-out

HM Treasury (2003) *Every Child Matters*, Cm 5860. London: The Stationery Office.

Hobbes, T. (1985 [1651]) *Leviathan*. New York: Viking Penguin.

Hobolt, S.B. (2016) 'The Brexit vote: a divided nation, a divided continent', *Journal of European Public Policy*, 23, 9, 1259–77, DOI: 10.1080/13501763.2016.1225785

Hohl, K., Stanko, B. and Newburn, T. (2013) 'The effect of the 2011 London disorder on public opinion of police and attitudes towards crime, disorder, and sentencing', *Policing*, 7, 1, 12–20. ISSN 1752-4512

Homeless Link (2018) *Facts and Figures*. Homeless Link, available at: www.homeless.org.uk/facts-figures

Houchin, R. (2005) 'Social exclusion and imprisonment in Scotland: a report', Scottish Prison Service, Glasgow Caledonian University. Published on SPS website.

Howard League for Penal Reform (2018) 'The rising tide: additional days for rule-breaking in prison', available at: https://howardleague.org/wp-content/uploads/2018/08/The-rising-tide-Addtional-days-for-rule-breaking-in-prison.pdf

HRW (2018) '"You don't want to breathe poison anymore" the failing response to pesticide drift in Brazil's rural communities', Human Rights Watch Report, available at: www.hrw.org/report/2018/07/20/you-dont-want-breathe-poison-anymore/failing-response-pesticide-drift-brazils

HSE (2019) *Workplace fatal injuries in Great Britain 2018* (Annual Statistics). Health and Safety Executive, available at: www.hse.gov.uk/statistics/pdf/fatalinjuries.pdf

Hudson, B. (2013) 'Criminal justice', in McLaughlin, E. and Muncie, J. (eds), *The SAGE Dictionary of Criminology* (3rd edn). London: SAGE.

Hughes, G. (2008) 'Community safety and the governance of "problem populations"', in Mooney, G. and Neil, S. (eds), *Community: Welfare, Crime and Society*. Maidenhead: Open University Press.

ICPR (2018) *World Prison Brief Data*. Institute for Criminal Policy Research, available at: www.prisonstudies.org/world-prison-brief-data

International Campaign for Bhopal (2014) 'What happened in Bhopal?', Bhopal.net, available at: www.bhopal.net/what-happened/

Intravia, J. (2018) 'Investigating the influence of social media consumption on punitive attitudes among a sample of U.S. university students', *International Journal of Offender Therapy and Comparative Criminology*, available at: https://doi.org/10.1177/0306624X18786610

IPRT (2012) *The Vicious Circle of Social Exclusion and Crime: Ireland's Disproportionate Punishment of the Poor*. Irish Penal Reform Trust, available at: www.iprt.ie/files/Position_Paper_FINAL.pdf

Jensen, T. (2014) '"Broken/Benefits Britain" in the attention economy: policing precariats and precarious policy', [presentation], *The Precarious Precariat Workshop*, Department of Sociology, London School of Economics and Political Science, 26 March 2014.

Jewkes, Y. (2010) *Media and Crime* (2nd edn). London: SAGE.

Jewkes, Y. (2011) *Media and Crime* (2nd edn). London: SAGE.

Jewkes, Y. (2013) 'Cybercrime', in McLaughlin, E. and Muncie, J. (eds), *The SAGE Dictionary of Criminology* (3rd edn). London: SAGE

Jewkes, Y. (2015) *Media and Crime* (3rd edn). London: SAGE.

Joffe, G. (2011) 'The Arab Spring in in North Africa: origins and prospects', *The Journal of North African Studies*, 16, 4, 507–32.

Jonson, C.L. (2012) 'The effects of imprisonment', in Cullen, F.T. and Wilcox, P. (eds), *The Oxford Handbook of Criminological Theory*. Oxford Handbooks Online, available at: www.oxfordhandbooks.com/view/10.1093/oxfordhb/9780199747238.001.0001/oxfordhb-9780199747238

Jupp, V. (2014) *SAGE Dictionary of Social Research Methods*. London: SAGE.

Katz, J. (2016) *The Macho Paradox: Why Some Men Hurt Women and How All Men Can Help*. Naperville, Illinois: Sourcebooks, Inc.

Kiley, S. (Presenter) and von Planto, C. (Producer) (2005) *India: Land of Missing Children* (Television series episode), in Gregory, F. (Executive Producer), *Unreported World*. London: C4.

Knepper, P. (2007) *Criminology and Social Policy*. London: SAGE.

Krahé, B., Möller, I., Huesmann, L.R., Kirwil, L., Felber, J. and Berger, A. (2011) 'Desensitization to media violence: links with habitual media violence exposure, aggressive cognitions and aggressive behavior', *Journal of Personality and Social Psychology*, 100, 630–46.

Krohn, M.D., Thornberry, T.P., Gibson, C.L. and Baldwin, J. (2010) 'The development and impact of self-report measures of crime and delinquency', *Quantitative Criminology*, 26, 509–25, available at: https://doi.org/10.1007/s10940-010-9119-1

Ksicinski, P. (2017) 'Crime and poverty: idle hands is crime's workshop', available at: www.paulksicinskilaw.com/blog/crime-and-poverty-idle-hands-is-crimes-workshop

Lea, J. (2015) 'Back to the future: neoliberalism as social and political regression', *Journal on European History of Law*, 6, 1, 109–17.

Lea, J. and Hallsworth, M. (2012) 'Understanding the riots', *Criminal Justice Matters*, 30–31, available at: https://doi.org/10.1080/09627251.2012.671013

Lea, J. and Young, J. (1984) *What is to be Done about Law and Order?* London: Penguin.

Lee, R.D., Fang, X. and Luo, F. (2016) 'Parental incarceration and social exclusion: long-term implications for the health and well-being of vulnerable children in the United States', in Bishop, J.A. and Rodríguez, J.G. (eds), *Inequality after the 20th Century: Papers from the Sixth ECINEQ Meeting (Research on Economic Inequality, Volume 24)*. Emerald Group Publishing Limited, 215 –34.

Levitas, R. (2005) *The Inclusive Society and New Labour* (2nd edn). Basingstoke: Palgrave Macmillan.

Levy, G. (2011) 'Titillation by the yard and scoops galore: an obituary for a 168-year-old very British institution', *Mailonline*, 8 July 2011, available at: www.dailymail.co.uk/news/article-2012436/News-World-shutting-Titillation-yard-scoops-galore.html

Lewis, P., Newburn, T., Taylor, M., Mcgillivray, C., Greenhill, A., Frayman, H. and Proctor, R. (2011) *Reading the Riots: Investigating England's Summer of Disorder*. London: The London School of Economics and Political Science and *The Guardian*, available at: http://eprints.lse.ac.uk/46297/

Lilly, J., Cullen, F. and Ball, R. (2015) *Criminological Theory: Context and Consequences* (6th edn). Thousand Oaks: SAGE.

Linebaugh, P. (2003) *The London Hanged: Crime and Civil Society in the Eighteenth Century*. London: Verso.

Loader, I. and Sparks, R. (2010) *Public Criminology?* London: Routledge.

Lynch, P. (2005) 'Homelessness, human rights and social inclusion, *AltLJ, 30*, 3, 116–9.

MacAskell, E. (2016) 'MI6 stood by bogus intelligence until after Iraq invasion', *Guardian* [online] 6 July 2016, avaialbale at: www.theguardian.com/uk-news/2016/jul/06/mi6-stood-by-bogus-intelligence-until-after-iraq-invasion

MacAskell, E. and Borger, J. (2016) 'Iraq war was illegal and breached UN charter, says Annan', *Guardian* [online] 16 September 2004, available at: www.theguardian.com/world/2004/sep/16/iraq.iraq

MacKinnon, C. (1987) *Feminisms Unmodified: Discourses on Life and Law*. Cambridge, MA: Harvard University Press.

MacNicol, J. (1987) 'In pursuit of the underclass', *Journal of Social Policy, 16*, 3, 293–318.

Maguire, M. and McVie, S. (2017) 'Crime data and criminal statistics: a critical reflection', in Liebling, A., Maruna, S. and McAra, L. (eds), *The Oxford Handbook of Criminology* (6th edn). Oxford: Oxford University Press.

Maher, L. (1997) *Sexed Work: Gender, Race and Resistance in a Brooklyn Drug Market*. Oxford: Oxford University Press.

Mailonline (2011) 'News-World-shutting-Titillation-yard-scoops-galore', 8 July 2011. Available at: https://www.dailymail.co.uk/news/article-2012436/News-World-shutting-Titillation-yard-scoops-galore.html

Markey, P. and Ferguson, C. (2017) *Moral Combat: Why the War on Violent Video Games Is Wrong*. Dallas: BenBella Books Inc.

Matza, D. (1964) *Delinquency and Drift*. New York: Wiley.

McLaughlin, E. (2013) 'State crime', in McLaughlin, E. and Muncie, J. (eds), *The SAGE Dictionary of Criminology* (3rd edn). London: SAGE.

McLaughlin, E. and Muncie, J. (eds) (2013) *The SAGE Dictionary of Criminology* (3rd edn). London: SAGE.

McLaughlin, E., Muncie, J. and Hughes, G. (2001) 'The permanent revolution: New Labour and the modernization of criminal justice', *Criminal Justice: An International Journal of Policy and Practice, 3*, 3, 301–18.

Merton, R.K. (1938) 'Social structure and anomie', *American Sociological Review, 3*, 367–682.

Messerschmidt, J.W. (1993) *Masculinities and Crime*. Lanham: Rowman and Littlefield.

Messerschmidt, J.W. (2000) *Nine Lives: Adolescent Masculinities, the Body, and Violence*. Boulder: Westview Press.

Millar, J. and Bennett, F. (2017) 'Universal Credit: assumptions, contradictions and virtual reality', *Social Policy and Society, 16*, 2, 169–82.

Mirza-Davies, J. and Brown, J. (2016) 'NEET: young people not in education, employment or training', HM Commons Briefing Paper. London: HM Commons.

Mississippi NAACP (2018) 'Number of offenders in the United States, by age and offense, 2012', available at: http://naacpms.org/sheriff-teaming-up-with-unions-to-offer-occupational-opportunity-to-felons/image2-2/

Moffitt, T.E., Ross, S. and Raine, A. (2011) 'Crime and biology', in Wilson, J.Q. and Petersilia, J. (eds), *Crime and Public Policy*. Oxford: Oxford University Press.

MoJ (2016) 'Statistics on women and the criminal justice system 2015', A Ministry of Justice publication under Section 95 of the Criminal Justice Act 1991, available at: https://assets.publishing.service.gov.uk/government/uploads/system/uploads/attachment_data/file/572043/women-and-the-criminal-justice-system-statistics-2015.pdf

MoJ (2017a) 'Proven reoffending statistics: definitions and measurement', Ministry of Justice, available at: https://assets.publishing.service.gov.uk/government/uploads/system/uploads/attachment_data/file/658384/guide-to-proven-reoffending-statistics-oct17.pdf

MoJ (2017b) 'Proven reoffending statistics quarterly bulletin, January to December 2015, England and Wales'. Ministry of Justice, available at: https://assets.publishing.service.gov.uk/government/uploads/system/uploads/attachment_data/file/633194/proven-reoffending-2015-q3.pdf

Mooney, G. and Neal, S.N. (eds) (2008) *Community: Welfare, Crime and Society*. Maidenhead: Open University.

Müller, K. and Schwarz, C. (2018) 'Fanning the flames of hate: social media and hate crime', CAGE Online Working Paper Series 373, Competitive Advantage in the Global Economy (CAGE), available at: https://econpapers.repec.org/paper/cgewacage/373.htm

Muncie, J. (2009) 'The construction and deconstruction of crime', in Newburn, T, (ed.), *Key Readings in Criminology*. Cullompton: Willan.

Murphy, T. (2015) 'The nomenclature of the undeserving poor: a history of marginalization', *Journal on European History of Law*, 6, 1, 103–8.

Murphy, T. (2019) 'Terror and trafficking in South Asia: a theoretical application', in Jaishankar, S. (eds), *Handbook on South Asian Criminology*. California: Taylor and Francis.

Murray, C. (1989) 'Underclass: the crisis deepens', *Sunday Times*, 22 May, 10–11.

Newburn, T. (2007) *Criminology*. Cullompion: Willan.

Newburn, T. (2008) *Handbook of Policing*. Cullompton: Willan.

O'Connor, R. (2017) 'How alcohol and drug treatment helps to reduce crime', Gov.uk [online], available at: https://publichealthmatters.blog.gov.uk/2017/11/02/how-alcohol-and-drug-treatment-helps-to-reduce-crime/

ONS (2016) 'Crime in England and Wales, quarterly bulletin' [Information Paper: Quality and Methodology], available at: www.ons.gov.uk/ons/guide-method/method-quality/quality/quality-information/crime-and-justice/quality-and-methodology-information-for-crime-in-england-and-wales.pdf

ONS (2018a) 'Crime in England and Wales: year ending March 2018', Office for National Statistics, available at: www.ons.gov.uk/peoplepopulationandcommunity/crimeandjustice/bulletins/crimeinenglandandwales/yearendingmarch2018

ONS (2018b) 'Crime in England and Wales: year ending Mar 2017', Office for National Statistics, available at: www.ons.gov.uk/peoplepopulationandcommunity/crimeandjustice/bulletins/crimeinenglandandwales/yearendingmar2017#quality-and-methodology

ONS (2018c) 'Crime in England and Wales: Annual Trend and Demographic Tables', Office for National Statistics, available at: www.ons.gov.uk/peoplepopulationandcommunity/crimeandjustice/datasets/crimeinenglandandwalesannualtrendanddemographictables

Open University (2008) 'Introducing social justice', DD208 Welfare, Crime and Society, module website [electronic materials].

Open University (2018) 'Understanding crime', DD212, module website [electronic materials].

Owenson, G.H. and Savage, N.J. (2015) 'The tor dark net', Global Commission on Internet Governance, (*20*), available at: https://www.cigionline.org/sites/default/files/no20_0.pdf

Oxfam (2014) 'The Rwandan genocide: twenty years on', *Views and voices*, available at: https://views-voices.oxfam.org.uk/2014/04/the-rwanda-genocide-twenty-years-on/

Park, R.E., Burgess, E.W. and McKenzie, R.D. (1925) *The City*. Chicago: University of Chicago Press.

Parsons, D. and Skinner, C. (2018) 'Kerala shows the risk of severe floods is still evolving', *The Conversation* [online], 22 August 2018, available at: http://theconversation.com/kerala-shows-the-risk-of-severe-floods-is-still-evolving-101880

Patton, D., Eschmann, R., Elsaesser, C. and Bocanegra, E. (2016) 'Sticks, stones and Facebook accounts: what violence outreach workers know about social media and urban-based gang violence in Chicago', *Computers in Human Behavior*, 65, 591–600.

Patton, D., Lane, J., Leonard, P., Macbeth, J. and Smith Lee, J. (2017) 'Gang violence on the digital street: case study of a South Side Chicago gang member's Twitter communication', *New Media & Society*, 19, 7, 1000–18, available at: https://doi.org/10.1177/1461444815625949

Pearson, G. (1983) *Hooligan: A History of Respectable Fears*. London: Macmillan.

Philips, J., Gelsthorpe, L. and Padfield, N. (2017) 'Non-custodial deaths: missing, ignored or unimportant?', *Criminology and Criminal Justice*, available at: https://doi.org/10.1177/1748895817745939

Phoenix, J. (2018) 'Understanding criminological theories', in Cooper, V. and Phoenix, J. (eds), *Criminological Theories and Concepts: Book 1*, Milton Keynes: The Open University.

Potter, G.W. (2017) 'Globalization', in Brisman, A., Carrabine, E. and South, N. (eds), *Criminological Theory and Concepts*. Abingdon: Routledge.

Power, A., Provan, B., Herden, E. and Serle, N. (2014) 'The impact of welfare reform on social landlords and tenants', available at: www.jrf.org.uk/sites/default/files/jrf/migrated/files/Welfare-reform-impack-FULL.pdf

Pratt, J. (2007) *Penal Populism*. Abingdon: Routledge.

Prideaux, S. (2010) 'The welfare politics of Charles Murray are alive and well in the UK', *International Journal of Social Welfare*, 19, 293–302.

Prison Reform Trust (2017) 'Bromley briefings prison factfile autumn 2017'. Prison Reform Trust [online], available at: www.prisonreformtrust.org.uk/Publications/Factfile

Ramaswamy, M. and Freudenberg, N. (2012) 'The cycle of social exclusion for urban, young men of color in the United States: what is the role of incarceration?', *Journal of Poverty*, 16, 2, 119–46.

Reiner, R. (2002) 'Media made criminality: the representation of crime in the mass media', in Maguire, M., Morgan, R. and Reiner, R. (eds), *The Oxford Handbook of Criminology* (3rd edn). Oxford: OUP, 376–418.

Reiner, R. (2007) *Law and Order: An Honest Person's Guide to Crime and Control*. Cambridge: Polity Press.

Reprieve (2018) 'Death penalty', available at: https://reprieve.org.uk/

Rufrancos, H.G., Power, M., Pickett, K.E. and Wilkinson, R. (2013) 'Income inequality and crime: a review and explanation of the time–series evidence', *Sociology and Crime – Open Access*, 1, 1, available at: www.equalitytrust.org.uk/sites/default/files/Income%20Inequality%20and%20Crime%20-%20A%20Review%20and%20Explanation%20of%20the%20Time%20series%20evidence_0.pdf

Rumgay, J. (2005) 'Twice punished: when women victims become offenders', *Criminal Justice Matters*, 60, 1, 16–38, DOI: 10.1080/09627250508553607

Savill, R. (2010) 'Vanessa George's nursery provided "ideal environment for abuse", *Telegraph* (online), 4 November 2010, available at: www.telegraph.co.uk/news/uknews/crime/8110275/Vanessa-Georges-nursery-provided-ideal-environment-for-abuse.html

Scraton, P. (2013) 'The legacy of Hillsborough: liberating truth, challenging power', *Race & Class*, 55, 2, 1–27, available at: https://doi.org/10.1177/0306396813499488

Scraton, P. (2016) *Hillsborough: The Truth* (updated edn). Edinburgh: Mainstream Publishing.

Short, D. (2017) 'Genocide and ecocide', in Brisman, A., Carrabine, E. and South, N. (eds), *Criminological Theory and Concepts*. Abingdon: Routledge.

Smith, A. (2019) 'Saudi Arabia executed 37 people and all the UK did was shrug. What will it take for the west to speak up?', *Independent* [online], 25 April 2019, available at: www.independent.co.uk/voices/saudi-arabia-death-toll-executed-mohammed-bin-salman-theresa-may-a8884721.html

Smith, E. (2018) *Key Issues in Education and Social Justice* (2nd edn). London: SAGE.

Sparks, R.F. (1982) *Research on Victims of Crime*. Washington DC: US Government Printing Office.

St Mungo's (2016) 'Stop the scandal: an investigation into mental health and rough sleeping', February 2016, available at: www.mungos.org/wp-content/uploads/2017/12/Stop_the_scandal_Feb20161.pdf

Steffensmeier, D. and Allan, E. (1996) 'Gender and crime: toward a gendered theory of female offending', *Annual Review of Sociology*, 22, 459–87.

Stop Genocide Now (2018) 'Syria', available at: https://stopgenocidenow.org/conflicts/syria/

Surette, R. (2014) *Media, Crime and Criminal Justice* (5th edn). Stamford: Cengage Learning.

Sutherland, E.H. and Cressey, D.R. (1947) *Principles of Criminology* (4th edn). Philadelphia: J.B. Lippincott.

Sykes, G. (1958) *The Society of Captives: A Study of a Maximum Security Prison*. New Jersey: Princeton University.

Taylor, J., Walton, P. and Young, J. (1973) *The New Criminology: For a Social Theory of Deviance*. London: Routledge and Kegan Paul.

Taylor-Gooby, P. (2012) 'Equality, rights and justice,' in Alcock, P., May, M. and Wright, S. (eds), *The Student's Companion to Social Policy* (4th edn). Chichester: John Wiley & Sons Ltd, 26–32.

The Sentencing Project (2018) 'Factsheet: trends in U.S. corrections', available at: https://sentencingproject.org/wp-content/uploads/2016/01/Trends-in-US-Corrections.pdf

Tibbetts, S. (2018) *Criminological Theory: The Essentials*. California: SAGE.

Tiihonen, J., Rautiainen, M-R., Ollila, H.M., Repo-Tiihonen, E., Virkkunen, M., Palotie, A., Pietiläinen, O., Kristiansson, K., Joukamaa, M., Lauerma, H., Saarela, J., Tyni, S., Vartiainen, H., Paananen, J., Goldman, D. and Paunio, T. (2014) 'Genetic background of extreme violent behavior', *Molecular Psychology*, 20, 786–92.

Tombs, S. and Whyte, D. (2008) *A Crisis of Enforcement: The Decriminalisation of Death and Injury at Work*. London: Centre for Crime and Justice Studies, King's College London.

Tombs, S. and Whyte, D. (2013) 'Corporate Crime' in McLaughlin, E. and Muncie, J. (eds), *The SAGE Dictionary of Criminology* (3rd edn). London: SAGE.

Tufail, W. (2015) 'Rotherham, Rochdale, and the racialised threat of the "Muslim grooming gang"', *International Journal for Crime, Justice and Social Democracy*, 4, 3 [online], available at: www.crimejusticejournal.com/article/view/766

Turk, A. (1969) *Criminality and Legal Order*. Chicago: Rand McNally.

UK Parliament (2016) 'Joint Committee on Human Rights report on the government's policy on the use of drones for targeted killing' (Second Report of Session 2015–16), available at: https://publications.parliament.uk/pa/jt201516/jtselect/jtrights/574/574.pdf

UK Parliament (2018a) 'Troubled families'. Public Accounts Committee (online), available at: www.parliament.uk/business/committees/committees-a-z/commons-select/public-accounts-committee/inquiries/parliament-2015/troubled-families-16-17/

UK Parliament (2018b) 'Rough sleepers and anti-social behaviour (England)', House of Commons Library [online], available at: https://researchbriefings.parliament.uk/ResearchBriefing/Summary/CBP-7836

UN (2018) 'Greater ambition, urgency needed to avert climate crisis, Secretary-General stresses at launch of new climate economy', available at: www.un.org/press/en/2018/sgsm19194.doc.htm

UNCESCR (2018) 'Committee on Economic, Social and Cultural Rights, concluding observations on the sixth periodic report of the United Kingdom of Great Britain and Northern Ireland', UN Doc E/C.12/GBR/CO/6, 24 June 2016.

UN General Assembly (1998) *Rome Statute of the International Criminal Court (last amended 2010)*, 17 July 1998, ISBN 92-9227-227-6, available at: www.refworld.org/docid/3ae6b3a84.html

UNODC (2016) 'Global report on trafficking in persons'. United Nations, Sales No. E.16.IV.6), available at: www.unodc.org/documents/data-and-analysis/glotip/2016_Global_Report_on_Trafficking_in_Persons.pdf

UN OHCHR (2018) 'What are human rights?', available at: www.ohchr.org/EN/Issues/Pages/WhatareHumanRights.aspx

Wacquant, L. (2005) *Punishing the Poor: The Neoliberal Government of Social Insecurity* (Politics, History, and Culture). Durham: Duke University Press.

Walters, G. (1992) 'A meta-analysis of the gene–crime realtionship', *Criminology, 30*, 4, 595–614.

Weissenborn, R. and Nutt, D.J. (2012) 'Popular intoxicants: what lessons can be learned from the last 40 years of alcohol and cannabis regulation?', *Journal of Psychopharmacology, 26*, 2, 213–220, available at: https://doi.org/10.1177/0269881111414751

Whittaker, D. (2012) *The Terrrorism Reader*. Abingdon: Routledge.

Wilkinson R.G. and Pickett, K. (2010) *The Spirit Level: Why Equality is Better for Everyone*. London: Penguin.

Wincup, E. (2013) *Understanding Crime and Social Policy*. Bristol: Policy Press.

Worthington, A. (2018) *Albums*, available at: www.andyworthington.co.uk/

Young, J. (2007) *The Vertigo of Late Modernity*. London: SAGE.

Zara, G. (2010) 'Farrington, David P.: the integrated cognitive antisocial potential theory', in Cullen, F. and Wilcox, P. (eds), *Encyclopedia of Criminological Theory*, SAGE Knowledge [online], available at: http://dx.doi.org/10.4135/9781412959193

INDEX